The Search for
BIG FOOT
Monster, Myth or Man?

Photo of a Female Bigfoot taken in Northern California.   *Credit: Wide World Photos.*

The Search for
BIG FOOT
Monster, Myth or Man?

PETER BYRNE
Founder, International Wildlife Conservation Society

Foreword by
Robert Rines
President, Academy of Applied Science, Boston, Massachusetts

ACROPOLIS BOOKS LTD./Washington, D.C. 20009

Grateful acknowledgment is made to the authors and publishers for permission to use the following:

"Mysterious Footprints" (pp. 13-14). Reprinted from *The New Book of Knowledge Annual* 1975, by permission of the publisher, Grolier Incorporated, New York.

"Dr. D.W. Grieve's Report on the Film of a Supposed Sasquatch" (pp. 152-157), by permission of Dr. John Napier.

"The First Russian Report on the 1967 Bigfoot Film Footage," by Doctors Dmitri Bayanov and Igor Bourtsev (pp. 158-163), and "The Second Russian Report on the 1967 Bigfoot Film Footage," by Dr. Dmitri D. Donskoy (pp. 164-166), by permission of History Institute of the USSR Academy of Sciences, Moscow.

"Preliminary Description of the External Morphology of What Appeared to Be the Fresh Corpse of a Hitherto Unknown Form of Living Hominid," by Ivan T. Sanderson (pp. 201-230), by permission of Mrs. Sabina Sanderson.

"Anatomy of the Sasquatch (Bigfoot) Foot," and "Additional Notes on Sasquatch (Bigfoot) Foot Anatomy," by Dr. Grover Krantz (pp. 232-254). Reprinted through the courtesy of Northwest Anthropological Research Notes, Department of Sociology/Anthropology, University of Idaho, Moscow, Idaho.

© Copyright 1975 by Peter Byrne

ACROPOLIS BOOKS LTD.
Colortone Building, 2400 17th St., N.W., Washington, D.C. 20009

Printed in the United States of America by
COLORTONE PRESS Creative Graphics, Inc., Washington, D.C. 20009

Library of Congress Cataloging in Publication Data

Byrne, Peter, 1925-
The search for Big Foot.

Includes index.
1. Sasquatch. I. Title.
QL89.2.S2B9   •   001.9'44   •   75-13943
ISBN 0-87491-159-1

THIS BOOK IS FOR C.J.B.

THE OLD MAN WHO STARTED IT ALL.

Contents

Foreword

THE INTRIGUE OF A SEARCH for an unknown species of man or animal, be it in the northwest wilds of the American continent or in the peaks of the Himalayas, sparks the souls and imagination of most people.

Couple such a concept with the relatively recent discovery of the coelacanth (a previously "extinct" prehistoric fish), and the much more recent discoveries of large, apparently unknown marine animals in northern Scotland's Loch Ness*, and of an unknown tribe of primitive people in the Philippines, and minds begin to open more freely to the possibility that the long list of prior accounts of the American Indians and settlers, and more current reported sightings by apparently wholesome citizens, bolstered by amazing film and a myriad of footprint records, might be heralding another fascinating discovery in our own time, country, and continent!

It was in this vein, at the urging of Tim Dinsdale, my dear friend and companion in the continuing quest for definitive pictures at Loch Ness, that both Tim and I, a couple of winters ago, journeyed to The Dalles on Oregon's Columbia River, to see for ourselves what the intrepid explorer, Peter Byrne, was actually up to in his search for Bigfoot or Sasquatch.

After trekking with Peter through the snows in the forests of Mount Hood and neighboring mountains (and with me nearly disappearing up to my neck in a snow blanket that was deceptively covering a deep crevasse), we came away entirely convinced that there were hundreds of square miles of wilds, perhaps never frequented by man, that could harbor a missing tribe, and that patently contained more than adequate food and shelter for same.

We tried to analogize between Byrne's "needle-in-a-haystack" problems and our not-so-different problems at the Ness in determining where to be and at what time, in order—hopefully—to detect what we are respectively seeking. Common aspects of habitual rounds of the domain, food-seeking at

---

*MONSTER HUNT, Tim Dinsdale, 1972, Acropolis Books Ltd., Washington, D.C.

specified times of the year, luring to exposure, and sophisti-
catedly photographing to document, were hashed over in great
detail around the campfire, in the dripping forests of the giant
Douglas fir.

Convinced of Peter Byrne's sincerity and dedication, and
thoroughly delighted with Peter's extreme expertise in animal
tracking and related skills, Tim and I determined to provide
what support we could to the Byrne expedition.

And to this end, through the efforts of the Academy of
Applied Science in Boston, of which we are all members, we
have been able to see to some funding, some photographic
equipment, some night equipment and personnel assistance,
contacts with the scientific community that could be available
for assisting in study of the live creature, and now help in
establishing a portable educational museum, currently in The
Dalles, that serves as an information-receiving headquarters
and a continuing educational display.

The historical and updated accounts of the exciting search
for the Bigfoot or Sasquatch that Peter Byrne here provides in
his own inimitable and refreshing writing style, should delight
the reader, and bring to the Byrne camp an ever-increasing
army of well-wishers and believers, so necessary for the lonely
pioneer who must defy convention and the mainly unimagina-
tive and usually self-appointed custodians of our current scien-
tific "knowledge."

ROBERT H. RINES, *President,*
The Academy of Applied Science,
Boston, Massachusetts

The Ultimate Hunt

PERHAPS THE REASON WHY MILLIONS OF people now find the Bigfoot legend so fascinating could be that it is, in this day and age, one of the last great unsolved and unexplained mysteries of this shrinking world of ours. People find excitement in reading about it, in hearing about it and of course in talking about it with other people who have had some experience with the phenomenon, who perhaps have seen a footprint or even, in some cases, have seen one of the giant primates. But if people find this vicarious association with the phenomenon exciting, how much greater the thrill if they could actually take part in the searches that are presently being conducted in the Pacific Northwest, actually go into the mountains and personally hunt the elusive giants? I am fortunate in being one of the few people who has hunted for the mysterious giant hominids of America's Northwest and to date the only man alive who has made a profession out of this extraordinary search and who, through the support of many dedicated associates and sponsors, continues that profession on a full time basis for twelve months of every year.

People have asked me, what is it that keeps you going, now, after four years, in a search that may go on for another decade? What spurs you on, keeps you out in the wild lonely mountains and binds you to a life in the backwoods of America's Pacific Northwest? What is the driving force that propels you relentlessly forward in a search that is not just for a needle in a haystack but for a moving needle that obviously does not want to be found?

The answer is difficult to put into words. Perhaps, with me, the reason is a simple one. Professionally and emotionally I am a hunter. Most of my life—some twenty years—has been spent as a professional big game hunter. I have hunted big game in both Africa and Asia, with a gun and, in recent years, after I gave up shooting, with a camera. (My professional hunting career ceased in 1968.) And to me, the title that I give to the search for the Bigfoot is one that I feel sums up its meaning most adequately. I call it the Ultimate Hunt—a hunt that is so difficult and so demanding that none but the most tenacious of men—or, as some of my friends put it, the craziest of men—would dare to follow it. The quarry in this hunt—the trophy, if one wishes to call it that—is nothing more than the rarest of all game, a possibly highly intelligent, highly mobile, totally nomadic, partially nocturnal creature with a habitat that measures more than 100,000 square miles and that embraces some of the most difficult and dangerous country in the world.

For sheer diversity there is nothing to equal the different types of terrain that this enormous area encompasses. The jungles of Assam, where I once hunted tiger and leopard, are dense and thick. But they are nothing compared to the near impenetrable scrub of the coast of British Columbia. The mountains of Kenya and the uplands of Mount Kilimanjaro have high rugged terrain where a lone hunter must watch the weather—as well as the mountain buffalo, rhino and elephant—if he is going to survive. But every year the highlands of Oregon and Washington, the central Cascades from 4000 feet upwards, claim victims, people who get lost and die of exposure and whose bodies are sometimes never found. The Nepal and Sikkim Himalaya is a huge area of predominantly mountain terrain, and we well realized its size when we—I and my companions of the Yeti expeditions—hunted the elusive snowmen there in the forties and fifties. But in size it cannot be compared to the habitat of the Bigfoot. The coast country of British Columbia alone could contain all of the Nepal Himalaya and the Sikkim and Bhutan ranges also.

The Ultimate Hunt. Now, unlike my safaris of previous years, it is a hunt with a camera and not a rifle. But though it may seem like an impossible dream, to me it is the ultimate challenge and one to which I am now totally dedicated. Every time that the phone rings at the Bigfoot Information Center in The Dalles, Oregon, there is the excitement of knowing that this could be the call that will lead my partners and me to the quarry. Every time a new sighting is made and we race to the scene, there is the thrill of knowing that this time we may get there quickly enough to track and find one of the giant primates while it is still in the area. Every forest road that we drive, every mountain that we climb, every forest that we penetrate, may have our impossible dream waiting on the other side of it, the ultimate prize of the true hunter and one to which I certainly intend devoting many more years of my life.

Peter Byrne

MYSTERIOUS FOOTPRINTS

The majestic Himalayas in Central Asia form a picturesque natural barrier that separates northern India from Tibet. Located among the valleys, peaks, and ridges of this vast mountain chain are the states of Nepal, Bhutan, and Sikkim. At their highest level the mountains rise like giant, snowcapped spires to well over 20,000 feet (6,000 meters). Mount Everest, the highest of the many towering peaks in the Himalayas, soars nearly 5.5 miles (8.8 kilometers) into the sky.

The people of the Himalayas look upon their mountain homeland with reverence. They believe that gods, spirits, and strange beings live on the remote forested slopes. And perhaps the people are right. Since the late 1890's, stories of the abominable snowman—a strange apelike creature—have filtered through the mountain ranges to the outside world. Several explorers who have climbed the rocky heights of the Himalayas have sighted footprints of a large, unknown creature in the snow. But no animal or mysterious beast has ever been found—dead or alive. The peoples of Tibet call this strange beast *yeti*, which means "dweller among the rocks," and they claim to have seen him many times. He has been described as being half-man, half-ape, and covered with long, fine blond or reddish hair, except on his hands, his face, and the soles of his feet. He has very long arms that reach to his knees, and he walks on thick legs in an upright position.

However, there is no real evidence that the yeti, or abominable snowman, exists. Many of the stories about the creature are based on the large, unidentifiable footprints that have been found in the snow. But these footprints could belong to almost any of the wild animals that live in the Himalaya range. The tiger, leopard, yak, and bear are found in the higher altitudes of the mountains. At certain gaits, bears place the hind foot partly over the imprint of the forefoot. This makes a very large imprint that looks as if it might be the print of an immense human being—or

a monster. The Himalayan langur, a monkey, with a long tail, bushy eyebrows, and a chin tuft, often leaves footprints that might also be mistaken for those of a large unknown animal. And sometimes the sun causes the tracks of an animal to melt into large footprints, thus giving the impression that a mysterious beast is roaming over the mountain slopes.

Explorers have also found that markings thought to be left by the abominable snowman could very well have been caused by lumps of snow or stones falling from higher regions and bouncing across the lower slopes of the Himalayas.

Whether or not the abominable snowman really exists is anybody's guess. But some people are convinced that it does. In the last several years many expeditions have trekked across the Himalayas in search of the creature. The explorers failed to discover anything except a few large footprints. They neither captured nor saw anything that resembled the snowman.

But strange beings resembling the abominable snowman have been sighted in other parts of the world. Bigfoot, a creature described as standing from 7 to 10 feet (2 to 3 m.) tall and weighing more than 500 pounds (220 kilograms), has been seen in the mountains of California, Oregon, and Washington, and in British Columbia in Canada. Hundreds of people have described the monster as apelike, with thick fur, long arms, powerful shoulders, and a short neck. He supposedly walks like a man and leaves huge footprints about 16 inches (41 centimeters) long and 6 inches (15 cm.) wide. That is why the Rocky Mountain Indians named the monster Bigfoot.

The Canadians think there might be a whole family of monsters roaming around. They call the creatures Sasquatch ("hairy men") after the legendary tribe of aboriginal giants in the folklore of the Indians of the Northwest Coast. The Chehalis Indians near Vancouver, British Columbia, believe that the monsters are the descendants of two

13

bands of giants who were almost exterminated in battle many years ago.

In 1957 a Canadian lumberman claimed that 33 years earlier he had been kidnaped by a family of hairy apelike creatures while on a camping trip near Vancouver Island. He was held captive for about a week before he escaped. When the lumberman reached civilization, he decided to keep the story of his strange encounter to himself, for fear nobody would believe him. But when sightings of strange monsters began to occur in the northwestern United States and Canada in the 1950's, he decided to reveal his experience.

One strange creature was even captured—at least on movie film—by a startled monster hunter in the mountains of northern California in 1967. And although the film is jumpy and unfocused, it shows the image of a tall, long-legged, apelike animal covered with dark hair.

In 1973 stories of yeti-like monsters spread throughout the United States. Giant apelike creatures covered with white hair and uttering high-pitched screams were seen and heard in Florida, Pennsylvania, and Arkansas. The residents of Murphysboro, Illinois, a small town on the Big Muddy River, reported several monster sightings. In response to the calls of one frightened eyewitness, the police searched a desolate forested area near the river. They discovered a rough trail in the bush and peculiar footprints fast disappearing in the mud. Grass was crushed and covered with black slime. Broken branches dangled from large trees, and small bushes and trees were snapped in half. Suddenly a shrill, piercing scream broke the silence of the night, and neighbors, police, and police dogs raced for safety. The sound of the scream, after all the stories they had heard, was enough to convince the searchers, and later the whole neighborhood, that something strange was in the area. Several further sightings were reported in the following weeks. Then the sightings stopped and it seemed as if the monster had just disappeared.

In addition to the many sightings throughout the United States and Canada, several unusual footprints have been found and preserved in plaster. The footprints, like those of the abominable snowman, are human in

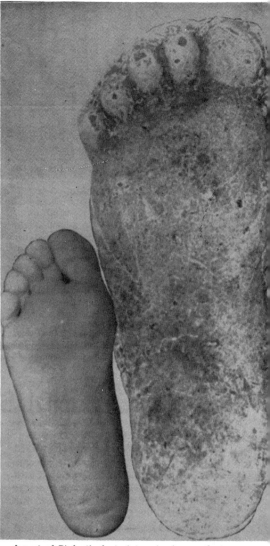

A cast of Bigfoot's footprint and a human foot.
Credit: Wide World Photos.

appearance, but much larger than any man could possibly have made. Anthropologists and zoologists who have listened to eyewitness accounts, studied the film, and examined the plaster casts of the footprints have reached only one conclusion: Whatever it is called—abominable snowman, yeti, sasquatch, or Bigfoot—it's difficult to prove that it doesn't exist.

14

Peter Byrne examining cast of footprint believed to be a Bigfoot's at the Bigfoot Information Center, The Dalles, Oregon. *Photos on this page courtesy of International TRAIL magazine, truck division publication of International Harvester Company.*

Richard Carlson, Deputy Sheriff of Wasco County, is the uniformed "informant" conferring at Center with Peter Byrne.

An extraordinary photograph of what might well be a giant Bigfoot in the woods of Northern California. The picture was one of a strip of negatives left in a photographic studio by a man named Zack Hamilton in 1960. The man left no forwarding address and never came back for the film and to this day no one knows where he is or who he was.

A number of Bigfoot sightings took place on a road in Skamania County in Washington. Eventually, in addition to a protective ordinance, the authorities put up road signs warning people to be on the lookout for the giant primates. Dennis Jenson beside one of the signs. Above, Peter Byrne with snow shoes and other equipment on his back.

Credit: International TRAIL magazine, truck division publication of International Harvester Company

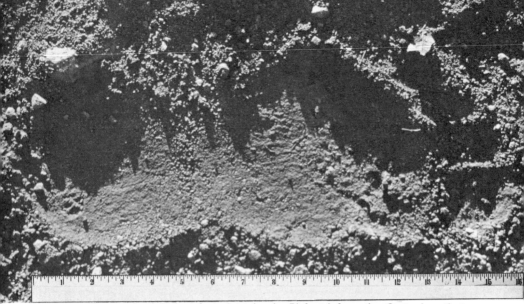

Photograph of Bigfoot footprint taken by Bigfoot Information Center Investigator. Footprint is sixteen inches long and is one of three thousand prints found in the dust of a logging road in the Cascade Mountains.

Dennis Jenson at strange holes in Eslacada after man said that he saw three Bigfeet digging for rodents. Depth of hole seen in photograph was more than six feet.

18

Dennis Jenson stands under tree where three men saw a Bigfoot. Jenson is 6 ft., 5 in. Branch above his head is over 7 ft., 6 in. and according to witnesses head of Bigfoot obscured lower portion of branch next to tree.

Byrne (center) and fellow Bigfoot searchers hiking the hills near The Dalles, Oregon. Mt. Hood is in the background.   *Credit: Nicholas Bielemeier.*

The Bigfoot Information Center in The Dalles, Oregon.
Credit: International TRAIL magazine, truck division
publication of International Harvester Company

Gorillas walk on all fours. Only man among the primates walks upright. Picture shows gorilla in normal locomotive position.   *Credit: George Holton*

Peter Byrne and his associate Celia Killeen setting up tripod-mounted viewer.
*Photos on this page courtesy of International TRAIL magazine,
truck division publication of International Harvester Company.*

Peter Byrne and Celia Killeen flying the Bigfoot flag in front of the Bigfoot Information Center.

Byrne and Ms. Killeen examining footprints in the snow.

The Checkamus River in British Columbia where a Bigfoot was seen in 1971.

Credit: Nicholas Bielemeier.

A large primate like a Bigfoot needs a lot of food. These salmon on a Pacific Northwest River, that have completed their spawning cycle and have died, are undoubtedly a source of food to the giant primates.

At this tiny lake high in the mountain of British Columbia two Bigfeet were seen eating water lily roots in 1972.

One of the search party vehicles [International Scout] on road above the Checkamus River gorge where Bill Taylor saw a Bigfoot in 1971. Above, Byrne radioing base from Observation Post near The Dalles, Oregon.

25

CIRCULATION 800
****

Bigfoot News

Number Eight

Published from The Bigfoot Information Center, P.O.Box 632,
The Dalles, Oregon 97058. Editors Peter Byrne & Celia Killeen. June 1975

EDITORIAL. From time to time we are asked what subjects, in addition to the Bigfoot phenomenon, we shall be covering in the BF News. The answer is, two other subjects. These are, the Loch Ness investigations and the Yeti, or Abominable Snowmen, of the Nepal Himalaya. We shall be writing about the work at Loch Ness, from time to time, because of our close association with the Academy of Applied Science, the Boston based academy that supports, with grants and with equipment, the work of the Bigfoot Information Center at The Dalles, Oregon. And we shall include in our news reports any up-to-date news that we receive on the subject of the Yeti, through our contacts in Kathmandu, Nepal, and Thimbu, Bhutan. Our interest in the Yeti, or Metakangmi, as the Tibetians call them, or Shookpa, as they are known to the Nepalese, goes back to the 1940s and 50s when we took part in the major expeditions that searched for them across the roof of the world, the high Himalaya of Nepal and Sikkim and Bhutan. In this coming year we hope to be able to provide our readers with special sections on the continued search for the elusive snowmen and also on the new work of the Academy of Applied Science at Loch Ness that begins in May.

The Bigfoot News continues to expand and as of this month 30 libraries, 60 schools and over 100 newspapers, radio stations and TV stations receive the newsletter monthly.

Continuing our examination of the various state laws under which a species such as a Bigfoot would find protection, we come this month to British Columbia, Canada. Inquiries to a senior official of the Fish and Wildlife Branch of the Department of Recreation and Conservation in the capital, Victoria, produced this answer: *"Only those species of animals listed in our Game Regulations may be hunted or killed. Therefore, if such a creature as a sasquatch or bigfoot were to be hunted or shot it would be illegal and, should the creature prove to be human, it would be murder."* The answer also contained a note to the effect that ignorance of the law in Canada, as elsewhere, cannot be accepted as an excuse for breaking said law, for Canadian citizens or anyone else, regardless of circumstances. THE EDITORS.

THE LATEST NEWS FROM THE PACIFIC NORTHWEST.

BRITISH COLUMBIA: Stuart Mutch (name incorrectly spelt in last issue) reports from Vancouver on the November sighting. Area visited by boat from Campbell River. No footprints found but definite disturbance in heavy brush on shore at site of BF encounter (BF News, December issue) Mutch camped in area for two weeks, then placed man in area for surveillance. Sighting considered genuine by Mutch, who has now returned to area again for more searching (January) with phone contact to Bigfoot Information Center through Campbell River. Will remain in area one month.
WASHINGTON: A report of loud screams by a camper near Northport. Man was familiar with bear and other animals, said sounds were most unusual. Report investigation by BF Information Center associates Robert Hewes and Ken Coon, of Colville who searched area from Elbow Lake, and via Sheep Creek and Crown Creek, without success. No footprints in area, no further reports.
OREGON: No new reports to date.
IDAHO : No new reports to date.
NORTHERN CALIFORNIA: At last we have some news of the proposed Lassen Park Bigfoot Expedition. Information Center Associate Loren Coleman, of San Francisco, advises us that sufficient funds for the venture were not forthcoming and that it has been abandoned.

THE BIGFOOT BOARD OF EXAMINERS

The Bigfoot Board of Examiners has now been firmly established in five US states and in British Columbia. A call to the Bigfoot Information Center in The Dalles (503.298.5877) will bring a competent and serious examiner to the source of any finding in the North West. Readers should call or write in all findings, no matter how seemingly unimportant they may seem. See the December issue for the terms of the $1000 reward that is offered for information leading to finds.

BIGFOOT IN THE NEWS

Saga Magazine, January 1975. Page 30.
Weyerhaeuser News, December, 1974.
Eugene Register Guard, Dec 19., 1974.
The Harvard Club, NY., lecture by bigfooter Russ Kinne, subject Bigfoot, January 21st.
Patriot Ledger, Quincy, Massachusetts, Dec 27th.
****

A MOUND OF EARTH

A huge mound of earth does not ordinarily excite curiosity, even if it rises to a height of 4 feet and measures 12 feet long and 10 feet wide. But when such a thing, as described, is found in the wilderness, far off any beaten trail and in a spot so difficult to reach that a machete was used to cut a path through dense undergrowth, it becomes a mystery. A companion and I stumbled on such a mound quite by accident near Alder Creek canyon, in Oregon state, several years ago.

The sight of the mound, when we discovered it, intrigued us and while pondering on a solution to its origin I climbed up on it. I found that my hiking boots sank several inches into the loose soil. The soil itself resembled dirt that has been torn up by a rototiller, mixed with debris. The complete absence of any growth, even a blade of new grass, was evidence that the phenomenon was of recent origin, for vegetation takes root swiftly in this type of rain forest.

The perimeter of the mound was rimmed by a very narrow margin of vegetation which had obviously been pushed upward when this huge pile of freshly turned earth had been built. The surrounding forest was composed of closely packed alders and dense undergrowth and it staggered the imagination to consider that the mound had been made by any forest creature. A gopher with a mound of this size would be as big as a buffalo.

I brought this mystery to the attention of the late Dr. Ivan T. Sanderson, a man who has explored many things that puzzle the realms of science. But he was at a loss to offer any explanation. The Oregon Journal published an account of our discovery and I was invited to luncheon by a group of geologists who wanted to discuss it. They provided me with an excellent bill of fare but I came away still seeking an answer to the riddle.

Perhaps a solution will never be found.(At this time efforts to relocate the mound have proved unsuccessful.) Still, sharing the adventure with Bigfoot News readers might inspire someone to shed light on a secret locked in the brooding silence of a lonely thicket.

BY KEITH SOESBE, PORTLAND, ORE. 1975.

THE A.A.S. INVESTIGATIONS AT LOCH NESS.

L to R: Robert Rines, President of the Academy of Applied Science, Boston, Mass. Martin Klein and Tim Dinsdale of the Loch Ness Investigation Bureau, with Side Scan Sonar apparatus on the LNI boat Water Horse, at Loch Ness.

Activities at Loch Ness were conducted this past year on a somewhat reduced scale, under the auspices of the Academy of Applied Science and in collaboration with Tim Dinsdale and former members of the Loch Ness Investigation Bureau, Holly Arnold and Dick Raynor. Impressive automatic underwater sonar detecting equipment coupled with stereoscopic underwater cameras and strobe apparatus are expected to enable the monitoring of Urquhart Bay commencing this next summer.

Since previous simultaneous underwater sonar and photographic contacts with large marine animals have been made during these months, and, in particular, when the salmon come up from the ocean to spawn in the rivers, it is hoped that clearer pictures and contacts will now be forthcoming that can enable a more reliable identification of the nature of these animals.

The Academy, of which both Mr Dinsdale and Peter Byrne are members, continues its extreme interest in the Bigfoot investigation and its desire to help in educational and investigatory programs at least to a limited degree until such time as the Loch Ness experiments are abundantly fruitful.
****

ARTICLE CONTRIBUTED BY ROBERT H. RINES.
Editors Note: For the interest of readers, Urquhart Bay has produced a number of sightings over the years and Loch Ness, an inland lake, is connected to the sea by the River Ness.

GORILLAS DO NOT EXIST, BY TOM PAGE.

While studying anthropology under Dr. David Brose, head of anthropology at Case Western Reserve University in Cleveland, Dr Brose one day made to me what was a startling statement. He told me that based on fossil records neither the lowland nor the mountain gorilla presently exist.

Even though we take the gorilla for granted, its discovery by the scientific world in the year 1847 is little over a century old. For over 400 years prior to its discovery there were vague reports from Africa of such a creature. But the reports were discounted as mere figments of wild imagination. Even now, if you want a skeleton specimen of the gorilla for research purposes, they are not easy to obtain. All hunting of the gorilla has been stopped and only those animals that die in captivity (zoos) are available and there are very few of those.

This lack of skeletal evidence is the same frustrating situation that confronts the Bigfoot investigators. As in the case of the Bigfoot phenomenon, the problem is that in order to have skeletal or fossil remains two very necessary conditions are needed. They are, I., The creature that dies, or is killed has to be entombed in such a way as to make its preservation possible. Dry or arid areas, tar pits, avalanches, earthquakes, volcanic eruptions and other similar natural phenomena can create such a condition. 2. Just as important as the preservation of a creature is the opportunity to later find the remains. Again we have to rely on nature to help. Erosion, and particularily water erosion, have been tremendously helpful in uncovering prehistoric bones. Without both of these very necessary conditions, preservation followed by discovery, the fossil history of any such creature can remain obscure. This is why Dr. Brose states that the existence of the gorilla is not supported by its fossil record and to a similar degree the same is true of the North American Bigfoot.

Many people are highly skeptical and question the lack of so-called " hard evidence " with regards to the Bigfoot question. Unless one is aware of the voluminous reports of sightings, footprints and other miscellaneous evidence on the subject, it might be felt that there is not enough to justify a continuation of the search for the creatures.

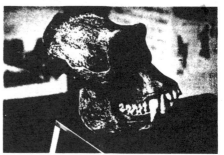

Skull reproduction, fully grown male gorilla at the Bigfoot Exhibition, The Dalles, Oregon.

However, such a volume of evidence does exist and when they discover this the skeptics are left with only one question to fall back on, the question of fossil remains. This is the question that I am asked, again and again. Why have no fossil bones been found? In my opinion there is a very reasonable answer to this. Like the moist forested areas where the gorilla are found, the rain-drenched forests of the mountains of the Pacific N.W., with their winter snows followed by summer suns, - the area where the majority of all Bigfoot evidence is discovered - could not be much worse for the preservation of fossil remains. The acidity of the ground, created by tree growth combined with a warm moist climate brings about the rapid decomposition of flesh and bone.

We know that as animals grow infirm from age, sickness or injury, they seek an place to hide and die. The natural camouflage of the N.W., the annual leaf fall plus the natural scavenger system of the forests sanitation department, from bears all the way down to worms and ants, very quickly returns everything to nature. Despite the lack of skeletal evidence, it is conceivable to me that creatures like the Bigfeet, obviously few in number, inhabiting so vast and remote an area as the coast ranges of the N.W. US and western Canada, could have gone undetected to the present day. With or without the skeletal record, the Bigfoot record has more than enough evidence to justify our continuing search.

EDITORS NOTE: Readers will be interested to know that although scientifically described in 1847., almost nothing was known about the gorilla until 1959-60., when studies were made by George Schaller and his wife. Again, the subspecies, the Mountain Gorilla, was not known to science until 1902.

A NEW NEWSLETTER FOR LOCH NESS BUFFS.

Tim Dinsdale, of the British Loch Ness Investigation Bureau, writes from Loch Ness: "Perhaps your readers would care to know that there is a good bi-monthly newsletter being put out about Loch Ness and Loch Morar investigation activities by one R.R. Hepple, Huntshieldford Cottage, St John's Chapel, Bishop Auckland, Co. Durham, England, zip code DL13.1RQ. Membership in the USA is $5 per year and I can recommend the letter as a good source of information on the Ness.

LOGGERS ON THE LOOKOUT FOR BIGFOOT.

Weyerhaeuser News, the monthly voice of the Weyerhaeuser Company, last month told its 57,000 employees to be on the lookout for Bigfoot sign in the forests and to report same, when found, to the BF Information Center in The Dalles, Oregon, without delay.

BIGFOOT ON THE MAPS, THE GEOGRAPHICAL RECORD.

Ape Canyon, one of the canyons draining Mt St Helens in Washington. Origin of name is story of encounter by miners, in 1924, with giant apes in canyon. Ape Cave, same area, named by survey team working in Ape Canyon. Bigfoot Creek, drains into Bluff Creek, Del Norte Co., N. California, near site of '67 film. Sasquatch Pass, in Homathko Icefield, at head of Bute Inlet, British Columbia coast. Also in B.C. coastal area, see Map 93-D., Ape Creek (52-125SW) Ape Glacier, (52-126SW) Ape Lake, (52-126SW) Ape Mountain, (52-126SW). Origins presently under investigation by S. Mutch.

LETTERS TO THE EDITORS.

Editors: Whatever happened to the Minnesota Ice Man? Does anybody really know, any of your 800 readers? Gerald Russell, Vienne, France.
We would welcome information on this subject.

Editors: During the Smithsonian TV special, one of the scientists talking about the 1967 film said that he "did not like the look of the white feet" of the subject of the footage, that they looked unreal. Can you comment on this for your readers? Jim Day, Agana, Guam.
The Smithsonian did very little homework on the '67 footage. The sand of the dry riverbed was a grey, off white colour. According to the photographers the creature was squatting in the water at the edge of the stream, when first seen. Our experiments, done at the site, suggest that the whiteness of her soles was caused by the white sand sticking to them. With wet feet we achieved the same result. We presume her feet were wet if she had just been in the water.

Editors: We saw where you were taken to task in a recent copy of the magazine Pursuit, for the paucity of reports which you publish and which you regard as genuine. Why do you not list more reports? Erhard Moritz, Sydney, Australia.
We do not list them because after examination we find 85% of them to be pure bunkum, or honest mistake on the part of the finders. A case in point is the 1974 Maple Valley sighting the author of which claimed to know the source of tunnels through which the BF travelled between Seattle and San Diego! David James, head of the British Loch Ness Bureau, uses a maxim which we often follow. When in doubt, throw it out.

NEXT MONTH IN THE FEBRUARY BF NEWS: *The missing town of Bigfoot. New eating places for the hungry Bigfooter. The Case of The Dismembered Dog, by Dennis Tenson. And more, with all the news from the Pacific Northwest. Bigfoot News, $5 annually, twelve times yearly.*

APE CANYON MURAL AT THE BIGFOOT EXHIBITION IN THE DALLES, OREGON

BIGFOOT
NEWS
P.O. BOX
632
THE
DALLES
OREGON
97058
TELEPHONE
503 / 298.5877.

Where the Conuma River enters the Tlupana Inlet on the West Coast of Vancouver Island. Here Muchalat Harry cached his canoe for the last time in 1928.

I

A Look Back into History

History shows that often the loudest skeptics are those who know nothing about the subject in question. They have not studied it and will not do so, for the very reason that they do not believe in it. Nevertheless they are prepared to take the time to pronounce judgment on it.
—IVAN SANDERSON, Columbia, New Jersey, December 1970

ACCORDING TO THE INDIANS, there were once a large number of Bigfeet living on Vancouver Island, a large island, 12,408 square miles in area, off the west coast of British Columbia. The Indians knew about them, feared them, and respected them, but granted that they were harmless. One of the Indians of the Nootka Tribe, who lived at Nootka in 1928, claims to have been carried off by them and held captive for some time.

The story, told to me by Father Anthony Terhaar of Mt. Angel Abbey in Oregon, is a curious one. Father Anthony, a much-loved missionary priest who traveled the west coast of Vancouver Island for many years, was living at Nootka at the time of the story and he knew Muchalat Harry very well.

Muchalat Harry was a trapper and something of a rarity among his fellow tribesmen. He was, according to Father Anthony, a tough, fearless man, of excellent physique. In the course of his trapping, he was wont to spend long weeks in the forest alone, something that the average Indian did not do in those days. The Indians of the coast were apparently a rather timid people and they seemed to regard the deep forest as the home and territory of the Bigfeet. When they went into the deep inland forest for any reason, they never went alone. Muchalat Harry was different from other Indians. He went in the forest alone and feared nothing.

31

Father Anthony Terhaar, who knew Muchalat Harry at Nootka on Vancouver Island in 1928.

Late one autumn Muchalat Harry set off for the woods with his traps and camping gear. His plan was to set out a trap line and stay in the woods for several months. He headed for his favorite hunting area, the Conuma River, at the head of Tlupana Inlet. From Nootka he paddled his own canoe to the mouth of the Conuma. There he cached the canoe and headed upstream on foot. Approximately twelve miles upstream he made his base camp and, after building himself a lean-to, started to put out his trap line.

One night, while wrapped in his blankets and clad only in his underwear, he was suddenly picked up by a huge male Bigfoot and carried off into the hills. He was not carried very far, probably a distance of about two or three miles, at the most. When daylight came he was able to see that he was in a sort of camp, under a high rock shelf and surrounded by some twenty Bigfeet. They were of all sexes and sizes. For some time they stood around him and stared at him. The males were to the front of the curious group, females behind them and young ones to the rear. Muchalat Harry was

32

frightened at first and his fear grew to terror when he noticed, he said, the large number of bones lying around the campsite. When he saw these he was convinced that the Bigfeet were going to eat him.

The Bigfeet did not harm him in any way. Occasionally one came forward and touched him, as if feeling him, and when they discovered that his "skin" was loose—it was in fact his woolen underwear—several came forward and pulled at it gently.

While they looked at him and examined him, Muchalat Harry sat with his back to the rock wall and did not move. He was cold and hungry, but his thoughts were only on escape. Some time in the late afternoon, curiosity on the part of the Bigfeet seemed to slacken and with most of the Bigfeet out of camp, probably food-gathering he thought, there came the opportunity that he needed. He leapt to his feet and ran for his life, never looking back. He ran downhill, toward where he guessed the river to be and sure enough, he soon came to his campsite. In what must have been blind panic he bypassed his camp and ran for twelve miles to where his canoe was cached at the mouth of the Conuma.

The story of Muchalat Harry's arrival at Nootka is described by Father Anthony as follows. It was probably three in the morning. He and his brother Benedictines were asleep and the village was quiet. Suddenly there was a series of wild cries from the waters of the inlet. Lights were lit and he and others hurried down to the water's edge. There, near-frozen and exhausted in his canoe, lay Muchalat Harry. He was barefoot and clad only in his wet and torn underwear and he had paddled his canoe through the winter night 45 miles from the mouth of the Conuma River.

Father Anthony and his companions carried the almost lifeless form up from the water's edge. It took three weeks to nurse Muchalat Harry back to sanity and good health. The nursing was done by Father Anthony, who took him into his own care, and he told me that during the course of this three weeks, Muchalat Harry's hair turned to pure white.

The story of the kidnapping came out slowly. At first Muchalat Harry would talk to no one. Then he told Father Anthony what had happened and, later, others. When he was fully recovered to health he was asked when he planned to go back to collect his belongings, the camp equipment, his pots and pans, his trap line and above all, his rifle, at the lean-to on the Conuma. In 1928 a trap line and all of its pieces must have been worth a great deal to an island Indian. A rifle alone would be regarded as a highly prized possession. But Muchalat Harry never went back to the Conuma. Not only did he never return there; according to Father Anthony, he never left the settlement at Nootka, never went in the woods again for the rest of his life. He preferred to lose all of his valuable and probably hard-won possessions rather than risk another encounter with the Bigfeet.

Late in 1972 I had occasion to visit Vancouver Island. I was on a routine investigating trip and when I found myself at Nainimo, not too far by road from the west coast and the scene of Muchalat Harry's adventure, I drove there. I stopped in Gold River and obtained from the Royal Canadian Mounted Police some maps and instructions on how to get to the Conuma River area. Nowadays there is a logging road that runs all the way down to the mouth of the river, and one Sunday morning, with the logging trucks out of the way, I drove there and made camp on the Conuma. I spent several days there, walking the river bed and exploring. I tried to make a rough determination of where Muchalat Harry might have had his lean-to and I found a place that offered a good campsite, twelve miles from the mouth of the river on the edge of a series of high bluffs. The salmon were running in the Conuma while I was there and all night long I could hear them splashing up the shallow waters of the river. In the morning black bear worked the river, getting the salmon that had come ashore in the night or had become tangled in the limbs of fallen trees that lay in the river. I counted six bears in several days. The country was generally wild and deserted and the actual mouth of the Conuma, where it flowed into the salt waters of the inlet, was one of the most beautiful places I have ever seen. Some of the forest close to the river had been logged off, but the logging work had moved on west and while I was there it was quiet. The days began with morning mists on the river and then warmed to the clear crispness of perfect autumn weather. Evenings were cool and damp and nights bright with a starlight that provided almost enough light to read. I found no sign of Bigfoot on the Conuma, nor any sign of Muchalat Harry's trap line or lean-to. I hardly expected to find anything of the latter, after forty-odd years. But even though Muchalat Harry was long gone, the river and the forest remained unchanged. The splashing salmon, the cold, clear water of the Conuma, the moss-covered banks, the shallow pools in the forest that the Conuma drained, that were the breeding places of the salmon, the river birds, the plodding bears, the deep silent waters of the inlet, all were as they must have been forty years before, when Muchalat Harry cached his canoe and made his camp there.

For most people the history of the Bigfoot phenomenon begins within the last decade or so, with stories of footprints being found in northern California and other parts of the Pacific Northwest. In actual fact it is much older and, in the northwest, can quite definitely be traced back to the 1850s. It is mostly to be found—as I and my associates have traced it—in the form of old newspaper stories of encounters, by various people, with large, ape-like creatures that were very possibly Bigfeet. A few of the stories are, of course, wildly apocryphal, the creation of imagination on the part of some of the early settlers. Others are much more credible.

The oldest of them all and one that is definitely "borderline" is from the Norse Sagas and describes an encounter by Leif Erikson and his men, during their first landing in the New World, with creatures that were pictured as "horribly ugly, hairy, swarthy and with great black eyes."

In the literature we must include, of course, the legends of the Indians of the Pacific Northwest—legends that have been handed down from father to son for hundreds of years, from northern California to north central British Columbia. Among the legends are the stories of the Giant Men of Mt. Shasta, the Stwanitie, or Stickmen, of the Washington mountains, and the Sasquatch, or giants, of the Salish Indian tribes of British Columbia.

Let us have a look at some of these stories in the light of their being "Bigfoot" evidence, starting at the earliest—Leif Erikson's strange encounter—and following them through to the present day.

Did the bold Leif and his Norsemen encounter Bigfoot? It is possible. It is more probable that the creatures that they encountered were simply Indians. The Norse word "skellring" is a term of contempt. It means, roughly, a "barbarian." But what caught my eye when reading Samuel Eliot Morison's account of the early Norse voyages, was the word "hairy." The Norse were a hairy people themselves, big men with matted hair and beards. Why did they remark on the "skellring" being hairy? Was it because they were very much hairier than the Norsemen, even covered with hair, perhaps? If the encounter had been between, say, Tibetans, who are not a hirsute people, and the "skellring," one could understand the reference to hairiness. But why the Norse mention? After a thousand years the mists of time have drawn their veil over the Norsemen and their heroic voyages into the New World, leaving us with an age-old question which we may never solve.

Leaving the Norsemen and taking a huge leap forward in time, we come to 1810 and the overland journeys of a Northwest Fur and Trading Company agent. His name was David Thompson and he was, as his diaries show, a bright young man who took an interest in what went on around him. His diaries also show him to be much traveled, and at one time when he passed down the great bend of the Columbia River where The Dalles is situated today, on one of his journeys he found what might well have been Bigfoot tracks. At the time of the footprint finding reported in his diaries, he was making his way across the Rocky Mountains at the place where Jasper lies today. The year was 1810 and the month was January. He was with a small party of Indian guides when he found the tracks. The prints were fourteen inches in length and some eight inches wide and they resembled, he wrote, the paw print of a big bear. But the nails seemed to be too short to be those of a bear and when Thompson talked with his Indian guides they told him that the prints were those of a "Mammoth"* (Thompson's word). He found another set of the same footprints in the fall of that year and he marveled at them, at their size and the Indians' telling him they were of a mammoth.

*Mammoth is a word still used by Indians of the Northwest to describe Bigfoot.

36

What made the footprints that he found? Was it an old grizzly bear with its claws worn down? Or a big Brown? The size of the prints were not out of proportion with those of one of the big bears. But if it was a grizzly would not his guides, Indians of the region, have recognized it as such? One wonders what Indian word it was that Thompson translated into mammoth. The Indians, old though their legends were, would hardly know of the Mammoth that once roamed the region, any more than they would have known of the modern elephant. That Thompson was intrigued by the tracks there is no doubt, for many years later he expanded his diaries into a narrative and in these later writings we still find him wondering what could have made those huge prints.

From 1810 we leap across another thirty years to 1840. From that year emerges a fascinating letter from a missionary living in northern Washington. We are indebted to Robert Ruby, M.D., of Moses Lake, Washington, for finding this letter and to the Holland Library of Washington State University for permission to publish it. Of particular interest in the letter—apart from the mention of "giants" that could well have been Bigfeet—are the notations concerning their strength ("they can carry two or three beams upon their back at once"), the size of their feet ("they say their track is about a foot and a half long") and their smell. As readers will know, many people who have been close to a Bigfoot have noticed the very strong smell that they seem to emit. Both Patterson and Gimlin, who made the 1967 Bigfoot footage, noticed this strong smell and think that it was this that caused their horses to bolt. As to the stone throwing, we have several mentions of this in our records as well as the famous story from Ape Canyon of rock throwing.

Date: April, 1840.
To: The Rev. David Green.
    Secretary of the American Board of Commissioners for Foreign Missions.
Dear Sir:
    I suppose that it is not necessary for me to say much as Mr. Eeles has given you all that is interesting. My health is very poor and I fear I shall be unable to pursue my labours as a missionary. We are, we hope, doing something in the language. It is, if I may be judge, very difficult and will require much hard study before we have much knowledge and

are prepared to make any direct or forcible appeal to them. I should not be at all surprised if this mission prove a total failure. How much more confidence I should have in its success if we had had real opposition to encounter from the Indians at its commencement. We, I fear, are destined to experience some opposition from the old chief I named in my letter last fall. He has been absent most of the time since. He soon after went off to Buffalo and has not yet to my knowledge returned. I left our place last Monday for this place (Fort Colville) and shall leave tomorrow for home, "Deo volente" which I expect to reach in two days.

It has been very sickly in this region the last part of the winter. Many have died. I do not know what can be done to save them from utter extinction. They seem as fated to fade away before the whites as the game of their country. There seems but one way that they can be saved and that is by settling them and civilizing them and this I fear they cannot bear. I sometimes think that it will be as injurious to them as their superstitions which are carrying them off very fast. Whatever is done for them must be quickly done, for there will soon be nothing to labour for. We need to be placed in such a situation that we can devote all our time and energies to them and when that is done we can do little on account of the few that we have access to. I think that I may safely say that the two tribes, Nez Perces and Flat Heads are as well supplied with ministers as New England, that is, there are as many preachers compared to the number of the people. We can only have access to a few at a time. If we travel and visit with them at their places we can have but little influence over them.

I suppose you will bear with me if I trouble you with a little of their superstition, which has recently come to my knowledge. They believe in the existence of a race of giants which inhabit a certain mountain off to the west of us. This mountain is covered with perpetual snow. They inhabit its top. They may be classed with Goldsmith's nocturnal class and they cannot see in the daytime. They hunt and do all of their work in the night. They are men stealers. They come to the people's lodges in the night when the people are asleep and take them, and put them under their skins and take them to their place of abode without even waking. When they wake in the morning they are wholly lost, not knowing in what direction their home is. The account that they give of these Giants will in some measure correspond with the Bible account of this race of beings. They say their track is about a foot and a half long. They will carry two or three beams upon their back at once. They frequently come in the night and steal their salmon from their nets and eat them raw. If the people are awake they always know when they are coming very near, by their strong smell, which is most intolerable. It is not uncommon for them to come in the night and give three whistles and then the stones will begin to hit their houses. The people believe that they are still troubled with their nocturnal visits.

We need the prayers of the Church at home. I am, My Dear Sir, Yours most truly and submissively, E. Walker (Elkanah Walker) Missionary to Spokane Indians.

38

In 1851 we find an account in the May 16 issue of the *Times-Picayune*, a New Orleans newspaper. The account appears to have been obtained from the *Memphis Enquirer*. It is also reported as having appeared in the *Galveston Weekly Journal*, of Galveston, Texas. News seemed to have been shared, or perhaps simply pirated, by newspapers in those days. Nowadays there are the wire services, UPI, AP, et cetera, but in the 1800s the only sources of news for many country papers, of events that occurred outside their own communities, were often other and larger newspapers. I was particularly interested in this story when I first saw it, for it is the only one occurring outside the Pacific Northwest that seems to be describing a Bigfoot. I spent many hours searching for the original *Galveston Weekly Journal,* in the city library of Galveston. I was unable to find it. One wonders if the area of the sightings in Arkansas could have held an isolated community of the creatures, one that the Indians had driven into some secluded pockets of forest. I do not know how extensive were the forests of Arkansas in those days, but they must have been considerable before the arrival and advance of the main bodies of pioneers and settlers with their axes and saws. Even today there are, I understand, areas big enough to hold much game and each year people still get lost in them, sometimes for days before being found.

Sitting in the public library in Galveston and listening to the muddy waters of the Gulf of Mexico lap listlessly against the shore, I came across an item of the May, 1851, issue of the *Weekly Journal*, an advertisement which offered "fast service to San Francisco and the West Coast." The service was via Cape Horn and the offer was for a "pleasantly quick ninety days to San Francisco." The writer, a born ad man no doubt, had either never traveled the Horn or else simply decided to ignore its rugged reputation. But thinking back on the distances involved and the slowness of travel in those days, I believe it unlikely that anyone in Galveston would have seen a news story in the July 4, 1884, issue of the *Daily Colonist,* a newspaper published in the port of Victoria, British Columbia.

The account, which is reproduced here, tells of the capture of what could well have been a young Bigfoot, taken by better: strange to say, here is a strong belief that the haunt of the Mammoth, is about this defile, I questioned several, none could positively say, they had seen him, but their belief I found firm and not to be shaken. I remarked to them, that such an enormous heavy Animal must leave indelible marks of his feet, and on feeding. This they all acknowledged, and that they had never seen any marks of him, and therefore could show me none. All I could say did not shake their belief in his existence.

January 6th. We came to the last grass for the Horses in Marshes and along small Ponds, where a herd of Bisons had lately been feeding; and here we left the Horses poor and tired, and notwithstanding the bitter cold, [they] lived through the winter, yet they have only a clothing of close hair, short and without any furr.

January 7th. Continuing our journey in the afternoon we came on the track of a large animal, the snow about six inches deep on the ice; I measured it; four large toes each of four inches in length to each a short claw; the ball of the foot sunk three inches lower than the toes, the hinder part of the foot did not mark well, the length fourteen inches by eight inches in breadth, walking from north to south, and having passed about six hours. We were in no humour to follow him: the Men and Indians would have it to be a young mammoth and I held it to be the track of a large old grizled Bear yet the shortness of the nails, the ball of the foot, and it's g.. . .. /e was not that of a Bear, otherwise that of a very large old Bear, his claws worn away; this the Indians would not allow.[1] Saw several tracks of Moose Deer 9 PM Ther - 4

Janu[ar]y 8th. A fine day. We are now following the Brooks in the open defiles of the secondary Mountains; when we can no longer follow it, the road is to cross a point of high wind, very fatigueing, and come on another Brook, and thus in succession; these secondary Mountains appear to be about 2 to 3000 feet above their base, with patches of dwarf pines, and much snow; we marched ten miles today; and as we advance we feel the mild weather from the Pacific Ocean. This morning at 7 AM Ther +6 at 9 PM +22. One of my men named Du Nord beat a dog to death, he is what we call a "flash" man, a showy fellow before the women but a coward in heart, and would willingly desert if he had courage to go alone; very glutinous and requires full ten pounds of meat each

[1] The measurements of this track — 14 inches × 8 — fall within those recorded for Grizzly Bears; the proportions are also correct. The shortness of the claws may be explained by the fact that Grizzlies' claws are worn very short during the open season and grow long again while the animal is hibernating. Any question as to why this particular Grizzly was not hibernating in January would seem to be answered from Henry's diary for 27 November, 1810, where he records that these bears "seldom den for the winter as black bears do but wander about in search of prey". (Coues, New Light,

The narrative of David Thompson, Agent, The Northwest Fur and Trading Company, 1810.

Daily Colonist.

FRIDAY MORNING, JULY 4th, 1884.

SHIPPING INTELLIGENCE.

PORT OF VICTORIA, BRITISH COLUMBIA.

ENTERED.

July 3—Str R. P. Rithet, Nanaimo
str Yosemite, New Westminster
Sch Annie Beck, Sooke
Str Queen of the Pacific, Pt Townsend
Str Olympian, Pt Townsend

CLEARED.

July 3—Str Dolphin, Sooke
Str R. P. Rithet, Nanaimo
Str Yosemite, New Westminster
Str Queen of the Pacific, San Francisco
Str Olympian, Pt Townsend

PASSENGERS.

Per ss 'LYMPIAN from Puget Sound—D J Fitzmathew, Misses Blair, E Alspaugh, Mrs B Evans, C M Buck and son, W H Cameron, H H Lang, Mrs D Evans, 2 infts and nurse, J A Ward and wife, Capt Hinde, D. W, H. Jaa and J Galbraith, Mrs Galbraith, Misses Galbraith, R B McMicking, F Fillicks and wife, Miss Skkimore.

Per ss QUEEN OF THE PACIFIC, fm San Fran.—Mrs Bushby and child, Miss L Denny, Mrs Page and San, Mrs Sperry and dau, Mrs Crane and 2 chdn, Geo Bushby, Miss Ordige, R D Chandler, wife and son, W F Parr, Mrs Bowker and son, C G Browning, J A McIlosky, J G Maguire, A Munro, C P Miller, Mesdames Iodisi, Villani, Bologna, Signors Villani, Bologna, Baldassa, W Marvin, C N Fellows, B F Magell, H Edvarda.

Per str YOSEMITE, from New Westminster—Miss fullich, Mr and Mrs Toomey, Mr and Mrs Innes, Miss tweet, Miss Nirri-, Mrs Much, Miss Harris, Miss Williams, E Vigor, A Glassford, E Mohun, Montgomery, Bartch, Mcdonald, Doyle, Cusic, Harvey, Byrne, Ismcock, Manson, Waterman, Sherman, Mason and Chinese.

CONSIGNEES.

Per str OLYMPIAN, fm Puget Sound—C Strouss, & R & T, H Wright, Neufelder & Ross.

New Westminster.

(Special to The Colonist.)

NEW WESTMINSTER, July 3. Custom receipts at this office the fiscal year ending 30th of June, 1884, was $94,-'28 56, a decrease of $16,567.02 as compared with the previous year, decrease caused by the increased imports from eastern provinces.

Constable Wiggins was brought up today before the police magistrate charged with assaulting one Richardson and was fined $75 and costs or three months' imprisonment.

WHAT IS IT?

A STRANGE CREATURE CAPTURED ABOVE YALE.

A British Columbia Gorilla.

(Correspondence of The Colonist).

YALE, B. C., July 3rd.
In the immediate vicinity of No. 4 tunnel, situated some twenty miles above this village, are bluffs of rock which have hitherto been unsurmountable, but on Monday morning last were successfully scaled by Mr. Onderdonk's employes on the regular train from Lytton. Assisted by Mr. Costerton, the British Columbia Express Company's messenger, and a number of gentlemen from Lytton and points east of that place who, after considerable trouble and perilous climbing, succeeded in capturing a creature which may truly be called half man and half beast. "Jacko," as the creature has been called by his capturers, is something of the gorilla type standing about four feet seven inches in height and weighing 127 pounds. He has long, black, strong hair and resembles a human being with one exception, his entire body, excepting his hands, (or paws) and feet are covered with glossy hair about one inch long. His fore arm is much longer than a man's fore arm, and he possesses extraordinary strength, as he will take hold of a stick and break it by wrenching or twisting it, which no man living could break in the same way. Since his capture he is very reticent, only occasionally uttering a noise which is half bark and half growl. He is, however, becoming daily more attached to his keeper, Mr. George Tilbury, of this place, who proposes shortly starting for London, England, to exhibit him. His favorite food so far is berries, and he drinks fresh milk with evident relish. By advice of Dr. Hannington raw meats have been withheld from Jacko, as the doctor thinks it would have a tendency to make him savage. The mode

of capture was as follows: Ned Austin, the engineer, on coming in sight of the bluff at the eastern end of the No. 4 tunnel saw what he supposed to be a man lying asleep in close proximity to the track, and as quick as thought blew the signal to apply the brakes. The brakes were instantly applied, and in a few seconds the train was brought to a standstill. At this moment the supposed man sprang up, and uttering a sharp quick bark began to climb the steep bluff. Conductor R. J. Craig and Express Messenger Costerton, followed by the baggageman and brakesmen, jumped from the train and knowing they were some twenty minutes ahead of time immediately gave chase. After five minutes of perilous climbing the then supposed demented Indian was corralled on a projecting shelf of rock where he could neither ascend nor descend. The query now was how to capture him alive, which was quickly decided by Mr. Craig, who crawled on his hands and knees until he was about forty feet above the creature. Taking a small piece of loose rock he let it fall and it had the desired effect of rendering poor Jacko incapable of resistance for a time at least. The bell rope was then brought up and Jacko was now lowered to terra firma. After firmly binding him and placing him in the baggage car "off brakes" was sounded and the train started for Yale. At the station a large crowd who had heard of the capture by telephone from Spuzzum Flat were assembled, each one anxious to have the first look at the monstrosity, but they were disappointed, as Jacko had been taken off at the machine shops and placed in charge of his present keeper.

The question naturally arises, how came the creature where it was first seen by Mr. Austin? From bruises about its head and body, and apparent soreness since its capture, it is supposed that Jacko ventured too near the edge of the bluff, slipped, fell and lay where found until the sound of the rushing train aroused him. Mr. Thos. White and Mr. Gouin, C. E., as well as Mr. Major, who kept a small store about half a mile west of the tunnel during the past two years, have mentioned having seen a curious creature at different points between Camps 13 and 17, but no attention was paid to their remarks as people came to the conclusion that they had either seen a bear or stray Indian dog. Who can unravel the mystery that now surrounds Jacko? Does he belong to a species hitherto unknown in this part of the continent, or is he really what the train men first thought he was, a crazy Indian?

What Some People Say.

That J. B. Ferguson & Co. are sole agents for Fairchild's Gold Pens for the province of British Columbia and have just received a large stock. Call and see them.

That a fresh lot of San Juan strawberries and a lot of chickens (broilers) were received this morning at Beauchamp's, Yates street.

A large stock of Seasides just received at J. B. Ferguson & Co.'s new book store—third door south of post office.

A few more Lawn Tennis Sets at J. B. Ferguson & Co.'s just opened.

That the King Tye Co. are leading manufacturers and importers of clothing, groceries, etc.

That for neatness and cheapness in repairing you should go to IRVING BROS.' Boot and Shoe Store, Government street, between Broughton and Courtenay. They make repairing a specialty.

That Clothing, Hats and Underclothing are very cheap at W. & J. Wilson's. Look at their prices and you will see that their stock is the best value in Victoria.

That the new Customs Excise Tariff with its refreshing, onerous facts, has arrived at last.   T. N. HIBBEN & Co.

That employers can be supplied with every class of labor by applying to Knights of Labor Bureau, Yates Street.

That you should go to John Weiler's, Fort street, and look at the beautiful Walnut and Ash Furniture, which has just arrived from the East. Do not miss the chance.

That for
    best value
        in clothing,
            furnishing goods,
                trunks, &c.,
                    go to the
                Mechanics' Store,
                    Johnson street,
                        W. G. CAMERON.

That the celebrated Val Blatzs Milwaukee is for sale at the "Senate."

That THOMAS NICHOLSON. Family Grocer, corner Douglas and Johnson streets, has a new stock of Groceries and Provisions, Lard, Hams and Bacon, packed by

The 1884 story of the capture of a young Bigfoot.

41

railwaymen near the town of Yale, British Columbia—in an area where several sightings of strange creatures had been reported by railwaymen in previous weeks, in the area of their work on the lines—and held for a period by them. The "creature" was apparently found on a railway line by some of the workers and they captured it by, as the writer so delicately puts it, "taking a small piece of loose rock and letting it fall" (on the wretched creature's head). This had the desired effect of rendering poor Jacko (as they called the creature) "incapable of resistance for a time at least." In other words, they smashed the wretched creature on the head with a boulder and knocked it out. The creature subsequently disappeared from the news. No one seems to know whether it died, or escaped, or was sold to a circus, as is rumored. My belief is that if the method of treatment while it was in captivity was in any way similar to the method of capture, it very quickly succumbed. In 1884, railwaymen were a rough and ready lot, and a quick exit to another part of this world, or to the next, was probably the best thing that could have happened to "poor Jacko."

From more than a thousand miles to the south and two years later comes the next story. It is contained in the January 2, 1886, issue of the *Del Norte Record* and is in the form of a letter from a correspondent in Happy Camp, California. The story, for which I am indebted to George Haas of Oakland, California, is an interesting one. Happy Camp is a small town in northern California and is not much changed since the time of the story. The Marble Mountain area, today the Marble Mountain Wilderness, is as wild and untamed as it was in 1886. In recent years I have trekked through it, caught fish in its lakes and camped in its silent forests. I have peered into many of its caves and into not a few of its old, abandoned mine shafts. I explored many of them long before I heard of the story. I never found anything there, no footprints in the caves, not any sign of a Bigfoot in the area. But that is not to say that there are no Bigfeet in the area now, or when Mr. Jack Dover, a "trustworthy citizen," claimed to have seen one in 1886.

Here is the Happy Camp correspondent's letter dated January 2, 1886.

I do not remember to have seen any reference to the "Wild Man" which haunts this part of the country, so I shall allude to him briefly. Not a great while since, Mr. Jack Dover, one of our most trustworthy citizens, while hunting saw an object standing one hundred and fifty yards from him picking berries or tender shoots from the bushes. The thing was of gigantic size—about seven feet high—with a bull dog head, short ears and long hair; it was also furnished with a beard, and was free from hair on such parts of its body as is common among men. Its voice was shrill, or soprano, and very human, like that of a woman in great fear. Mr. Dover could not see its foot-prints as it walked on hard soil. He aimed his gun at the animal, or whatever it is, several times, but because it was so human would not shoot. The range of the curiosity is between Marble mountain and the vicinity of Happy Camp. A number of people have seen it and all agree in their descriptions except some make it taller than others. It is apparently herbivorous and makes winter quarters in some of the caves of Marble mountain.

In 1891, Theodore Roosevelt traveled through Yellowstone Park and heard various stories of Bigfoot sightings. One of these he retold in THE WILDERNESS HUNTER, published in 1893. Roosevelt calls it a ghost story, and recounts it as told by a "grisled, weatherbeaten old mountain hunter, named Bauman, who was born and had passed all his life on the frontier."

When the event occurred Bauman was still a young man, and was trapping with a partner among the mountains dividing the forks of the Salmon from the head of Wisdom River. Not having had much luck, he and his partner determined to go up into a particularly wild and lonely pass through which ran a small stream said to contain many beaver. The pass had an evil reputation because the year before a solitary hunter who had wandered into it was there slain, seemingly by a wild beast, the half-eaten remains being afterwards found by some mining prospectors who had passed his camp only the night before.

The memory of this event, however, weighed very lightly with the two trappers, who were as adventurous and hardy as others of their kind. They took their two lean mountain ponies to the foot of the pass, where they left them in an open beaver meadow, the rocky timber-clad ground being from thence onwards impracticable for horses. They then struck out on foot through the vast, gloomy forest, and in about four hours reached a little open glade where they concluded to camp, as signs of game were plenty.

There was still an hour or two of daylight left, and after building a brush lean-to and throwing down the opening their packs, they started up stream. The country was very dense and hard to travel through, as there was much down timber, although here and there the sombre woodland was broken by small glades of mountain grass.

At dusk they again reached camp. The glade in which it was pitched was not many yards wide, the tall, close-set pines and firs rising round it like a wall. On one side was a little stream, beyond which rose the steep mountain-slopes, covered with the unbroken growth of the evergreen forest.

They were surprised to find that during their short absence something, apparently a bear, had visited camp, and had rummaged about among their things, scattering the contents of their packs, and in sheer wantonness destroying their lean-to. The footprints of the beast were quite plain, but at first they paid no particular heed to them, busying themselves with rebuilding the lean-to, laying out their beds and stores, and lighting the fire.

While Bauman was making ready supper, it being already dark, his companion began to examine the tracks more closely, and soon took a brand from the fire to follow them up, where the intruder had walked along a game trail after leaving the camp. When the brand flickered out, he returned and took another, repeating his inspection of the footprints very closely. Coming back to the fire, he stood by it a minute or two, peering out into the darkness, and suddenly remarked: "Bauman, that bear has been walking on two legs." Bauman laughed at this, but his partner insisted that he was right, and upon again examining the tracks with a torch, they certainly did seem to be made by but two paws, or feet. However, it was too dark to make sure. After discussing whether the footprints could possibly be those of a human being, and coming to the conclusion that they could not be, the two men rolled up in their blankets, and went to sleep under the lean-to.

At midnight Bauman was awakened by some noise, and sat up in his blankets. As he did so his nostrils were struck by a strong, wild-beast odor, and he caught the loom of a great body in the darkness at the mouth of the lean-to. Grasping his rifle, he fired at the vague, threatening shadow, but must have missed, for immediately afterwards he heard the smashing of the underwood as the thing, whatever it was, rushed off into the impenetrable blackness of the forest and the night.

After this the two men slept but little, sitting up by the rekindled fire, but they heard nothing more. In the morning they started out to look at the few traps they had set the previous evening and to put out new ones. By an unspoken agreement they kept together all day, and returned to camp towards evening.

On nearing it they saw, hardly to their astonishment, that the lean-to had been again torn down. The visitor of the preceding day had returned, and in wanton malice had tossed about their camp kit and bedding, and destroyed the shanty. The ground was marked up by its tracks, and on leaving the camp it had gone along the soft earth by the brook, where the footprints were as plain as if on snow, and, after a careful scrutiny of the trail, it certainly did seem as if, whatever the thing was, it had walked off on but two legs.

The men, thoroughly uneasy, gathered a great heap of dead logs, and kept up a roaring fire throughout the night, one or the other sitting on guard most of the time. About midnight the thing came down through the forest opposite, across the brook, and stayed there on the hill-side for nearly an hour. They could hear the branches crackle as it moved about, and several times it uttered a harsh, grating, long-drawn moan, a peculiarly sinister sound. Yet it did not venture near the fire.

In the morning the two trappers, after discussing the strange events of the last thirty-six hours, decided that they would shoulder their packs and leave the valley that afternoon. They were the more ready to do this because in spite of seeing a good deal of game sign they had caught very little fur. However, it was necessary first to go along the line of their traps and gather them, and this they started out to do.

All the morning they kept together, picking up trap after trap, each one empty. On first leaving camp they had the disagreeable sensation of being followed. In the dense spruce thickets they occasionally heard a branch snap after they had passed; and now and then there were slight rustling noises among the small pines to one side of them.

At noon they were back within a couple of miles of camp. In the high, bright sunlight their fears seemed absurd to the two armed men, accustomed as they were, through long years of lonely wandering in the wilderness to face every kind of danger from man, brute, or element. There were still three beaver traps to collect from a little pond in a wide ravine nearby. Bauman volunteered to gather these and bring them in, while his companion went ahead to camp and made ready the packs.

On reaching the pond Bauman found three beaver in the traps, one of which had been pulled loose and carried into a beaver house. He took several hours in securing and preparing the beaver, and when he started homewards he marked with some uneasiness how low the sun was getting. As he hurried towards camp, under the tall trees, the silence and desolation of the forest weighed on him. His feet made no sound on the pine needles, and the slanting sun rays, striking through among the straight trunks, made a gray twilight in which objects at a distance glimmered indistinctly. There was nothing to break the ghostly stillness which, when there is no breeze, always broods over these sombre primeval forests.

At last he came to the edge of the little glade where the camp lay, and shouted as he approached it, but got no answer. The camp fire had gone out, though the thin blue smoke was still curling upwards. Near it lay the packs, wrapped and arranged. At first Bauman could see nobody; nor did he receive an answer to his call. Stepping forward he again shouted, and as he did so his eye fell on the body of his friend, stretched beside the trunk of a great fallen spruce. Rushing towards it the horrified trapper found that the body was still warm, but that the neck was broken, while there were four great fang marks in the throat.

The footprints of the unknown beast-creature, printed deep in the soft soil, told the whole story.

The unfortunate man, having finished his packing, had sat down on the spruce log with his face to the fire, and his back to the dense woods, to wait for his companion. While thus waiting, his monstrous assailant, which must have been lurking nearby in the woods, waiting for a chance to catch one of the adventurers unprepared, came silently up from behind, walking with long, noiseless steps, and seemingly still on two legs. Evidently unheard, it reached the man, and broke his neck by wrenching his head back with its forepaws, while it buried its teeth in his throat. It had not eaten the body, but apparently had romped and gambolled around it in uncouth, ferocious glee, occasionally rolling over and over it; and had then fled back into the soundless depths of the woods.

Bauman, utterly unnerved, and believing that the creature with which he had to deal was something either half human or half devil, some great goblin-beast, abandoned everything but his rifle and struck off at speed down the pass, not halting until he reached the beaver meadows where the hobbled ponies were still grazing. Mounting, he rode onwards through the night, until far beyond the reach of pursuit.

The Roosevelt story is interesting in that it is the only record—if indeed it is a record—of violence on the part of a Bigfoot. The injuries suffered by the man who died suggest a bear, rather than a Bigfoot. At the same time the footprints that Bauman saw were not, according to him, those of a quadruped, a bear.

Comes the new century and with it a spate of Bigfoot findings that begin in Coos County, in western Oregon's coast range country. A newspaper article in the *Lane County Leader*, April 7, 1904, talks of several incidents in that area. It mentions the miners of that time and in quaint jargon tells of their sighting a "wild man" and adds, "They have seen him and know whereof they speak." I can find no other written reports from the Coos County area, but I have had several oral reports of "findings" in the last few years, the latest being in the summer of 1971. I spent some weeks in the area in 1972 and talked with the local people. There was nothing very definite in the way of new sightings or footprint findings, but the area, if one can believe all that one hears of it, does seem to have produced some evidence over the years.

In 1960 I went to Kelso, in the state of Washington, to see an elderly man named Fred Beck. Mr. Beck lived alone in a small cabin, was retired and was the only known survivor of what has become known as the Ape Canyon incident. The date of the incident was 1924 and Mr. Beck was the central figure in the incident. As the story went, he and three others had a mining claim in the canyon. On several occasions they found, he told me, large man-like footprints in the sand and gravel of the canyon bed. They wondered about what made them but the pressure of work prevented them from worrying too much about the prints. Then, one day, one of the men saw what he thought was a large ape, peering at him over the top of a big rock. The man, Beck's companion, ran to the cabin that they had built close to the mine and got a rifle.

He fired a shot at the creature, which disappeared. A few days later, Beck himself saw one, walking ahead of him along

Supplement
to
The Lane County Leader

VOL. XV   COTTAGE GROVE, OREGON, APRIL 7, 1904   No. 51

SIXES WILD MAN AGAIN.

Visits the Cabins of Miners and Frightens the Prospectors.

At repeated intervals during the past ten years thrilling stories have come from the rugged Sixes mining district in Coos County, Oregon, near Myrtle Point, regarding a wild man or a queer and terrible monster which walks erect and which has been seen by scores of miners and prospectors. The latest freaks of the wild man is related as follows in the last issue of the Myrtle Point Enterprise: The appearance again of the "Wild Man" of the Sixes has thrown some of the miners into a state of excitement and fear. A report says the wild man has been seen three times since the 10th of last month. The first appearance occured on "Thompson Flat." Wm. Ward and a young man by the name of Burlison were sitting by the fire of their cabin one night when they heard something walking around the cabin which resembled a man walking and when it came to the corner of the cabin it took hold of the corner and gave the building a vigorous shake and kept up a frightful noise all the time—the same that has so many times warned the venturesome miners of the approach of the hairy man and caused them to flee in abject fear. Mr. Ward walked to the cabin door and could see the monster plainly as it walked away, and took a shot at it with his rifle, but the bullet went wild of its mark. The last appearance of the animal was at the Harrison cabin only a few days ago. Mr Ward was at the Harrison cabin this time and again figured in the excitement. About five o'clock in the morning the wild man gave the door of the cabin a vigorous shaking which aroused Ward and one of the Harrison boys who took their guns and started in to do the intuder Ward fired at the man and he answered by sending a four pound rock at Ward's head but his aim was a little too nigh. He then disappeared in the brush.

Many of the miners avow that the "wild man" is a reality. They have seen him and know whereof they speak. They say he is something after the fashion of a gorilla and unlike anything else either in appearance or action. He can outrun or jump anything else that has ever been known; and not only that but he can throw rocks with wonderful force and accuracy. He is about seven feet high, has broad hands and feet and his body is covered by a prolific growth of hair. In short he looks like the very devil.

Chittem Bark Claims in Demand.

A correspondent at Greenleaf, Lane county writes as follows:

"Chittem claims" are in demand, and a good many homesteads are being located where there are canyons containing the tree, the object being to peel the bark and abandon the claims, as there is no valuable timber on them, and they are of no value as homes under present conditions.

One man who has squatted on a claim in a canyon debouching into Chickahominy creek, is peeling the bark with a drawing knife and drying it in his cabin. He hired 1600 pounds hauled to Eugene a couple of weeks ago and sold it for 9 cents a pound, though by this process of peeling much of the inner bark is lost, so that the bark is not of the best quality

Early newspaper clipping with information on Bigfoot activity in Western Oregon, April 1904.

a narrow trail high above the canyon. He was hunting at the time and carrying a rifle. He promptly shot the creature in the back. It turned on the trail and fell into the canyon. He did not see it again. That night and for several nights afterwards the cabin was the target of showers of rocks that fell on its roof and against its walls from the surrounding trees. Beck said that he and his companions rushed out with guns several times to see who or what was throwing the stones. They saw and heard nothing. As soon as they went inside the stoning started again and after a few nights of this, unnerved, they left the cabin and returned to Kelso.

Subsequently a group of men formed an expedition and went into the canyon to find the "giant apes" that Beck and his companions reported. They found nothing. The canyon, which appears to have been unnamed prior to the incident, was then given the name Ape Canyon and this is the name under which it is marked on all maps to this day.

Beck told me that he never returned to the canyon and that the mining claim was abandoned. He did not know, when I talked with him in 1960, what had happened to the other members of his 1924 party. He seemed to me to be honest and to be telling a true account of something that actually happened.

Early in 1961 I visited the canyon with two friends, Monte Bricker of Portland and Shearn Moody of Galveston, Texas. We planned to spend a week in the canyon and to search it from end to end. Unfortunately after only one day Monte had an accident. He scalded his foot in a pot of hot water on the camp fire and had to be taken out. Shearn Moody and I returned later and flew the canyon in a helicopter and still later I walked it out, from end to end. It is a wild, somewhat inhospitable area, and when I was told recently that it was "probably young boys, out for a lark," who were responsible for the stone-throwing in 1924, I could hardly suppress a smile. I was also informed, again recently, that it was well known that a local man had been responsible for the footprints in Ape Canyon in 1924. But what he was doing away out there in the wilderness, and who or what the creature was that Beck claims to have shot, is still unexplained. Someone

Map of Mount St. Helens area showing Ape Canyon.

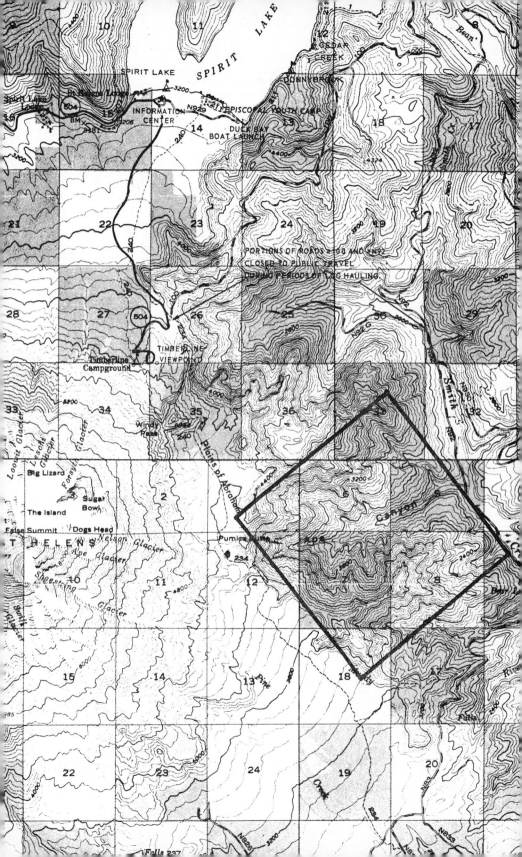

LOCATION NOTICE

KNOW ALL MEN BY THESE PRESENTS, That _Fred Beck_
P. O. Kelso Wash

.....................the undersigned citizen.... of the United States, ha......

this _18_ day of _Sep._ , 192_2_, located and claimed

and by these presents do.......locate and claim. by right of discovery and location. in compliance with the

Mining Act of Congress. approved May 10, 1872. and all subsequent Acts, and with local customs, laws and

regulations, _1500_ linear feet and horizontal measurement on the _Surface_

.... lode, vein, ledge or deposit along the vein thereof, with all its dips, angles and varia-

tions, as allowed by law, together with _300_ feet _east_ side

and _300_ feet on the _west_ side of the middle of said vein

at the surface, so far as can be determined from present development; and all veins, lodes, ledges or

deposits and surface ground, within the lines of said claim _600_ feet running _south_ from

center of discovery shaft, and _900_ feet running _north_ from center

of discovery shaft; said discovery shaft being situated upon said lode, vein. ledge or deposit, and within the

lines of said claim, in _Spirit Lake_ Mining District _Skamania Co_

described by metes and bounds as follows, to-wit:

COMMENCING at this discovery post, being the center of the vein or claim, and upon which this Notice

is posted; thence _South_ feet _600_ , to a post marked _South_ center end; thence

west feet _300_ , to a post marked _S.W._ corner; thence _1500_ feet

north , to a post marked _N W_ corner; thence _300_ feet

east , to a post marked _north_ center end; thence _300_ feet _east_ , to a

post marked _N E_ corner; thence _1500_ feet _south_ to a post marked _S E_

corner; thence _300_ feet _west_ , to _south_ center end.

This claim is further described as follows: _this notice being about
80 feet north from discovery shaft
ledge running along the canon dive_

This claim to be known as the _Vander White_

Discovered _August_ , 192_2_   _Fred Beck_ {SEAL}
Located _Sep 18_ , 192_2_   .... {SEAL}
    Witnesses: .... {SEAL}
Marion Smith   .... {SEAL}
....   Locators........

Copy of the mining claim of Fred Beck in Ape Canyon, the Vander White Claim, dated September 18, 1922.

LEGEND OF APE CANYON

The Mt. St. Helens area is said to be inhabited by large, hairy, ape-like creatures.

In 1924, a group of miners working a mine on the east side of Mt. St. Helens returned to their homes in Longview with stories of being attacked by mysterious apemen. It seems that while in their cabin "huge creatures being at least seven feet tall and covered with long black hair" showered them with large boulders. The next morning they encountered the creatures and shot at them. One of the creatures was believed slain, but its body rolled over a cliff and into a deep ravine, destined to be known as Ape Canyon.

Searching parties were immediately mobilized from the Longview area to visit the mountain region to seek out the headquarters of the apemen. These parties, however, found no trace of the apemen but did find the cabin with huge boulders around it and the inside torn to shreds.

Gorg Totsi, editor of the *Red American*, a weekly Hoquiam publication, published an explanation of the legend of the apes several years ago. He said these creatures were the ferocious Selahtik Indians, a tribe of renegade marauders, much like giant apes in appearance, living like animals in caves in the High Cascades.

Ape Canyon is located on the southern end of the Plains of Abraham. From Timberline Campground, on Mt. St. Helens' north side, follow Timberline Trail #240 over Windy Pass to Pine Creek Trail #234. Follow Trail #234 south for two miles.

The legend of Ape Canyon and the incident with the miners in 1924 is today included in official U.S. Forest Service literature.

Byrne (left) and fellow Bigfoot searchers hiking the hills near The Dalles, Oregon.
Credit: Nicholas Bielemeier.

Map of west side of Vancouver Island showing Muchalat Inlet and the site of the
Indian Village of Nootka and also the Conuma River.

might, one day, come across the bones of Fred Beck's "mountain devil" as he called it. But it is doubtful, after all this time. The remains of the cabin are still there and were seen in 1972 by some "Bigfoot searchers." And somewhere close by is the old mine shaft. So the cabin was there, the mine was there, and I believe Fred Beck and his worthy companions were there. As to whether the Bigfeet were there and were responsible for the vengeful stone-throwing is a matter that must remain, for the time being, or at least until someone goes in there and finds and digs up the bones of Fred Beck's "mountain devil," a mystery.

II

A Look at the Present

The exact answer to the origin of the genus homo has yet to be found but I believe that it will be found in the relatively near future.
—RICHARD E. LEAKY, speaking at Foxcroft School, Middleburg, Virginia, March 1975

THERE ARE MANY MORE fascinating accounts of Bigfoot encounters from the late 1800s and all the way through to the present day—too many to tell here. Some of them are told in detail in other chapters of this book. For others perhaps a brief mention will serve.

The following report* comes to us from Mr. and Mrs. Robert L. Behme of Magalia, Butte County, California:

BIGFOOT SIGHTED ABOVE PARADISE, BUTTE COUNTY, CALIFORNIA

You may be interested to know that my husband and I have seen what we believe to be a Bigfoot in Butte County, California. To our knowledge, nothing of this nature has been seen here before.

On April 16 (1969) about midnight, we were driving along the road from Paradise to Stirling City. The surrounding country is thickly wooded, well watered and criss-crossed by deep canyons. As we drove around a long curve our headlights shone on what appeared to be a man in a fur suit, crossing the road. For one moment we had a front view as he turned toward the car, then walked into the darkness. Our impressions are that he was over six feet tall, completely covered with short, black hair which seemed to be flecked either with white hairy patches or mud. His face was white and hairless although the features appeared as a blur. The eyes did not glow in the light as would the eyes of an animal. The head was small and came to a peak at the top. He was heavily built with particularly heavy legs. He did not run, but shuffled away with a definite limp, once turning his head to look back at our car. The following morning I returned to the area to look for footprints

*Credit Mr. George Haas, of Oakland, California.

55

but could find nothing. The ground near the road is rock, gravel and hard clay.

We have lived in this area for nearly ten years. My husband is a writer and photographer specializing in outdoor stories for such publications as *Field and Stream* and *Sports Afield*. I mention this with the hope that you will believe we are reasonable people, not given to hallucinations brought on by the novelty of a back-woods road at midnight. Naturally we have given a great deal of thought to what it could have been, other than Bigfoot. A bear is out. There are bears in Butte County, but all are smaller and do not cross highways on their hind legs—especially when one is apparently sore. The idea of a hoax occurred to us. Chico State College is about thirty miles away and this is the sort of involved trick that might appeal to college students, except that on a week-night, during a non-hunting or fishing season, at midnight, this is a very lonely road. The chances of a motorist passing until morning are slim. We even thought of the possibility of someone bent on robbery expecting that a motorist would stop at such an apparition. But again the lack of traffic makes this very unlikely.

By Mrs. Robert L. Behme

A woman who lives in The Dalles saw a Bigfoot on the road that runs up the Klickitat Valley in Washington, in 1969. It was night and the creature seemed to be standing still while she passed. A deputy sheriff of The Dalles Sheriff's Department saw one on the Wind River in Washington in 1959. He was fishing at the time and watched it approach him through the trees· and then, on seeing him, turn and walk away. A young man doing fire watch service at one of the fire towers in the Timothy Lake area in Oregon saw one in 1970. It was early morning and the Bigfoot was walking up the road toward the tower. Suddenly it turned off the road and walked into the trees and was not seen again. Two young men, summer camping in an area near The Dalles, saw one just before dawn one morning. Small, falling stones awakened them and they looked up to see it standing on a bank above their heads. They had a shotgun, so they fired at it in fright and then ran for their lives. Apparently they missed, for no carcass was found. A deputy sheriff of the Greys Harbour County Sheriff's Force saw one walking along a forest road in 1971. He stopped his patrol car and watched it for a few minutes, before it turned off the road and walked into the trees. A logging contractor watched three of the creatures digging for rodents in a rockpile in the high mountains near Tarzan Spring, in the Clackamas River watershed, near Estacada, in Oregon. The trio consisted of a male, a female and a young one. The male did most of the work, lifting rocks weighing more than three-hundred pounds while digging. With Tom Page and Dennis Jenson, associates of the Bigfoot Information Center in The Dalles, Oregon, I visited the area of the incident in 1972. We saw the hole in question and counted many other holes in the high broken ridges above the Clackamas River. A brief study of the rodents of the area showed them to be marmots, which would hibernate in the winter, at the time the logger said he saw the Bigfeet.

Two fishermen saw a Bigfoot swimming across a lake, one of the small lakes near Priest Lake in northern Idaho. Its arms were underwater and so they were unable to see just what stroke it was using to propel itself through the water. It climbed out of the water, shook the water from its arms only and then disappeared into the lake grass. This was in 1970. Four young people, traveling in a car to Portland early one morning in 1969, saw one sitting on a high rocky bluff near The Dalles, Oregon. They stopped the car, got out, and watched it for four or five minutes. It was still sitting there when they left. The time was just after five in the morning. The president of a heavy equipment company in Portland saw one while fishing in northern California in 1960. He was with a companion and they became separated. He heard noises in the brush and looked up to see the Bigfoot walking through some small pines about thirty yards away. Apparently it had seen him for it was already walking away. The pines, young trees in a plantation, stood about six feet in average height and the head and shoulders of the creature showed clear above them. Later, when he looked for his companion, he found that the man had returned to camp. His companion later told him that he had wished to continue fishing but had an uncanny feeling that he was being watched. He grew uneasy and had returned to camp alone.

Many of the reported sightings have been subjected to intensive investigation, by scientists and laymen associated with the Bigfoot Information Center in The Dalles or by independent groups of part-time searchers and investigators. Instead of coming to an end, as they might do in the face of annoying scrutiny if they were hoaxed, the incidents have continued. Each year has produced its quota of both sightings and footprint findings and to date the number of sightings has remained constant at an average of about four a year. The record shows five for 1971, three for 1972, four for 1973, four for 1974 and three for 1975.

The Bigfoot Information Center, the central office of the present search and investigation project in the Pacific Northwest,* has now expanded its activities to include a Bigfoot Board of Examiners, a group of trained and experienced Bigfoot investigators whose task it is to examine all reported incidents in the Pacific Northwest and then submit their findings to the Information Center. In addition the Center has increased its associate membership. Its loose-knit group of watchers and reporters living throughout the northwest now numbers over one thousand. For an indication of the rapidly expanding activity of the Center and its research team, both the full-time team working from The Dalles and the associate investigators, one has only to look at the number of reports that were received and investigated by the Center in 1974. The record number that were reported and investigated by the team does not necessarily indicate an increase in the actual number of incidents. Rather it shows that the expanding word of the Center has reached out to people previously unaware of its existence and of the fact that there is now an established clearing-house where their stories, no matter how far-fetched they may sound, will be given serious and confidential processing. In the year 1974, on learning about the Center, people who had been shy about their sightings or other findings, or who had been held back by the fear of ridicule, came forward and informed the Center researchers. In all cases their findings were investigated and even where the reports turned out to be negative, e.g., bear prints, or even large human prints, or, in the case of two sightings, large roadside tree stumps seen by car lights at night, the Center researchers made sure that all reports were given at least some attention and that the people who provided the information were properly thanked for coming forward as they did.

*Sponsored by the Academy of Applied Science of Boston, Massachusetts, and the International Wildlife Conservation Society, Inc., of Washington, D.C.

One of the first sightings in 1974 took place while winter snow still lay deep on the ground. Just west of The Dalles the freeway, Highway 80, carrying traffic east and west between Portland and Pendleton, sweeps past the cluster of houses and trailers that is Rowena. At four o'clock on a freezing morning in mid-January, Deputy Sheriff Harry Gilpin, of The Dalles Sheriff's Department, was concluding a routine patrol. He was heading east towards The Dalles and driving at approximately sixty mph as he approached the big highway sign that signals the exit to Rowena. While he was still about 150 yards from the sign, he saw, in the extreme limits of the patrol car headlights, something which he described as "very tall, probably about seven feet," close to the center of the highway and the steel center rail that separates the double lanes of the east-west traffic. It looked vaguely like a man and it was walking away from the center rail, to the north. Gilpin, who is skeptical about the existence of the Bigfeet, is not certain at all what it was that he saw. He will not state definitely that it was a Bigfoot. He admits that he was tired and that whatever it was, it was already moving out of the limit of his patrol car headlights when he saw it. But he is puzzled as to what a man would be doing on the freeway at that hour. A very tall man. On a very cold morning.

The next report that we received at the Center came from Florence, a little fishing town west of Eugene on the Oregon coast. Late in the evening of March 8 one of our younger associates, Mike Kuhn, of The Dalles, called to say that there had been a sighting at Florence that morning, by a schoolboy. He gave us details that included the schoolboy's home address and telephone number. The boy's name was Nick Wells, age nine, and we called his mother and talked with her. She confirmed that her son claimed to have seen a Bigfoot that morning while on the way to school. She said that she honestly believed him to be telling the truth. She added that some of the other schoolboys, his companions, claimed to have found footprints. I left at once, taking with me Celia Killeen, co-editor of the *Bigfoot News* and my assistant at the Center. The distance to Florence is about three-hundred miles and we drove most of the night, arriving there at eight-thirty the following morning, our trusty* Scout loaded with camping gear and provisions for a week.

We found the Wells' home and interviewed Nick, the boy who said that he had seen the Bigfoot. It was a Saturday and, school being closed, he agreed to accompany us to the place where the incident occurred. Nick told us that the previous morning, at about 8:45, he had seen a large, brown, hairy figure walking in the heavy scrub that fringes the road near the school. He said that the creature stood about six feet in height and was moving slowly. When it saw him it stopped, growled at him, and then moved on. It did not chase him, as subsequent newspaper reports claimed, but simply walked into the deep brush. Nick told us that he took one look and ran for his life, and his schoolteachers later confirmed that he arrived at the school white-faced and panting. We searched the area Nick indicated, and found only shoe prints. It appeared that during the midday break from school, the previous day, some fifty or more boys had come down to the area to "see the Bigfoot." Any footprints that the creature might have made were long buried under an army of shoe impressions. We camped in the area for three days and searched the sand dunes north and south of Florence and the mud flats on both sides of the Siuslaw River. All that we found was some of the densest brush ever seen, the penetration of which, in the inevitable and constant coastal rain, made the Florence incident a memorable one. Later, assessing the sighting, we were of the opinion that the boy told the truth about the sighting and that he very probably did see a Bigfoot. The Siuslaw River cuts through the coastal range at Florence and the country north and south of the township, within the coastal mountains, is mostly heavily timbered and devoid of human habitation.

About a month after the incident we received a note from Mrs. Wells thanking us for our visit and for a copy of our report, which we had mailed to her. She enclosed with her note a most interesting letter, from a Mr. C. E. Dixon, of Bremerton, Washington, to young Nick Wells. Mr. Dixon

*An International Harvester four-wheel-drive Scout. I.H. Scouts are used exclusively by the Information Center teams in their search and investigation work in the rugged country of the Pacific Northwest.

wrote that he had never seen a Bigfoot but that he had seen tracks in the same area, in 1905. The letter, written in a fine strong hand, said that in April of 1905, the year of the Lewis and Clark Fair, he and a companion were in the vicinity of Florence, mainly to have a look at the ocean, which neither of them had ever seen. They had walked "twenty miles by trail to Florence" and there obtained the help of an old Indian, Indian Charlie, to get them across the mud flats. It was in the flats close to the present site of the town, that they found several sets of huge "humanlike" footprints. At that time they had never heard of Bigfoot and so they put them down as grizzly prints. What puzzled them was the size of the tracks. They had no measuring tape and so they cut a stick and later measured the stick. The tracks were eighteen inches in length and there were no claw marks. Mr. Dixon concluded his letter by telling Nick, "Even if your Bigfoot should turn out to be a grizzly, that is something to brag about, for the grizzly is supposed to be extinct in this country."

Twice during the summer of 1974 an Indian boy, night fishing for sturgeon in the Columbia, claimed to have seen a Bigfoot. Both occasions were in the very early morning, just after first light, and both took place just east of Stevenson, Washington, close to the first tunnel through which the Stevenson–White Salmon road runs. The Bigfoot, we were told, was seen standing in the shallows, up to its waist in water and motionless. On each occasion, when sighted, the creature had left the water and retreated into the bushes. Searches of the area by Information Center investigators produced no footprints. But on each occasion strong Columbia gorge winds had smoothed the dry summer sand and both searches took place more than a week after each claimed sighting. After the sighting we kept the area under periodic surveillance. No further sightings have been reported in that area into 1975.

The *National Observer* for Thursday, August 22, gave the author a birthday present with a report of an unusual sighting in British Columbia. The story ran as follows: "Wayne Jones still isn't sure what it was that he says he saw standing next to a building at his boys' camp on Harrison Lake up in British

Columbia one night a few weeks ago. It looked somewhat human, it walked on two feet, it had a rounded head with large ears, it stood nearly eight feet tall, and its whole body, except face and hands, was covered with hair." The story went on to say that the new sighting was another "tantalizing piece in a puzzle for [Peter] Byrne, who has been looking for the storied Bigfoot in the Pacific Northwest since 1970."

We heard of the incident at the Information Center three days after it happened. We probably would have heard of it sooner, but Wayne Jones, the young man who claimed the sighting, did not talk about it to reporters and asked his fellow directors at the camp to keep the matter quiet.

We were fortunate at that time in having one of the Center's more active researchers, Stuart Mutch, working on some other leads about one-hundred miles away toward the coast. We immediately contacted Mutch and asked him to fly into Camp Dunbar and investigate the incident.

Camp Dunbar is a British Columbia government-operated camp for emotionally disturbed children. It lies on a peninsula of land at the north end of Harrison Lake, a long narrow lake north and east of Vancouver in southern British Columbia. Access to the camp is by boat, via the lake, or by plane, to a narrow landing strip in the camp. The purpose of the camp is to provide quiet and peaceful surroundings, in a natural setting of woodland and water, as part of the rehabilitation program for children with emotional problems. Situated as it is in an isolated place, the camp has few visitors and the setting is one that is generally regarded by the government as conducive for and totally suited to the ideals and objects of the program.

Our investigator, Mutch, flew into Camp Dunbar to interview Wayne Jones, the director who claimed the sighting. He learned that Jones had been sitting by a campfire in the evening, about nine. Suddenly a Bigfoot had appeared out of the heavy forest behind his campfire. It walked slowly toward the fire and then stood and looked at him. Jones kept quite still. The creature, manlike in stance and in facial appearance, was in view for perhaps three or four minutes. At a distance of about thirty-five feet it stood and watched Jones and the fire. It did not appear to be threatening. It made no aggressive movements. Its face, Jones said, was curiously human and not at all apelike. Suddenly, some of the camp's children came running through the trees. The Bigfoot turned and moved quickly toward the edge of the forest. It moved into the forest and disappeared. Some of the children saw it. Later, some footprints were found.

Mutch flew into the camp a few days after the sighting and talked with one of the camp directors. Jones was not in camp at the time. When he landed a dozen or so of the children came up and surrounded the plane, talked to him and told him about the incident. But Mutch also noticed two men, and a little later a third, standing back along the edge of the airstrip, holding high-powered rifles and watching him. None of them approached and Mutch became apprehensive. Later he learned that they were there to hunt and kill the Bigfoot. They were Canadians, from Harrison Hot Springs and from Richmond. Why they were allowed into a camp of emotionally disturbed children with loaded high-powered rifles, to hunt and kill something that had done no harm, had not threatened anyone, and had not even frightened any of the children, was not clear. Mutch stayed for a short time and then flew out. He did not see any of the footprints and thus the full value of the sighting is not determined at this time. However, Jones' story is generally believed by the other camp directors and his reputation as an employee of the British Columbia state government is believed to be high.

Not far from The Dalles, but in Washington state, north of the Columbia, is the little township of Willard. Willard has a timber plant with one of the last sluice or water transporters in this country, down which the mill shoots its cut timber to a second plant, twenty-five miles away on the Columbia. Northeast of Willard is a small campground called the Oklahoma Campground. In mid-August a fisherman from White Salmon, a young man just a few weeks out of the army, drove up to Oklahoma Campground and then walked north a short distance to where a stream runs parallel to the campground road. The campground itself is set in the heart of the rugged country that is the central Cascades, and north of it the road comes to an end. The young man planned to spend a day fishing and he picked an area with which he was familiar, that he had known since boyhood. He turned off the road

63

and started to walk down to the stream. On the opposite side of the stream was another road that had been severed cleanly by the stream, leaving a jutting fragment of roadway that ended abruptly at the stream's bank. On this roadway, right on the edge, according to the fisherman, squatted a Bigfoot. The young man stopped, took one look and then turned and ran for his car. As he turned he saw the Bigfoot rising from the ground and starting to walk away. The frightened fisherman reached his car, jumped in, locked his doors, and drove wildly for Willard and the nearest telephone. From Willard he telephoned the Sheriff's Office in Stevenson. The deputy who took the call promised to investigate and later two deputies went to the area. They found nothing and a subsequent investigation by Information Center investigators also produced nothing. However, the young man's story had a ring of truth to it and it is indeed possible that it was a Bigfoot that he saw and that its reaction to him was exactly the same as his reaction to it, a fast exit into the deep forest of the mountains north of the campground.

The general pattern of Bigfoot sightings and footprint findings is centered in the coast ranges and the Cascade Range of the Pacific Northwest and the coast ranges of British Columbia. This is what is known to the cognoscenti of the Bigfoot fraternity as the First Area of Evidence, or Area I. For a hundred and fifty years this pattern has seldom changed. When it has, when evidence of Bigfoot activity in other areas has appeared, it has been restricted to what is called Area II and this restriction is one that is confining and definite. Area II includes only south central and southwestern British Columbia and one area of north central Idaho. There are no records in the files of the Bigfoot Information Center, either from sightings or from footprint findings or other evidence, of any *credible* Bigfoot activity outside of these areas. Within Area II evidence is sparse. Idaho, in spite of its wild and rugged mountains and wilderness areas, has produced no evidence for nearly ten years, and southern British Columbia has produced very little. One of the few recent sightings reported to us at the Center from Area II took place in southwestern British Columbia in 1974. It was reported to us by a young couple who must, at their own request, remain nameless but who personally came to the Information Center's Exhibition in The Dalles and told us the story.

They were driving at night, just north of Castlegar in British Columbia, a town not far north of the Washington border. The weather was clear and visibility was good. As they came around a corner on the Castlegar–Silverton highway, they saw a huge, dark brown or black, hairy figure standing on the edge of the hardtop. Both occupants of the car saw it at the same time and both were shocked at what they saw. They were adamant in their description that the creature was not a grizzly bear. They saw its arms, clearly, hanging by its side and they saw its head, well-rounded and not at all bearlike. The creature stood perfectly still as they passed. They did not stop. They did not turn around and go back. Theirs was an eerie feeling, seeing that giant lonely creature standing solitary on that bleak roadside. They felt, with a gentle philosophy which we admired, that perhaps it was best left alone.

The large-scale map that hangs in the Bigfoot Exhibition in The Dalles includes the states of Washington, Oregon and Idaho. Clearly marked, with red and yellow markers, are all of the sightings and footprint findings that the Information Center has recorded and investigated in the last four years. The markers range out of northern California and follow the mountain chains into southern Oregon. From there they divide, as do the mountains themselves, soon after they pass the California border. The northwest mountain range that flows into Oregon splits in two at this point. A line drawn east-west through the city of Eugene marks the end of the main range and, in the upper drainage of the great Willamette River valley, the chain breaks east and west, one arm becoming the coast range and the other the Cascade range. The lines of markers that indicate the range of the Bigfeet also divide at this point. (Indeed, if they were to continue up and into the heavily populated valley of the Willamette, with its farms, road systems, cities and industrial areas, we would be very skeptical about them.) One line of markers is seen to continue through the Cascades, staying close to the high backbone of the east-west watersheds, out of which grow mountains that are place names to Oregonians, like Bachelor, the Three

Sisters, Jefferson, Hood. Crossing the northern border of Oregon they continue into the Washington Cascades, passing between and around Mt. Adams, Mt. Saint Helens, Mt. Rainier and Baker. From there they leave the United States and merge with the coast ranges of British Columbia. The second set, the western set as they might be called, lie in the heart of the coast ranges and they dot the chain all the way through Oregon and into Washington until they eventually wind into the Olympic Peninsula and come to an end hard against the San Juan Straits.

The Olympic Mountains have had their share of sightings and footprint findings, and the Exhibition map shows a dozen or so pins that mark incidents and findings reported to the Information Center over the years. One such sighting was reported in the Olympics late in 1974. Two young men from Port Angeles, Richard Taylor and Larry Followell, were doing some night driving on the Hurricane Ridge Road, not far from Port Angeles. Taylor thinks that he saw the creature first. Perhaps if Followell had seen it quicker he might not have crashed. As it happened, he saw it when there seemed no way to avoid it. It was close to the center of the road and it was a matter of swerve and avoid it or hit it head on. Followell swerved, left the road, hit a big rock and wrecked his car. Both men finished up in the nearby Olympic Memorial Hospital with injuries and both swore statements of the sighting to local police. Olympic Park Rangers went to the scene of the incident to search for any sign of the Bigfoot. No footprints were found, but this was not surprising for the ground was frozen hard. The month was December—deep winter in the Olympics.

Of all the sightings that took place in 1974 probably the most extraordinary, certainly one of the most exciting to the research team, was a double sighting that took place in the Hood River National Forest, about thirty miles west of The Dalles, in July.

Jack Cochran, forty-three, lives in Parkdale, in the Hood River valley, in Oregon. By profession he is a logging crane driver. He is married, with a family. In his spare time Jack is an artist in the field of woodcarving and his models of animals, bears, deer, and men, are fine examples of the woodcarver's art. In his community at Parkdale, Jack is regarded as a man of standing and integrity. Living not far from Jack, on the road between Mount Hood—a small roadside community—and Parkdale, is Fermin Osborne. Fermin is a logger by trade, age about fifty-five, married, with a family, and originally from Tennessee. He has lived in the Hood River valley for about fifteen years and is regarded in his community and by his employers as a man of reliability and honesty.

On the day of the first sighting Jack Cochran and Fermin Osborne were working at a logging operation on Fir Mountain, a 3000-foot hill in the Hood River National Forest about twenty miles south of the town of Hood River. They were concluding the work of an operation that had cleared an area of about five acres. With them at the time was one other man, age twenty-two, named J. C. Rourke, also a resident of the Hood River valley. The weather was clear and the hillside on which they worked, with an eastern exposure, was beginning to take the full light of the morning sun. Jack's job at this time was to lift broken logs and debris into piles for subsequent burning and at the time of the first incident he was working with his crane and seated in a cab with glass windows, about fifteen feet above the ground. There was considerable noise from the crane machinery and from the crash of the falling logs as they were dropped into piles. Jack's companions, Rourke and Osborne, were working to his left and a little behind him.

While the huge steel jib of the crane was swinging across his front, Jack's eye suddenly caught sight of a figure, standing at the edge of the trees that fringed the clearcut area of the logging operation, at a distance of about sixty-five yards. Jack Cochran has sharp eyes, for when he is not woodcarving, or working in the forest, he spends his time hiking and hunting. The figure caught his attention because there should not have been a figure there. One of the things that a crane driver has to be most careful of in his work is people, and a professional crane man always has his eye peeled for his co-workers. A false move with the ponderous loads that a big logging crane swings through the air and a man can be crushed in an instant.

The first thing that Jack did when he saw the figure standing at the edge of the trees was to look back for his two co-workers. He quickly ascertained that they were both where they should be, behind him and well clear of the crane. Who then was the fourth "man" and what was he doing there? To shade his eyes Jack swung the boom of his crane up and to the right, blocking the sunlight that was streaming in from his left. Then he saw the figure more clearly and when he did he slowed his engine and stepped out of his cab.

The figure was manlike and was standing quite still, seemingly watching the crane and its operation. It was dark in color and except for the face the general pattern of color that covered the whole body was uniform. The body itself was massive, with broad, muscular shoulders and it seemed to stand about six to six-and-a-half feet in height. Its covering appeared to Jack to be thick black hair and its arms hung by its sides. While he watched, the Bigfoot—which Jack immediately guessed it to be—turned and walked slowly into the woods. It put one arm up against a tree as it passed, presumably to balance itself. Jack saw it move into the trees and then turn to the right and disappear. He did not see it again. He described its movement as smooth, flowing, like the movement of a big man in fine physical condition. The other two men did not see it.

Next day, at about the same time, the working conditions were repeated. Jack Cochran was in his crane cab and Fermin Osborne was working with his young companion, J. C. Rourke, some distance away. This time, however, Jack was keeping a sharp watch on the edge of the trees. He knew what he had seen and he wanted to see it again if he could. Again it was a warm day and the increasing heat of the morning sun eventually persuaded Osborne and his companion to take a break from their hot and dusty work. They sought the edge of the trees and, leaving the clearcut area, walked into the shade of the forest edge. The place that they chose was about fifty yards west of where Jack Cochran had seen the Bigfoot the previous day.

Osborne was in the lead as they entered the edge of the tree line, with Rourke close behind. Suddenly, just ahead and to the left, they saw a huge shape rising out of the bushes and starting to move away from them and toward the left. There is a slope in the trees at this point, with dense coniferous growth and a carpet of pine needles and stick debris. The creature moved up the slope and Osborne saw it clearly, for there is almost no undergrowth in this particular area and the dark, tall, manlike figure stood out clearly to his view. His companion, Rourke, behind him, did not have as clear a view as Osborne did but he also saw the figure.

Osborne, as befits a working logger from Tennessee, is basically a simple man, with a simple man's understanding of nature and things natural. His description of what he saw amply illustrates this fact. He does not pretend to know exactly what it was that he encountered in the Fir Mountain forest. He describes the creature as being about six feet in height, covered with thick black hair and with massive shoulders and body. The legs were very thick and, under the hair, he thinks, very muscular. The creature walked upright. At no time did he see its face, for it walked away from him and did not look back. It walked with a smooth but rapid stride and Osborne was surprised at the speed with which this stride began to take it out of his range of vision and away from him. It made no sound and there did not appear to be any smell from the creature. It did not run, but within a few seconds it had reached the top of the slope and begun to move down the other side.

The reaction of most people who encounter a Bigfoot seems fairly standard. The usual pattern is one of shock, surprise, often followed by near-panic and rapid flight. That this is quite unnecessary seldom matters to the witness. That the Bigfeet have never harmed anyone, or even threatened anyone, is quickly forgotten in the shock of the sightings, and all that one remembers is what Hollywood and the slick magazines and the comic books have told us about gorilla-like monsters that tear men to pieces and carry women off to a fate worse than death. Osborne's reaction was quite different from the norm, and he did something that—as our records show—no one else has ever done. He saw that the creature was moving out of range and he wanted to have a better look at it. So he ran after it, leaving young Rourke standing open-mouthed at the edge of the trees. He reached the top of the hill as the Bigfoot started to move into the dense scrub on the other side and, perhaps to vent his frustration at not getting a better look at it, or perhaps to try and make it turn, so that he could see its face, he picked up two big rocks and threw them after it. It did not turn and he did not see its face. It simply passed quickly into the scrub and out of sight and he did not see it again.

Later, all three men were questioned about the sighting by investigators from the Information Center accompanied by visitors to the Center, among whom were David and Jane Hasinger of Philadelphia, and Nicholas Bielemeier, an associate of the Center and a professional photographer from Hood River. Jack Cochran, in his account of the sighting, gave a clear and precise description of what he saw and of how he saw it. He is fairly sure that what he saw was a Bigfoot. He cannot think what else it might have been. It was certainly not a bear and it was not a man. And it was not a deer or a mountain lion or an elk, the only other large animals that one might find in the Fir Mountain area. Jack is a man with extensive experience in the Cascade forests and he is not a man to make a mistake on something like that, an opinion which is confirmed by many who know him in the Hood River valley.

J. C. Rourke is not sure of what he saw. He says, in all honesty, that he did not see it clearly enough to be able to state, definitely, that it was a Bigfoot. He did see something, of that he is sure, but what it was he does not know.

Fermin Osborne's account of the incident is straightforward and simple. He does not know that the creature he saw was a Bigfoot. He does not know what it was. In fact the actual words that he used to describe it to us, in our interviews with him later, were, "some kind of a goddam monster." But he is sure that he saw his "monster," that it was there, flesh and blood, real, live and not anything that he had ever seen or heard of in the woods to that day.

Our investigation of the incidents was as thorough as time and money would allow. We went to the area with all three of the men and spent many hours examing it. Then we camped in the area and searched it for a week. We saw where the creature had walked. There were heavy scuff marks and

70

indentations in the soil and on the slopes of the hill in the forest. We saw the boot prints where Fermin Osborne ran after it and we found the two hollows in the soil where he picked up the rocks that he threw at the creature. We found some broken sticks and we saw stones, embedded in the soil, partially dislodged in their sockets by the weight of a soft but heavy foot. All of us who interviewed the men, including David and Jane Hasinger, were convinced that they were telling the truth and that they did indeed see a member of the species that has come to be known as Bigfoot, on that sunny summer morning, on Fir Mountain in the Hood River National Forest.

The year 1974 also produced its quota of footprint findings. During the summer months and into the fall, three sets were found. One set was found by a group of girl hikers in the Three Sisters mountains, in the Oregon Cascades. Another set was found high on Mount Jefferson, just north of the Three Sisters, by an engineer from Pascoe, Washington. A third set was seen and examined by forest workers north of Mount Adams in Washington state. All three sets were reported to the Information Center by associates of the Center, and photographs and casts were examined by members of the Center and of the Bigfoot Board of Examiners.

There are many more examples of encounters with the Bigfoot. But the ones described in this chapter are of particular interest because in each case the people involved were interviewed by researchers from the Center and in most cases the actual place of the encounter was also searched, examined, and photographed. Where the examinations produced evidence that thoroughly supported the account of the witness and if the incident was of recent date, extensive searching was carried out in the area of the incident. In some cases, as in these descriptions, the names of the witnesses were released to the public and the press. In others, where the witnesses did not wish to have their names made public, the policy of confidentiality that is maintained by the Information Center was strictly maintained.

As to the other, the literally hundreds of sightings and footprint findings that have come into the Information Center in The Dalles, some of them are undoubtedly farfetched. But many of them appear to be genuine accounts of actual happenings or real finds. Whatever credibility one may allow them, the odd thing is that there is so little variation among the accounts, in the basic description of the subject matter. Basically the subject has been a large, fully haired, upright-walking, man-like figure. Color description has varied, of course, as have height estimates. But there the variation ceases and one cannot help thinking that if all of the stories, all of the accounts from the early 1800s onwards, were imaginary or simply fabricated, there would be a wider and consequently less credible area of description. No one has ever seen one walking on all fours, for example. Why not? If the account is going to be of something that one has imagined, why *not* have him, or it, walking on all fours? Surely the story will be just as believable—probably it will actually sound more believable—if the storyteller has his imaginary creature on all fours. Why have him, or it, so uninterestingly tame and dully shy? Why not aggressive and dangerous, charging on sight and uttering savage growls and snarls? Surely a huge, hairy, gorilla-like creature would be expected to act like this and surely this is the description that one's listeners would expect and would find most exciting in a story about an encounter? If one is going to be so bold as to say that one has actually encountered a Bigfoot, surely one is not going to spoil a good story with a dull and unconvincing account of a shy giant that simply turned and walked away and did nothing. This is not what the modern audience wants at all. This is not the stuff of which legends are made.

But, oddly enough, this is all that the audience is liable to get in an account of a Bigfoot incident. In the 160 years of Bigfoot history and in all of the accounts that are not included in this book but which go to shape the historical background of the phenomenon, all of the stories have a sameness, a repetition that, were the subject matter not so interesting, would make them dull reading indeed. Looking back at them one cannot help thinking that the authors of these fanciful stories, creating them as they did out of their own imaginations and with all of the license that imaginative storytelling allows, were singularly lacking in creative wit. Unless, of course, unbelievable as it may seem, the stories are all true.

III

From the Bizarre to the Believable

*Rivers . . . 'tis rivers are the friend of
the hunter as well as a safe spot for
the savage when he's afraid of rocks
and shadows.*
—ALFRED HORN (Trader Horn),
Johannesburg, South Africa, 1927

DENNIS JENSON* AND I HAD BEEN down in Hoopa, California, and a bright fall day in October 1971 saw us driving up Highway 199 in southern Oregon on our way back to base in The Dalles. We stopped briefly in the little townlet of O'Brien, not far north of the California border, where I mailed some letters. O'Brien consists of a post office-cum-gas station, a cafe, and a few houses back off the highway. I remembered coming in there once in 1960, during the first searches, and stopping for a coffee at the cafe. The waitress was talking about Bigfoot, as were so many people in those days. I asked her if she knew anything about it, or had ever seen one or spoken to anyone who had seen one. No, she had never seen one. No, she had never met anyone who had. And as far as she was concerned the whole thing was ridiculous. Why, she added, there was even some crazy Englishman cruising around the country with one of them science fiction dart guns, trying to find one. She had read about him in the papers. His name was Brin, or Bruin, or Burn, or something like that. We left O'Brien and drove our worthy Scout on up 199 and that evening made camp on the north bank of the Illinois River in southern Oregon, about half a mile back from the highway in a small sandy flat with scrub timber and clumps of tall river grass. It was a pleasant campsite, with clean fresh water in the Illinois and ample driftwood for a

---

*Dennis Jenson, 35, of Marcus, Washington, has been a field worker and associate of the Bigfoot search project since 1971.

cooking fire and, later, a camp fire. The evening was clear and dry and the air had that crisp feeling to it that says winter is coming. A few deer moved in the scrub around the campsite and the only sounds were the occasional rumble of a truck on the highway and the calling of night birds. We drank a little scotch together, cooked and ate our dinner, and afterwards sat at the fire with mugs of coffee and talked about the Bigfeet.

Jenson had, at that time, more field experience than any-one else in the Bigfoot search and his accumulated knowledge of the general subject, and of the people associated with it, was considerable. He had many interesting stories to tell of his experiences when he worked with Roger Patterson after the 1967 film incident (see Chapter VII) and of his own background. Some of them were quite serious and some of them hilarious. Even the serious ones, interspersed as they were with Jenson's escapades with the fairer sex, had their amusing sides. Once, visiting a farmer who was to be inter-viewed in connection with a sighting, Jenson arrived at the farmhouse to find it empty. It was a hot summer's day and so, instead of waiting in the sun, he walked into the barn, crawled up into the hayloft, and went to sleep. He was awakened by the farmer's bosomy daughter about an hour later, forking hay down for the cattle and, incidentally, nearly sticking Dennis with the pitchfork in the process. He ex-plained that he had come to see her father and talk to him about the recent incident near their farm. The young lady listened to his story and then took him up to the house to meet the old man. The old man, a crusty backwoods farmer of the Washington coast range, took one look at Jenson's Levis, with hay sticking out of them at every point and his daughter's hair, also full of hayseed from the forking, and reached for the family shotgun. Jenson fled.

We talked late that night, hunched over the driftwood fire, and climbed into our sleeping bags on the river sand, as a thin moon sank across the Siskiyou Forest to the west. But before the fire died Jenson brought another name out of his hatful of experience. It was the name of a man who lived not far from where we were camped and he thought, as I did when I

74

recalled the name myself, that it might be worth visiting him. The name was Flumpf.

Next morning we set out to try and find Mr. Flumpf. We drove into the town of Wonder and then backtracked to Selma. There was a gas station owner in Selma who knew Flumpf, and from him we obtained directions to Flumpf's cabin in the woods west of Selma. A few hours later we found the cabin and sure enough Mr. Flumpf was at home.

I forget what it was that we had heard about Flumpf. Something to the effect that he had had an experience with a Bigfoot or that he knew something about them that others did not. In any case whatever it was seemed to be worth investigating and so here we were at his cabin, about three miles back in the Siskiyou Forest.

As we entered the wooden garden gate, a small man with bright piercing eyes who had been sitting on the verandah, came down to meet us. It was Flumpf. He asked us what we wanted and when we told him that we were doing an investigation of the Bigfoot mystery—a full-time serious investigation—he stopped and looked at both of us very closely. For a moment no one spoke. Then he leaned forward and in a near whisper said, yes, we had come to the right place indeed, for no one could tell us the things that he could tell us about the Bigfeet. Jenson and I glanced at each other as we followed Flumpf to the verandah of his house, where he bade us to be seated. Mr. Flumpf then told us about the Bigfeet, the Bigfeet as he knew them and as surely no one else did.

The Bigfeet were from Venus, he told us, and they came and went quite regularly in Venusian rocket ships. They came to earth to rest, on a sort of R&R basis and they usually came in small family groups. He, Flumpf, was in constant communication with them, not only in the woods surrounding his cabin but also with the Venusian headquarters and the rocket ship base. As owner of the local land and the only person living in the woods for some miles in any direction, Flumpf had been taxed with the job of looking after the visitors, keeping them happy with small food offerings and protecting them from the curiosity of strangers to the area. The present family, he told us, looking across at the densely wooded hillside opposite his cabin, was a case in point. They indicated that they liked certain types of food and not everything that he left for them. They had met with him half a dozen times since their arrival and they had explained a difficulty that they had in which he might be able to help. This was to find a husband for their unmarried daughter. She was about eighteen and, Flumpf said, just about ready to take a husband. Flumpf had indicated to them his willingness to be a candidate in matrimony, should a suitable mate not be available elsewhere. The prospective bride, we gathered, was not uncomely and, according to Flumpf, had indicated to him her pleasure at the proposal. How she had done this Flumpf did not actually say.

The rocket ships landed and took off on the sand flat in the river below his house. This was also where he met the families and where he put out the food offerings. There was another ship due in very soon and Flumpf was at this very moment standing by for a radio signal from the Venusian rocket base with its arrival schedule.

People have asked me, from time to time, what has been the hardest part of my search, the most difficult time, the one that put the most strain on me. I answer without hesitation, having an Anglo-Irish sense of humor, that it is often in trying to keep a straight face in circumstances like these. We did, on this occasion, manage to get to the gate and into the car before we collapsed, but Jenson, at other times so dependable, behaved very badly on this occasion. Somehow, while we were listening to Flumpf on the verandah, he slowly managed to move his chair, inch by inch, until he was in a position behind and to the left of the speaker. From there his face could not be seen by Flumpf but it could be seen by me and while Jenson closed one eye, both eyes, scratched his ears, pursed his lips and contorted his mouth in a long apelike series of silent guffaws, I was unable to do anything but keep a blank face. It was most unfair.

We concluded our visit to Mr. Flumpf with what we thought was a professional touch. We did go down and look at the sand bar behind his house, where the rocket ships allegedly landed. Alas, we found no Venusian footprints, no scorch marks from flaming rocket tubes, and no outer space beer cans or other galactic debris.

Albert Ostman, of British Columbia, has a rather different story to tell of his adventures with the Bigfeet. Ostman insists that he was picked up and carried away by a Bigfoot, to a Bigfoot lair, one night in 1924.

Albert Ostman is now in his mid-eighties. At the time of his experience he was thirty-four. He was a logger, or lumberjack, and indeed this is the trade that he followed all his life. In that year, 1924, he decided to take a little vacation and go prospecting. He chose Toba Inlet and he went there on a Union Steamship boat, disembarking at Lund. There he engaged the services of an Indian who canoed him to the head of Toba Inlet.

The Indian told Ostman many stories about gold brought out by a white man from a lost mine that supposedly existed at the head of Toba Inlet. This white man spent a great deal of time drinking in saloons, but he never seemed to run short of ready cash—he would just make a short trip to his mine and come back with bags of gold. However, he went back to the mine once too often, and he was never seen again. There were those who believed that a Bigfoot had killed him. Ostman had never heard of Bigfoot at that time, so he inquired of his Indian guide what they were like. The Indian told him, "The Sasquatch are big people living in the mountains."

Ostman was not inclined to believe the Indian's story, putting it down to legend and superstition, but the Indian assured him that, though the Bigfeet were few in number, they did indeed exist.

Ostman and his guide made camp at the mouth of a creek at the head of Toba Inlet. The Indian ate with him, but insisted upon setting out for Lund that same night, with the tide. Ostman told him to return in three weeks' time, that he would be waiting in the same spot.

Next morning, Ostman set out on a northeasterly route, looking for a deer trail into the mountains. He took his 30-30 Winchester rifle, a pick that had an axe on its other end, and his pack. The pack contained cans of sugar, salt, and matches, a side of bacon, a bag of beans, some prunes, pancake flour,

canned goods, hardtack, a quart sealer of butter, three cans of snuff, and shells for the rifle. He cached some of his food so that he would have it when he returned, rolled up his sleeping bag, together with some cooking utensils, and set off.

He climbed through the mountains until midafternoon, when he came to a place that was flat, sheltered, and had good water. It was quite high up, and he had a beautiful view out over the foothills and the water. He prospected there, but found nothing.

The next day was like the one before—Ostman found a lovely campsite, and, as he was tired, decided to spend several days there. He had just settled down into what he intended to make his permanent camp, when things began to happen.

The first night, his equipment was disturbed, but nothing was taken. Ostman dismissed the disturbance as the work of a porcupine, and thought no more about it. He went prospecting during the day, shot and cooked a squirrel for his supper, and settled down for the second night.

In the morning, his pack had been emptied out, and some prunes and pancake flour were missing. Now Ostman was curious. He found no tracks, but he knew that the culprit could be neither a porcupine nor a bear, since a porcupine could not have reached the pack, and a bear would have made more of a mess.

The third night, Ostman determined to find out just what was playing merry hell with his belongings, so he arranged everything just so, closed the pack, and climbed into his sleeping bag fully dressed, except for his shoes, which he put into the bottom of the bag. He kept his rifle close by, fully intending to stay awake to catch the intruder.

Some time during the night, Ostman says, he was awakened by something picking him up bodily and carrying him off, still in his sleeping bag. He was unable to get out of the bag, nor could he reach his knife and defend himself. He could feel the rise and fall of the ground, so that he knew when his captor was going up or downhill. At one time, Ostman was dragged along the ground. He was carried thus for about three hours. Then he was unceremoniously dumped out on the ground and, emerging from the bag, he found himself con-

Toba Inlet, on the British Columbia Coast, scene of the Ostman incident.

fronted with four large Bigfeet, who stood around him chattering to each other.

At first, while it was still dark, he could not see them clearly. Then, as the dawn came out of the east, he was able to examine these curious creatures. The Bigfoot group, according to Ostman, consisted of a large male, a large female, and two smaller specimens that Ostman called children. They looked like humans to him, rather than apes. In fact, Ostman used the word "people" in referring to them. He thought that the young ones ("a boy and a girl") seemed frightened of him, and that the large female did not seem overjoyed to see him.

The male, he says, was about eight feet tall and barrel-chested, with huge arms and legs. He had what seemed to be exceptionally long forearms and large hands with short fingers. The fingernails were short and broad and he was covered with hair all over, as were the other members of the family. The only parts of the body that were bare of hair were the soles of the feet, the palms of the hands, the nose, and the eyelids. He estimated the weight of the male at over 700 pounds, and the female at close to 550 pounds.

Ostman stayed with the family for several days. The male had taken Ostman's pack along, so he had plenty of food (including all three cans of snuff) and he was quite comfortable, except for wondering how he would elude his captors. He was able to walk around the Bigfoot habitat—an area of about eight or ten acres, Ostman thought—and he discovered the sleeping quarters of his jailers. It was like a cave in a tree, the floor of which was covered with moss, and Ostman could see several items that seemed to be blankets, woven of cedar bark and packed with dry moss.

Ostman began to make friends with the young ones, in hopes of enlisting their assistance in an escape attempt. By the sixth day, the young male was quite at ease with Ostman, watching him cook and eat his food, and showing quite a bit of interest in his snuff-taking. He weighed about 300 pounds, and had a large chest (Ostman estimated it to be fifty to fifty-five inches). His jaws were wider than his forehead, and his hair was about six inches long all over. He was very agile; one of his favorite pastimes was to grasp his feet with his hands and bounce along on his hind end, apparently attempting to see how far he could go.

At last the older male, who had prevented Ostman from leaving at one point, began to show some interest in the snuff. After watching Ostman for some time, he reached out and took the snuffbox from him. Apparently thinking that it contained food, he emptied its contents into his mouth and swallowed it.

Within a few minutes, the Bigfoot was in extreme discomfort, rolling on the ground and screaming in pain. Ostman determined that this was his chance for escape and, taking his rifle, he made for the opening in the canyon wall. The female attempted to come after him, but he fired a shot over her head and she ran back to the lair. He got away and, after several days of wandering, managed to reach a logging camp on what is called the Salmon Arm of Sechelt Inlet. From there he made his way back to Vancouver.

There was a great deal more detail in Ostman's original account of his experience and, to my way of thinking, the more detail there is, the more believable a story is. Ostman was subsequently asked to make a statement before a Justice of the Peace and he did this—to support his story and to convince others that he was telling the truth—at Langley, British Columbia, in August, 1957, before Lieutenant Colonel A. M. Naismith, J. P. He was then interviewed by the same magistrate, who, in a separate statement, said that he found Albert Ostman to be in full possession of his mental faculties, of pleasant manner, and with a good sense of humor. Naismith added that, after examining Ostman, he was left with the impression that Ostman certainly believed the story himself and that his examination and cross-examination failed to bring out any evidence to the contrary.

Is Ostman's story true? Personally, I think that if we are to allow that the Bigfeet exist, then it could be. The discovery of a live Bigfoot that matches Ostman's description of his captors will prove that he has told a true story. Curiously enough, his description matches very closely the figure that is seen in the 1967 footage made by Roger Patterson. And it was given by him, in writing, in 1957, some ten years *before* the Bluff Creek filming.

IV

A Nervous Afternoon for the Welch Brothers
A Disturbed Meeting at The Dalles
A Nasty Fright on a Lonely Road

*When you have eliminated the impos-
sible, whatever remains, however improbable, must be the truth.*
—SHERLOCK HOLMES to his
Immortal Companion, Dr. Watson

IN THE PRECEDING CHAPTER we have looked at two
Bigfoot stories. The first one is usually good for a laugh or
two when told in detail. The second is different. Its age
precludes a thorough investigation and all that I can say is
that people who have interviewed Albert Ostman believe him
to be telling the truth. Ostman, on request, signed an affidavit
in the presence of a magistrate who subsequently noted that
he appeared a sane and sensible person. In this chapter we
deal with three more stories. They are simply three accounts
of sightings that I have picked out of the many hundred that
are on file at the Information Center in The Dalles. All three
have been exhaustively checked, and interviews with most of
the people involved in them have been recorded. This compre-
hensive checking system, a part of the daily routine of the
Information Center, in these three cases gives them a ring of
truth that is hard to ignore.

The first story is about two mining prospectors, Canadians,
who in 1965 found themselves in wild mountain country at
the head of Pitt Lake, in British Columbia, looking for minerals. Ron and Loren Welch worked for a large mining concern and their job was to locate mineral sources and stake
claims on them for their company.

The country to the north of Pitt Lake is rugged and
inhospitable. Many stories have come out of the area of lost

mines, of impassable gorges, and of men who have gone in there and disappeared, never to be seen again. Pitt Lake itself is a body of water subject to sudden and violent storms and it has drowned many people. Generally speaking it is not a country for amateurs.

But the Welch brothers were professional prospectors and their knowledge of survival in the wilderness was born of many years of experience. They were not the kind of men to go into the British Columbian wilderness unprepared, just as they were not the kind of men to imagine something like a Bigfoot. Theirs was a hard-headed approach to a profession that did not allow for flights of fancy, did not allow for anything, in fact, but hard work and plenty of it.

One afternoon they were trekking northeast, close to the shores of a small lake. There was snow on the ground and the lake was frozen. There was light timber in the area. The weather was clear, with a thin sun and no wind. They stopped to rest and have a smoke, taking off their packs and placing them against a rock. They sat for a while and were smoking and talking quietly when one of the brothers noticed a movement among the trees about a hundred and fifty yards away. Both brothers looked up and saw, standing and watching them, a very large, hairy, dark-coloured man-like creature.

The creature, they said, simply stood and watched them and they gained the impression that it was as curious about them as they were about it. The only movement that it made was with its arms, which hung down by its sides and which swung slightly as its body swayed a little. It seemed to be about eight feet tall and very heavily built. It seemed to have almost no neck. It was thickly covered with hair all over, and the color was a uniform, dark brown, almost black. The face seemed to be hairless, but it was difficult to say at the distance at which they saw it. The backs of the hands seemed to be lighter in color. They were either less hairy or the actual hair on the backs was a paler shade.

The brothers kept quite still and they say that they watched the creature, as it watched them, for probably several minutes. Then suddenly it turned and walked away, its massive body quickly disappearing into the trees. They did not see it again but later that day, when they came back through

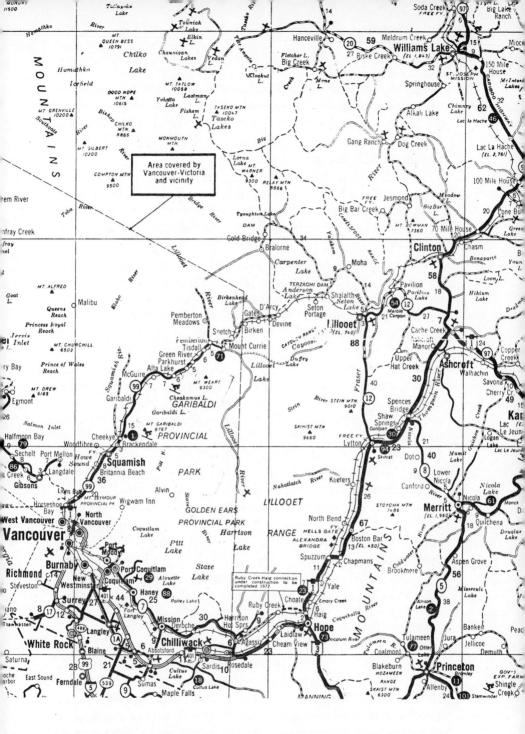

Map of Pitt Lake area, British Columbia, where the Welch Brothers claim their sighting of a Bigfoot in 1965.

the same area, they were nervous at the thought of meeting it and instead of taking the same route back they walked out on the frozen ice and down the middle of the lake. The ice was thick enough to bear their weight but not, they hoped, strong enough to bear the weight of Bigfoot.

Next day, still working in the same area, they found a set of footprints. The prints were old and melted out to a length of twenty-three inches. They found a second set of ten inches in length. The second set came to and went from a small lake where the ice had been broken and the snow swept back. The hole was four or five feet in width and quite like one that the International Wildlife Conservation Society (I.W.C.S.) team found in a lake in northern Washington in 1971.

The Welch brothers returned to their homes in Vancouver and Victoria and for a while kept quiet about what they had found. They knew that people would view their story with great skepticism, but it was difficult not to talk about it, and after a while it leaked out. For a few days nothing happened; then the *Vancouver Sun*, a large-circulation newspaper of some influence in British Columbia, called one of the brothers about the sighting. Both brothers had agreed not to talk to the newspapers and now the problem arose about publicity. Eventually the persistent *Vancouver Sun* agreed to a compromise. If they could have the story they would not print the brothers' names. They got the story but their reporter quite frankly did not believe it. The brothers suggested that he fly out to the area and have a look at the footprints but the newspaper balked at the cost of chartering a helicopter. Annoyed at the skepticism of the newspaper and its staff, one of the brothers offered to pay for the charter of the helicopter. The *Sun* agreed and a few days later one of the *Sun's* reporters flew with one of the Welch brothers to the area. There he and the helicopter pilot saw the footprints. By this time they were melted out and deformed by wind and sun effect. But the reporter returned satisfied with his story and satisfied with the integrity of the two men. The *Sun* subsequently published the story and there the matter came to an end. The Welch brothers have never returned to the area of the sighting, and to the best of my knowledge there have been no organized expeditions or searches for what they saw

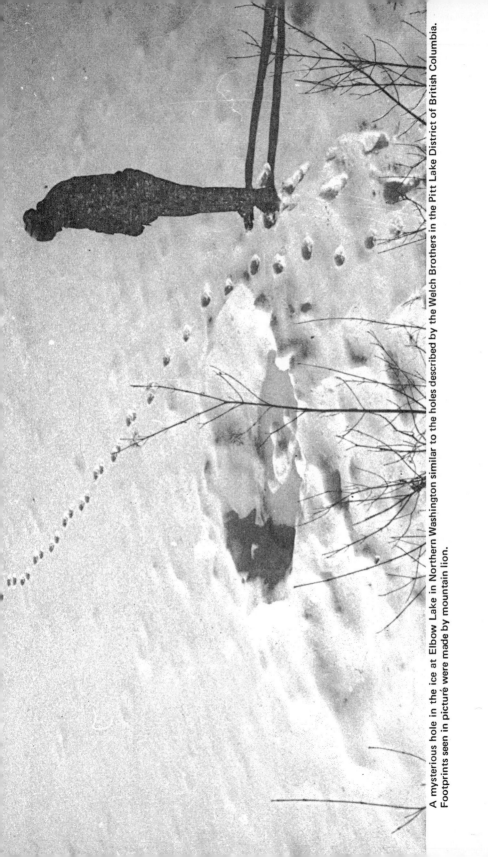

A mysterious hole in the ice at Elbow Lake in Northern Washington similar to the holes described by the Welch Brothers in the Pitt Lake District of British Columbia. Footprints seen in picture were made by mountain lion.

in those rugged ranges of the Garibaldi mountains, to the north of Pitt Lake.

The Dalles is a town of some ten thousand people lying on a bend of the Columbia River, in northern Oregon, about eighty miles east of the city of Portland. It was originally called Les Dalles. The word "dalles" is French and means stepping stones, or flagstones, and it presumably referred to the flag-like stones that lay across the bed of the Columbia River at this place and which can still be seen just below The Dalles dam today. The name was given to the area by early French settlers and traders working the Columbia River. History records that the first settler in The Dalles was a Frenchman named Joseph Lavendure. He arrived in 1847. He left again in 1848 and settled in California.

The Dalles is the county seat of Wasco County and so it houses all of the bureaucratic offices that are normally found in the principal town of a medium-sized county, including state, county, and city police. There are the normal number of schools, shops, clubs, churches, garages, and motels that one finds in the average American town of this size. There is even that fast-disappearing institution, a shoe shine shop, owned and operated by an elderly Greek who dispenses a mixture of gossip, wisdom, and small philosophy for all comers at twenty-five cents a time.

The Dalles has a reasonably moderate climate but summers can climb into the 100s and stay there for days and winter snaps can be as cold as northern Washington, where I spent an icy first winter in the United States. Lewis and Clark, the explorers, and David Thompson, the Northwest Fur and Trading Company agent of Bigfoot note, passed through the present site of The Dalles in the early 1800s but there were no permanent settlers in the area until 1847. After the establishment of Fort Lee a town began to grow and by 1852 there was a small and expanding community. A charter was granted to Fort Dalles, as it was called, in 1857. Soon after the name was changed to Dalles City and later still to The Dalles. The city had the first newspaper between the Missouri River and the Cascades, the *Journal*. By the late 1800s The Dalles was a flourishing community.

Wood carving of a Bigfoot in Willow Creek, California.   *Credit: Russ Kinne.*

Today the city is pleasant and quiet. The town has many old wooden houses that lend it a certain charm and dignity and the mighty Columbia, flowing quietly through the bend on which the town is situated, reminds one of the colorful past that is the history of northern Oregon. There are a few Indians in The Dalles now, but the tribe—the Celilo—that once lived on the bend of the river and fished its waters for salmon and sturgeon are almost all gone. They called the Columbia the Wauna, a beautiful word that is somehow more fitting than its present name. In years gone by the Celilo fished the Wauna with hand nets and salmon was a major part of their diet. The building of the dams at Bonneville, Cascade Locks and The Dalles put an end to their livelihood on the river.

The city of The Dalles lies on the northern border of Oregon, and the Columbia River is the borderline between Oregon and Washington. The area of Washington that lies to the immediate north of The Dalles is mostly open pastureland with sweeping hills that climb west and north to the Cascades. Almost due north is Mount Adams, a mountain that the Indians called Klickitat. The name means "galloping horse" and said quickly, three times, the word does have the ring of galloping hooves. The ranges that run out of the southern watershed of Klickitat are called Rattlesnake Ridge, Toppenish Ridge, and Horse Heaven Hills. East of The Dalles is generally open country that runs all the way to the Wallowa Mountains, the home of Chief Joseph of nineteenth century fame. To the south is more open country, wheat land and farming land with a scattering of small towns that include Dufur, Shaniko, Antelope, and Madras. West is the gorge of the Columbia and it is a deep and spectacular gorge, with three- to four- thousand-foot walls in places and many beautiful waterfalls whose long white plumes pour through the dense green foliage of the hillsides. It is also a funnel for the wind that rushes in, sometimes for days on end, onto the flat-bottomed valley that holds the city. Some old timers jokingly call The Dalles "Windy City II."

At the eastern end of the city is a long, flat hill about 800 feet in height, variously known as Strawberry Hill, Raspberry Hill, or Table Mountain. Half a mile short of this hill the city comes to an end in a sprawl of trailer courts and sales lots, garages and some farmland. The eastern slope of the hill contains a quarry owned by Arlie and Jack Bryant, father and son partners in a rock crushing business. On the west side of the hill is an abandoned asphalt plant owned by two brothers, Howard and Stanley Stinson. Land on the top of the hill is divided in ownership between these two families and a third owner, Ernie Kuck. The land to the west, below the hill, land that stretches for a thousand acres west and south, is owned by a Mr. and Mrs. William Marsh. The Marshes, long-time settlers in The Dalles, with land ownership going back several generations, call their land Hidden Valley and their one thousand-odd acres is mostly basalt rock and stunted oak tree country, with short grass and shallow ravines that hold deer, pheasant, quail and, occasionally, bear. There is some water here and there in small springs.

Fringing and enclosing the northwestern edge of this whole area is a hill that is called Crate's Point. It is named after John Crate, one of the first settlers in the area, a Hudson Bay Company man who married an Indian girl and by her fathered a large family, some of the descendants of which still live in the area today. This hill begins at the river, crosses The Dalles to Portland Freeway, crosses the old highway, and then climbs rapidly to a height of 2020 feet. The lower reaches of this hill are rocky and bare, with sparse grass and scattered small oaks. There is much rock, broken and tumbled, and in places there are narrow, shallow ravines. On the western edge of the hill there is a high cliff that drops sheer to the old highway and a series of man-made terraces that hold a dozen or so trailer homes. As the hill climbs, the vegetation increases, and on the crown of the hill is a dense growth of oak interspersed with clumps of scattered pine. The pine mostly fringe the very top of the hill and one can see in their twisted and bent shapes the force of the wind that rushes down the Columbia gorge and unendingly assails the hill. The older maps of the area show a small town, high up on Crate's Point Hill, called Ortley. But Ortley is long gone, deserted, and today there is nothing left of it but a couple of buildings used for machinery storage by Mr. and Mrs. George Johnson, who own the hilltop land. Oldtimers say it was the eternal wind

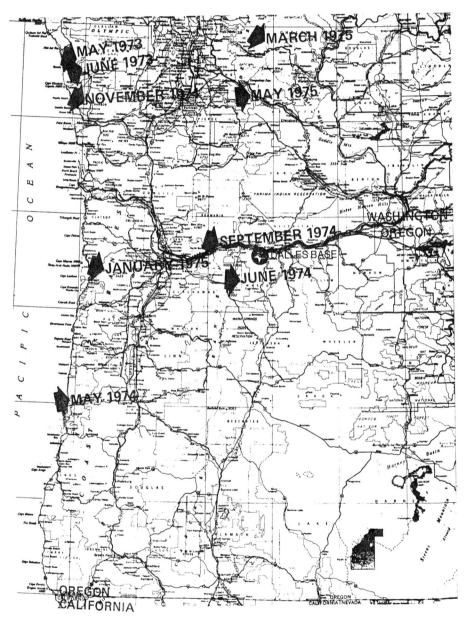

Map of Northern Oregon showing location of The Dalles in relation to Portland, Washington State, etc.

92

Pinewood Trailer Court and the area in The Dalles where the 1971 sightings took place.
Credit: Russ Kinne.

that drove the people of Ortley out of their homes and down to the warmer and less windy climes in The Dalles.

Between the land enclosed by Crate's Point Hill and Table Mountain and roughly facing the center of it, situated on the old highway and lying between that highway and the main freeway, is a trailer court. It is called the Pinewood Trailer Court, and it consists of a couple of dozen trailers, a swimming pool, some rather ragged flower beds, and an office.

In midsummer, 1971, on a fine afternoon with bright sunshine and a clear sky, the three businessmen-owners of the trailer court were having a meeting in the trailer court office. The time was about three-thirty and all three were deeply engrossed in the affairs of the trailer court, when one of them happened to look up and see a Bigfoot walking among the rocks in the meadow directly opposite the office. It was, apparently, clearly visible through the trailer window.

The meadow that lies opposite the trailer court is about 400 yards in length, roughly east to west, and 200 yards in width, roughly north to south. The old highway, also called the Rowena Highway, borders the north side of the meadow and the south side is bounded by a cliff of broken basalt rock about fifty feet high. The area has thick grass and a scattering of small oak trees. The rock cliff is broken in several places that allow access for the nimble-footed to the upper meadows, the larger areas that stretch all the way down into Hidden Valley. The cliff itself comes to an end almost opposite the trailer court office and it was at the end of this cliff, walking among the broken rock, moving slowly, seemingly slightly bent over, hesitating, appearing, disappearing, and finally going from sight behind the end of the little cliff, that the three businessmen from Portland saw what they believe was a Bigfoot.

The Sheriff's Department of The Dalles, headed by a man of many years' law enforcement experience, Sheriff Ernie Mosier, is an efficient, well-run organization. In the matter of the Bigfoot and the investigation being headquartered in The Dalles, I would describe the general attitude of the department as interested, helpful, cooperative, and open-minded. Among the deputies who took a particular interest in the Bigfoot phenomena and in our investigation in 1971 were Richard

94

Carlson, Jack Robertson, Larry Tillinghusen, and Bob Hazlett.

The man usually assigned by the department to investigate officially the reports of Bigfoot footprints and claims of Bigfoot sightings, was, in midsummer, 1971, Deputy Richard Carlson. Carlson is intensely interested in the Bigfoot phenomenon and this interest spurred him to offer and supply much help to my investigating team. Backing the interest was an open-minded attitude toward the phenomenon, an attitude that befitted an intelligent officer of a law enforcement agency. On June 2, 1971, Deputy Carlson wrote a routine report for the Sheriff's Department. The report reads as follows: Wasco County Sheriff's Office, The Dalles, Oregon. Date: 6.2.71. Subject: Alleged Sighting of Bigfoot. Officer's Report, Rich Carlson. The report describes how Carlson, after hearing of the sighting supposedly made by the three men, called them in Portland. He spoke to Dick Ball, Jim Forkan, and Frank Verlander. All three made statements to the effect that they had seen what they thought was a Bigfoot. Verlander in particular was adamant about what he saw. He told the deputy that he definitely saw it, that it was very large, very wide, and probably close to seven-and-a-half or eight feet in height. Forkan and Ball confirmed the story.

In this same week, in The Dalles and more or less in the immediate area of Crate's Point, other people made similar claims of sightings. There was a maintenance man at the trailer court, one Joe Mederios, who said that he saw it twice. There was a music teacher and his wife, Mr. and Mrs. Richard Brown, and two others. All gave very much the same description, the only difference in agreement being on height. But all said that it was very tall, and no one thought that it was under six-and-a-half feet.

One of the part-sponsors of my investigation at this time was Tom Page of Ohio, businessman and member of the Explorers Club. Page was intrigued by The Dalles sightings to the point where he decided to fly out and take part in the interviewing of the people concerned. He called to tell me that he was bringing his attorney with him, Mr. Wayne Newton, a trial lawyer from Mentor, Ohio. Page wanted to have Newton talk with some of the witnesses and gauge the credibility of their stories.

The three of us drove to Portland to talk with the owners of the Pinewood Trailer Court. Frank Verlander, for reasons of his own, refused to see us, but Jim Forkan and Dick Ball allowed us several hours of interviews and were most cooperative and helpful in telling us their stories. We interviewed each man separately and taped most of their conversation. Wayne Newton did most of the questioning and proved himself to be an astute, quick-thinking, and highly intelligent man. On our return to The Dalles we also interviewed the Browns, who at that time lived at the trailer court. Before Tom Page and Wayne returned to Ohio, we managed to add to the list two other people who claimed sightings, one of them Bob Gimlin, partner in the 1967 footage event.

Later we sat down to analyze the results of our talks with The Dalles group. We read our notes again and discussed the sightings for many hours. The gist of our findings was this: that we, all three of us, were reasonably convinced that Dick Ball and Jim Forkan and their companion Verlander—although we did not personally hear his account of it—saw something that might have been a Bigfoot. The "something" that they saw was man-like in appearance, walking upright, seemingly quite large, grey or dark grey in color. They saw it at a distance of between 260 and 270 yards and they watched it for approximately twenty seconds. The sighting was in good light and both Forkan and Ball had some experience in hunting and with Pacific Northwest wildlife. When interviewed they were quite sure, for instance, that it was not a bear that they saw, or any other animal. Again, their experience of the outdoors persuaded them to admit, in all honesty, that they were not absolutely certain what it was that they saw. It looked to them like a Bigfoot or at the least what they imagined a Bigfoot would look like. But we were quite satisfied with the truthfulness of their story, even if the nonavailability of one member of the party, Verlander, did detract somewhat from its completeness.

Tom Page and Wayne Newton were not able to interview Joe Mederios. (He had left the trailer court when they arrived in The Dalles, but I had seen him soon after the sightings that he claimed and I was satisfied with his truthfulness. I believe that he saw something but, as with the Portlanders, what he saw is another matter.) They were able to interview the Browns, however, as I have already mentioned and on the analysis of the results of this interview we did have a division of opinion. Newton was not satisfied with the Browns' story. There was detail in it that he did not like, detail that did not fit in with the sighting. To him it lacked credibility. But Page and I were reasonably well satisfied, as was Jenson, later. We believed their story to be truthful and we think that they gave us a true account of having seen something. Whether it was actually a Bigfoot is another matter. In their case, the sighting took place in the evening, with poor lighting conditions that could have induced error.

The first year of its investigation, the I.W.C.S. team was based at Evans, Washington, close to the Canadian border. For the second year we moved to The Dalles, in Oregon, not so much because of the sightings that supposedly had taken place in the area as for its strategic location. The Dalles is on the edge of the main Cascade range, and through a network of roads the range is accessible to the north, west, and south. The town is also on the extreme northern border of Oregon and is thus equidistant between the state of Oregon, to the south, and the state of Washington, to the north. It is also, because of its position, halfway between British Columbia to the north, and northern California to the south, all supposedly Bigfoot habitat area, as suggested by the pattern of evidence. Geographically, The Dalles makes an excellent base for an investigation that must cover all of this vast area.

What we were concerned with at The Dalles and what we considered a most important part of our investigation of the alleged sightings, was the reason, or reasons, why a creature like a Bigfoot would come there in the first place. All wild creatures have a natural reason for whatever they do and the reason is usually a simple one, like the need for food, seasonal migration, mating urges, et cetera. We felt that if indeed it was a Bigfoot that the various witnesses claim to have seen at The Dalles, that there must be a very good reason for its coming there. We also felt that if we could discover this reason, that we would be making a great step forward in our search for the truth.

There is some food in the general area of Crate's Point, in

97

the meadows and higher up on the hill itself. Jenson and I found wild cucumbers growing in patches in June and July of 1971. There were also wild potatoes and wild onions on the hill. But there was very little else and what there was hardly seemed enough to attract a large primate.

We looked for other reasons. An ancient river crossing place? An ancient route, from the south, along the ridges that run east of Mount Hood? A migration route? A meeting place? A mating area? None of these seemed to fit and the reason, was, simply, the character of the vegetation of the area. All wild creatures need cover. They need it as much as they need food and water. The mole has his tiny tunnels and grass-covered runways. The elephant has his forests. The tiger his grass jungles. In particular the big primates need cover and one has only to look at the habitat of gorilla, or chimpanzee, or orang, to see this. But The Dalles, at least the area where these sightings supposedly took place, has almost no cover. The forests that roll all the way from the coast, the great stretches of coniferous trees, come to an end at the top of Crate's Point Hill. From there on, down across the meadows of Hidden Valley, up over Table Mountain, into The Dalles itself and then on beyond The Dalles for more than a hundred miles, the land is almost bare of cover of any kind. There are ravines with scrub timber, patches of oak and small trees. But there is no real cover, the kind that a large, shy, wild creature, be it White-Tailed Deer or Bigfoot, must have.

Just west of The Dalles there is ample timber for cover. It grows right down into the deep gorge of the Columbia River and it provides protection for all kinds of game. Again, the river is actually narrower in several places west of The Dalles, if one is thinking of routes that might go to crossing places. There is also more food in the heavily forested areas to the west, much more than at The Dalles. There are many other factors that have to be taken into consideration, for all of them have a place in the "Why The Dalles?" puzzle, a puzzle that still, after all this time, has us wrinkling our brows. Jenson's solution, "It's probably just sentiment. He just likes to come every year and sit and look at the river from Crate's Point," I find unsatisfactory.

The third story takes us to British Columbia, and thinking

of the area which produced the story I am taken back to the high ranges of the Nepal Himalaya. Deep in the heart of the peaks that the Nepalese called the Mahalangur Himal—the mountains of the great monkeys—there is a high and permanently frozen pass. The wind whistles through it for three hundred and sixty-five days of every year and the temperature never rises far above zero. A British expedition, with grim humor, named it Brass Monkey Pass and if the reader does not know why they gave it this name, I suggest that he take a trip there and spend an hour or so on the pass. He will quickly find out.

When the winter winds blow up the gorge of the Checkamus River in southwestern British Columbia and you have been huddled for ten hours on some bleak rock, watching for a sign of a Bigfoot, you know what the British were thinking when they named their Himalayan pass.

As any outdoorsman knows, each mile per hour of wind speed means one degree less of temperature. When the temperature is already close to zero and the wind is blowing twenty knots, only bears, madmen, and Bigfoot searchers go out in the midday freeze. The weather was like this when I first went to the Checkamus, in December 1971, to examine the place where William Taylor, highway maintenance foreman for Squamish area, British Columbia, almost ran into a Bigfoot one bitterly cold afternoon in the winter of 1971.

Bill Taylor has now been transferred to another area of British Columbia, but at the time of the incident his headquarters and his home were at Pemberton, about a hundred miles north of Vancouver. On the afternoon in question, at about three o'clock, Taylor was driving north towards Pemberton. He had been down to meet a man coming up from Squamish with spares, and was now on his way back to Pemberton. About six miles south of Alta Lakes, the main Pemberton–Vancouver highway runs east of the Checkamus River and about a thousand feet above it. Along the river, also on the east side of it but much lower and closer to the river, runs a railway line. There is a sharp curve in the road, below which the railway line crosses the Checkamus, and about half a mile south of this curve there is a man-made cleft in the hillside through which the road runs. Taylor had come through this cleft and was coming out of the curve when he saw the Bigfoot.

His first impression was that it was a bear, for it was down on all fours close to the bank of the left, or west side of the road. Then it stood upright and as he drew his truck to a sudden halt, it walked quickly across the road to the opposite bank. It climbed this bank, watching him as it did so. Then it went over the top of the bank, which is about twenty feet high at this place, and, walking upright, disappeared.

Before he was transferred from the Squamish area I went to see Taylor at his home in Pemberton. I found him to be an intelligent, rational man of considerable credibility. He told me his story in direct, simple fashion. He told me exactly what happened and nothing more, and I found it very difficult not to believe him. He wanted no remuneration for the story and no publicity locally. His home, a large trailer unit, was clean and tidy and his family impressed me with their pleasant and friendly attitude. Later, without Taylor's knowledge, I checked on his background with local Canadian police, his employers, and some of his friends. All said the same thing. Good working record, good family man, sane, sensible, no abnormalities and not given to flights of fancy.

Taylor told me that the creature that he saw was at least seven feet tall and probably weighed 300 to 400 pounds. It was of massive build and had a large, protruding stomach. It was dark reddish brown in color and completely covered by hair with the exception of the face. He guessed that the hair on its body was four inches in length. It was about a hundred yards away when he first saw it and by the time he brought the truck to a halt, it was about thirty yards from him The time was early afternoon, about two-thirty, and the day was clear, with light overcast and no sun. It was very cold and he thinks that it was well below zero in the exposed area of the road above the Checkamus River. He thinks that it must have fallen off the bank, or jumped down and landed on all fours because it seemed to rise awkwardly when it got to its feet. It walked upright all of the time that he watched it and only once, when it was climbing the steep bank on the east side of the road, did he see it put a hand down. It seemed to do this to steady itself, as a man will when climbing a steep place. It did not run, but walked rapidly across the road and it kept its head turned towards Taylor and its eyes on him until it reached the bank. Taylor described the look as menacing (as did Patterson of the Bluff Creek Bigfoot he said he saw) and although he was perfectly safe, in the steel cab of a big solid truck, with both doors securely locked, he said that he felt the hair on the back of his neck begin to prickle and a cold feeling creep over him that was, simply, fear. He does not attempt to hide this. He quite frankly admits that the huge creature that he saw and that seemed to glare at him as it crossed in front of him, scared him very badly indeed. He wasted no time in getting away from the place and back to his home. Later his work took him through this area many times, but it was several weeks before he could force himself to get out and walk around at the place where he had seen the Bigfoot on that lonely mountain road.

Three "sighting" stories. The Welch brothers at Pitt Lake. The Portland businessmen at The Dalles. Bill Taylor on his mountain road above the Checkamus. Three stories of sightings of huge, hairy primates, walking upright, manlike, gigantic, creatures from another world. What are we to believe of them? What conclusions can we draw? What can we really say when we sit down and analyze the stories in all their detail and, more important, the character and the credibility of the storytellers? I think that the reader will agree that there are only three conclusions that make sense. These are, A) that the storytellers are lying; B) that they were, at the time of the supposed "sighting," hallucinating; C) that they are telling the truth.

Were they lying? It is possible but not probable, for a man who lies—and in this case the man would be lying about a story that he himself had concocted—usually has a motive. That motive is sometimes money, sometimes publicity, sometimes private personal reasons that are the creation of a warped and unstable mind. None of the storytellers involved in these three incidents seemed to have any motive for lying. None of them showed any desire for monetary return for their stories. All of them, without exception, shunned publicity. (The Welch brothers would not even allow their names to be connected with the story when it first appeared in

Vancouver newspapers.) And all of them, again without exception, seemed to me in my private interviews, and to others with whom they talked, to be of sound mental attitude.

Then, were they hallucinating? Did they simply imagine that they saw a large grey, or brown, hairy creature, walking around in the middle of the day? Was it perhaps auto-suggestion created by the general publicity that the newspapers had been giving to the public on the subject of the Bigfoot over the years, an inner semi-secret desire to see one, a desire strong enough eventually to produce the mind state that convinced the owner that he was actually seeing a Bigfoot? Somehow, I doubt this. The credibility rating that I would give to all of the people concerned in these three sightings is high. None of them struck me as being men of frivolous mental attitude. All of them, in fact, seemed very much the opposite. In the case of the Welch brothers, their way of life was hardly one that would allow for mental frivolity. Rugged environments have a nasty habit of chastising men who lack mental discipline. As to Taylor, his position of roads foreman and his long record of good service hardly seem to fit with a man who imagined seeing large hairy primates on the highways, unless they were really there. As to Forkan and Ball, an inquiry into their background showed them to be longshoremen, union men, hard workers who made their living in an atmosphere that would hardly tolerate men given to vivid imagination. Their background included the rough and tumble life of the Portland dockyards, a way of life that allows for the survival of only the determined worker and the basic thinker. I think that in their case, as in the case of the Welch brothers and Taylor, hallucination is ruled out. Unfortunately for the skeptics, this leaves us with only one remaining alternative, which is that all of them were telling the truth. Again, unfortunately for the skeptics, I find myself having to accept this conclusion, with just one small stipulation, which is that all of them were hoaxed by some other person or persons unknown. A stipulation that suggests, I must admit, the highly improbable.

Is it possible that they were hoaxed by some other person? Hoaxed by an arch-Piltdowner who not only keeps different colored sets of fur suits in his closet but is also prepared to travel thousands of miles at the drop of a hat, just for the doubtful privilege and self-gratification of showing himself for a few seconds to some hard-working and rather disinterested woodsman? Someone who would boat his way up the turbulent waters of Pitt Lake and then, with ingenious navigation, manage to locate himself in the precise place where the Welch brothers were going to be at a given time? A place that they probably did not know themselves and which certainly no one else was going to know? (Prospectors working for big mining concerns are under rules of the strictest secrecy concerning mining claims.) Could it be someone so mentally backward as to find reward in sitting on the edge of a freezing mountain road in the wild hills of British Columbia, waiting for a roads maintenance man to come along and have a quick look at him? Could it be someone with such disregard for his own safety that he would walk out in the open fields of The Dalles, in broad daylight, in a country that literally bristles with guns and people who use them, not a few of whom, unfortunately, have said that they will use them on a Bigfoot if they see one? Open fields that offer, for a hoaxer, no safe line of retreat and where the nearest cover is over a mile and a half away? Somehow, I doubt it. Thus we are left with what will be, for the skeptics, the totally unacceptable conclusion, that they were telling the truth and that what they saw was a real living creature, a real Bigfoot.

I have told these three stories in some detail because they are among the better accounts that the I.W.C.S. team has produced in its investigation of the Bigfoot phenomena. There are many other stories and many of them are equally credible. Mrs. Gruber, of Evans, Washington, saw one walking down to the Columbia River near her home, one afternoon in 1968. It walked through the trees, she said, and as she climbed into her car and raced away in fright, it disappeared toward the river. George Hildebrand, of Republic, Washington, claims to have seen one on the Republic Road, just west of Sherman Pass, on a winter's morning in 1971. It jumped off the road into the snow when it saw his car approaching, a huge, dark-haired creature that looked like a giant man, he said. (We got to the scene of this sighting three days later and there were still footprints in the snow where the Bigfoot had left the road. Heavy new snow prevented us from following the prints.) Louis Awhile, of White Salmon, Washington, saw one cross the highway just east of Beacon Rock, in Washington, in 1973. His young daughter, who was with him at the time, also saw the creature and was badly scared by it. Mr. and Mrs. Martin Heinrich, of· Portland, saw one on the Lewis River in 1968. They were fishing from a boat at the time and watched it for several minutes before it saw them and walked quickly into the trees. Frank Luxton, another British Columbia highways foreman like Bill Taylor, saw one cross a lonely road north of New Hazelton, in British Columbia. There are many other claimed sightings in the I.W.C.S. files and while some of them are not sufficiently documented and others are obviously imagination or honest mistake (bears, tree stumps at night and so forth), too many of them have the ring of truth to them to be ignored.

Skamania County, in Washington State, has officials who are the first to take a long and serious look at the incidents that have taken place in their own county and at the credibility and responsibility of the people involved in them. The result has been a county ordinance that imposes a fine of up to $10,000, or imprisonment, or both, on anyone attempting to injure or kill a Bigfoot, a creature that they believe should top the list of endangered species in the world today, a belief with which I and my associates concur.

Text of Skamania County's Bigfoot Ordinance

Affidavit of Publication

ORDINANCE NO. 69-01

Be it hereby ordained by the Board of County Commissioners of Skamania County:

WHEREAS, there is evidence to indicate the possible existence in Skamania County of a nocturnal primate mammal variously described as an ape-like creature or a sub-species of Homo Sapiens, and

WHEREAS, both legend and purported recent sightings and spoor support this possibility, and

WHEREAS, this creature is generally and commonly known as a "Sasquatch," "Yeti," "Bigfoot," or "Giant Hairy Ape," and

WHEREAS, publicity attendant upon such real or imagined sightings has resulted in an influx of scientific investigators as well as casual hunters, many armed with lethal weapons, and

WHEREAS, the absence of specific laws covering the taking of specimens encourages laxity in the use of firearms and other deadly devices and poses a clear and present threat to the safety and well-being of persons living or traveling within the boundaries of Skamania County as well as to the creatures themselves,

THEREFORE BE IT RESOLVED that any premeditated, wilful and wanton slaying of any such creature shall be deemed a felony punishable by a fine not to exceed Ten Thousand Dollars ($10,000.00) and/or imprisonment in the county jail for a period not to exceed Five (5) years.

BE IT FURTHER RESOLVED that the situation existing constitutes an emergency and as such this ordinance is effective immediately.

ADOPTED this 1st day of April, 1969.

Board of Commissioners of Skamania County. By: CONRAD LUNDY JR., Chairman.

Approved: ROBERT K. LEICK, Skamania County Prosecuting Attorney.

Publ. April 4, 11, 1969.

STATE OF WASHINGTON } ss.
COUNTY OF SKAMANIA }

Roy D. Craft _____, being first duly sworn on oath, deposes and says: That he is the Publisher, Editor or Manager of the SKAMANIA COUNTY PIONEER, a weekly newspaper, which has been established, published in the English language, and circulated continuously as a weekly newspaper in the City of Stevenson, and in said County and State, and of general circulation in said county for more than six (6) months prior to the date of the first publication of the Notice hereto attached, and that the said Skamania County Pioneer was on the 7th day of July, 1941, approved as a legal newspaper by the Superior Court of said Skamania County, and that the annexed is a true copy of ....Skamania County Ordinance....

No. 69-01 Prohibiting Wanton Slahing

of Ape-Creature and imposing Penalties

as it appeared in the regular and entire issue of said paper itself and not in a supplement thereof for a period of ......two.......

............consecutive weeks commencing on the ....

4th ......day of ......April ...., 19....69...., and ending

on the .....11th............... day of .....April..........., 19..69...,

and that said newspaper was regularly distributed to its subscribers during all of this period.

That the full amount of $...11.05.......... has been paid in full.

Roy D. ....

Subscribed and sworn to before me this ....

day of ....April.......................... 19...69...............

_.._
Notary Public in and for the State of Washington

The Skamania County Ordinance that was issued to prevent a Bigfoot from being hunted, captured, or shot.

V

No Place to Hide?

Only a pukka shikari* will ever catch a Yeti. The Yeti is much given to traveling. He is also very cunning.
—TENZING NORGAY, at Rathong Camp, Sikkim, September 1956

I AM CONSTANTLY AMAZED at the number of people who approach me and tell me, quite seriously, that there is absolutely no such thing as a Bigfoot, and the simple reason for this—surely you should have learned this by now, Mr. Byrne— is that there just isn't anywhere for them to hide. The rivers are full of fishermen. The hills are full of deer hunters. The mountains are full of elk hunters, and cougar hunters, and foresters and loggers and timber cruisers and ecologists and Boy Scouts and Girl Scouts and trekkers and campers and cross country skiers and rock climbers and horse riders and of course, Bigfoot hunters. All of the available land on which houses can be built has been built on. All of the available land for farming has been farmed. Most of the timber has been cut down and between the logging companies and the U.S. Forest Service there just isn't anywhere, anymore, where there is not a road with a truck or a pickup roaring up and down it. The high peaks all have fire lookouts, for fire control. The high ridges all have telephonic relay stations. There is a radar or radio or electronic device of some kind on every hilltop. Planes of all sizes fly across the mountains all the time and those that are being used on fire control work contain men who are actively watching the ground beneath them. Some may be carrying wildlife agents engaged in the work of animal counting in which case they will be studying

*A true hunter.

the ground and its wildlife population with care. Some may be carrying timber cruisers,* who will be watching the timber with equal care, evaluating it for cutting. Even private planes, simply passing over the mountains from A to B, often fly only a few thousand feet above the forest, at altitudes that allow clear views of the treetops and, in the clear spaces, of the wildlife therein. In other words, and surely you can see this, Mr. Byrne, creatures of that size simply have nowhere to go, nowhere to hide. This proves, as any simpleton can see, Mr. Byrne, that the things simply cannot exist.

Normally the people who expound this theory do not have the time to hear or do not want to hear any argument. They have delivered their ultimatum. They have expounded what anyone but a complete fool can see is the truth. That their argument is based on almost total ignorance of the real situation would never, ever occur to them. That they have no understanding of the incredible vastness of the coast ranges is something that they prefer to close their tiny minds to, now and in the future. That there just might be a Bigfoot and that in actual fact he might have a very large habitat that is perfectly suited to his needs, is something that they would consider quite unfair to have proved to them.

How is it that animals, or even people, can occupy an area and remain so well hidden for so long? What factors are involved that enable them to do this? There are many, but basically the reason is that they simply do not want to be found—they simply do not wish to have contact with man. With most animals, of course, there is a plain and simple reason. They are shot, or shot at, by man. Man is regarded by all of the animals, certainly all of those who have had contact with him, as the ultimate predator. No other creature on the face of the earth since time began has been so successful at eliminating his fellow creatures and his fellow men. And so man's fellow creatures know that if they are going to survive they are going to have to hide and to remain hidden.

There is a saying that you may find what you are searching for if you search hard enough but that you will not find that for which you are not searching. This saying can be applied to the Bigfoot. Part of the reason why one has never been found, in the fullest sense of the word, is that with the

*Men who are agents of lumber companies, whose job it is to examine and assess the value of timber in areas to be logged.

exception of my own expeditions no one has ever searched for the creatures on a full-time basis. The finding of the Tasaday tribe of the Philippines in 1972 is a case in point. This incredible stone-age group was not discovered mainly because no one was looking for them. They in turn were not really hiding. If they were, they would have taken steps to ensure that they remained hidden. Another example, though on a somewhat different scale, is the amusing story of the Portland Park Hermit. In 1969 two boys noticed a man going into a clump of bushes into Washington Park, Portland's municipal park. They followed, and when he saw them, the story goes, he chased them. They informed the park authorities, who came to the scene to investigate. In a small clump of bushes, in an island of shrubbery in the center of the park, officials were stunned to find a cabin, complete with bed and all home comforts. Washington Park has a total area of 149 acres and employs twelve gardeners and maintenance men who work each day in the park from nine to five. There are also several office staff workers and a superintendent. Each day the park has an average of fifty visitors and in summertime this figure increases to 300. A large number of children use the park and play in the open grass areas and in the bushes and clumps that separate the flower beds and lawns. The park authorities were startled to find that one of their bush clumps held a homesite! They were even more surprised to learn that the owner, an elderly hermit, had been living there undiscovered for fifteen years.

In the southwest jungles of the Kingdom of Nepal, an area where I hunted for many years, there lived a large male black panther. The panther had as his habitat an area of about sixty square miles, and in this he lived and hunted. In one village, a small village subsequently destroyed by smallpox, the natives had seen him once, during very heavy rain, in the middle of the monsoon. They told me about him and I made a mental note that one day I would go after him with a camera. I felt that I would eventually have a chance to see him myself, for I hunted his area for nine months of the year and spent many hours just sitting and watching wildlife, a favorite occupation of mine in those days. I saw his pug marks many times and also his kills, or rather the remainder of them. I found his dens and on numerous occasions I heard him call in the night, the heavy sawing noise that is the hunting call of the leopard. Had I made a determined effort at searching for him, with either camera or gun, we might have come to grips within a week or so. Had I informed the Nepalese authorities of his presence, they would have hunted for him, for he would have been a prized trophy with his dark green eyes and black velvet coat. But I told no one and for many years he and I shared the same jungles, I publicly and he very privately, very secretly, unseen by the eyes of man. The Kala Cheetua, the natives called him, the black leopard.

Six years after I had first heard of him I saw him one day, in broad daylight, running for his life from a great forest fire. I saw him as he crossed a clearing at a distance of about thirty yards, bounding through the air in a beautiful blur of motion. He was in sight for about three seconds and then he was gone. I never saw him again, though I lived in the area for many years. But the evidence, his pug marks, told me that he shared the area with me.

In Idaho, in late 1970, two men were lost in the mountains. There was deep snow and extreme cold and when their pickup bogged down and left them stranded, they found themselves in serious trouble. For some time they stayed with the vehicle. Then one man set off on foot to try and get help. The man who stayed behind eventually succumbed to the cold. The man who set out to try and find help came across a cabin and found some food in it and was able to survive. Both men were the subject of a massive hunt in which several hundred men, supported by air search, took part. Every effort was made to find the missing men, and the men themselves, particularly the man who holed up in the cabin, made every effort to contact the searchers and to let them know their whereabouts. The searchers had a fair idea of where the men had disappeared and concentrated their search on a comparatively small area. The pickup, though half buried in snow, was visible from the air but was never seen by the air searchers. After two weeks of effort that included hundreds of man-hours of footwork, the search was abandoned. Fifty-eight days later the second man found his way out to a road and was picked up and rescued. Lesson? The northwest wilderness hid both these men and the combined efforts of both the lost men to be found, and the searchers to find them, were in vain.

Since I came to the Pacific Northwest, just four years ago, no less than six planes have been lost in the tangled wilderness of the coast ranges. In this same period four planes that crashed in previous years have been found.

The high forests of the Marble Mountain Wilderness area in California provided one find, a small two-seater that had been missing since 1969. Lost in a storm while on a flight from Eugene, Oregon, to Bodega Springs, California, the plane was found one hundred miles south of where searchers had operated—and given up—some twenty months previously. All hope of finding the craft and its two passengers had been abandoned when hikers in the Abbot Lake area, deep in the wilderness, found pieces of wreckage that led to its discovery.

On December 10, 1944, a pilot named George Wilbur Carroll took off from Billings, Montana, to fly to Seattle. Carroll planned to be home for Christmas and had loaded the back of the plane with Christmas presents for his wife and children. The plane, a Ryan B-I Brougham, a sister plane to Charles Lindbergh's aircraft, the *Spirit of St. Louis*, was last seen flying over Superior, Montana. After that it completely disappeared. For many years it was believed that Carroll had missed the Washington coast in fog and flown into the Pacific. Then, in November 1971, two U.S. Forest Service workers found aircraft wreckage in a snow-covered ravine near Lookout Pass, on the Idaho-Montana border. In the wreckage they located a number, NC-6955, and reported it to the Federal Aviation Administration. The FAA identified the plane as Carroll's Ryan Brougham and thus solved a mystery that the wild mountains of the Northwest had kept unsolved for twenty-seven years.

And so, the rivers are full of fishermen. The hills are full of deer hunters. The mountains are full of elk hunters and bear hunters and cougar hunters and so many others that it just is not possible for anything to hide out there or for anything to remain hidden for more than, say, a day or two at the most. You can't tell us, Mr. Byrne, that something like a Bigfoot could actually find a place to live and hide, in the United States, in this modern day and age?

111

Invariably when the subject of the Bigfoot comes up among skeptics I am also served, in addition to the "no place to hide, nothing to eat, too cold in the winter" theories, two other little gems of modern skepticism. One is the Loch Ness monster phenomenon. The other is the mystery of the Yeti, or Abominable Snowmen. On the subject of the Loch Ness monsters I do not have a great deal to say. I have been to the brooding Scottish lake that is the Ness and have peered through the mists like many another, hoping for a glimpse of the elusive monsters. But I have had no personal part in the search and investigations that have been carried out at the lake over the past few years. However, two of the principal searchers are not only friends of mine but also associates in the Bigfoot project and from them I have first-hand knowledge of the work that has been done and which now, in 1975, is continuing at the lake. The first of these is Robert Rines, President of the Boston-based Academy of Applied Science and head of the American team that has done such sterling work at Loch Ness since 1970. Working with Dr. Rines is an Englishman, Tim Dinsdale, head of the photographic section of the British Loch Ness Investigation team.

I first met Tim Dinsdale at the home of Ivan Sanderson in New Jersey, in 1972, in the company of old Nepal hands Gerald Russell and Ron Rosner. At intervals in a fascinating weekend's conversation on such diverse subjects as Yeti, Bigfeet, the Bermuda Triangle, UFOs, Shookpas, and Okopogos, Tim told me of his thirteen-year search for the monsters at Loch Ness, a search that started with a sighting and a piece of now famous 8mm film, and has continued, without ceasing, to the present day. He also told me about the work of the Academy of Applied Science under Dr. Rines and of their findings to date.

In 1970 a team of scientists from the Academy of Applied Science in Boston went to Scotland to commence research at Loch Ness. There they were joined by Tim Dinsdale and together they put into effect a meticulously planned investigation of the thousand-year-old phenomenon, an investigation based on sound scientific principles and detailed planning.

For the first tests at the lake the Academy used a standard Klein Associates Model Mk-300 Side Scan Sonar. The sonar was used in two modes. One was the conventional towed configuration to examine the bottom slopes of the lake. The other was in the form of a fixed mode, to make positive determination of moving targets.

These first tests produced three important discoveries. They were, 1) that there were large moving objects in the lake. 2) That there was abundant fish life in the lake that could support a large fish-eating creature. 3) That there were large ridges or caves in the steep walls of the lake which could conceivably harbor large creatures.

These tests set the stage for further search and investigation. In 1972 Dr. Rines returned again to Loch Ness. Working with other Academy members he put into action a plan that in August of that year produced their first success, an extraordinary photograph of a section of one of the huge lake creatures. The photograph was supported by sonar findings that indicated that not one but two of the leviathans had swum within range of their search gear. The photograph, which showed a very large fin-like appendage, was later examined by sonar experts at the Massachusetts Institute of Technology and by Woods Hole Oceanographic Institute. The examination showed there were two of the giant creatures and that they were from twenty to thirty feet in length, with several humps and fins and with long tails. This expert examination of the evidence plus the quite impeccable credentials of the Academy group removed any doubt as to the authenticity of the findings and, in the minds of most people, firmly established the existence of the Loch Ness creatures as an accepted fact.

In the meantime, the work at Loch Ness continues. One aim of the Academy of Applied Science is good, clear, color pictures of one or more of the creatures, on the surface, both movie and still. That the creatures do surface from time to time is accepted. Some witnesses even claim to have seen them on land, some distance back from the water, suggesting that they are amphibians. Dr. Rines went underwater for his first pictures and Dinsdale assisted him in his efforts. But Dinsdale's own efforts are directed toward surface photography and the modus operandi of the lone Britisher, when he is not assisting Dr. Rines, is a small boat loaded with camera equipment in which he quietly floats for hours, days, weeks at a time, patiently waiting. In 1975, after some thirteen years of patient watching and waiting, Dinsdale writes, in answer to one of my letters, "Thank you for your encouragement. Sometimes the water-hunt wears me down to the point where I feel like falling overboard on purpose. But then, like you, I believe that confrontation is coming. It's just a matter of sticking it out."*

As mentioned, I have taken no part in the Loch Ness searches and when writing about them can only write of the work of others. But in the case of the Yeti, the snowmen abominable, I can contribute a little more. I was not only one of the first searchers for the elusive Himalayan primates but in the long run probably spent more time investigating that particular phenomenon than anyone else.

I cannot remember where or when I first heard of the snowmen. I seem to recall my father telling me bedside stories about them, years ago, and spinning yarns about the swirling mists of the high Himalaya and the giant hairy men that inhabited those inhospitable regions. My first personal experience with the phenomenon was in conversations with Sherpas and Lepchas in Darjeeling, the mountain vacation town in northern India, during a vacation from Royal Air Force duties in 1946. What I learned then inspired me with a desire to learn more and eventually, I hoped, to take an expedition into the mountains and find the mysterious creatures. Back in London after demobilization I started to do some research on the one-hundred-year-old mystery and one of the first things that I learned was that apart from some mentions of primate creatures, in early Chinese manuscripts dating back to 200 B.C., creatures that might have been Yeti, there is really very little record before 1832. In that year the British Resident at the Court of Nepal in Kathmandu wrote in an article that some of his men, while on a collecting expedition, were frightened by a rakshas. The word rakshas is of Sanscrit origin and like the other name for the Yeti, shookpa, is still in use among the northern tribes of Nepal today. The Resident, Mr.

---

*Dinsdale continues his work at Loch Ness, patiently investigating, studying, photographing, and awaiting a close look at the object of his quest.

B. H. Hodgson, an esteemed naturalist of his day, described the creature that his men had seen as walking erect, covered with long dark hair and tailless. Fifty-seven years later a British explorer, Major L. A. Waddell, found some sets of huge footprints in the snows at 17,000 feet in Sikkim, neighboring country to Nepal and also in the Himalayan chain. His porters told him that the prints were those of a shookpa, or Yeti, and Waddell duly reported the fact on his return to London. Another report came out of Sikkim in 1914. This time the origin was a British Forestry Officer and his find was also footprints. J. R. P. Gent referred to the creature that made the prints as the sogpa, apparently a local pronounciation of the name shookpa. The reports continued through the late 1800s and into the early 1900s. Lieutenant-Colonel C. K. Howard Bury, leader of the Mount Everest Reconnaissance Expedition of 1921, reported huge footprints on the Lhokpa Pass at an altitude of 20,000 feet. In 1925 a British photographer, N. A. Tombazi, a gentleman of impeccable credentials and a fellow of the Royal Geographical Society, reported seeing a Yeti-like creature in the area of the Zemu Glacier at an altitude of 15,000 feet. The creature was moving through a stand of dwarf rhododendron bushes. (Twenty-three years later, in 1948, on one of my first expeditions, I found footprints in this same area.) Then came Eric Shipton's find, a single, large, thirteen-inch footprint on the Menlung Glacier in 1951 and soon a host of famous names became associated with finds, including John (now Lord) Hunt, Sir Edmund Hillary, Frank Smythe, H. W. Tilman. The well-known anthropologist, Prince Peter of Greece, in whose former home in Kalimpong, India, I spent many pleasant hours, studied the question of the Yeti for many years and eventually concluded that there must be some basis in fact behind the many reports of sightings.

In 1954 a British newspaper, the *Daily Mail*, sponsored the first Himalayan Yeti expedition. The party, which included my friends Gerald Russell and Ralph Izzard, spent many months clambering up and down the Himalaya without finding a Yeti. Three years later, in 1957, I came into the picture with the first American Yeti Expedition Reconnaissance.

My introduction to the Himalaya was during the aforementioned trip to Darjeeling, in 1946. In early 1947 I left the Royal Air Force and joined a British Tea Company with offices in Eastcheap, London and estates in north Bengal. In those days companies were liberal with the amount of vacation time they allowed their young gentlemen assistants and just a year later I was able to take a month's leave of absence. I left for Sikkim by car—an ancient Austin Seven—and then with two Sherpas set out on foot from Gangtok. My goal was Lachen and the Green Lake region in northern Sikkim, which I reached in some ten days of hard hiking. It was close to the Zemu Glacier that I found the single footprint, in the hard snow at the edge of a small frozen pool. My Sherpas, two older men, were, I recalled, very nervous about the finding and reluctant to stay in the area. We returned by way of the Sikkim-Nepal border, along the eastern edge of the Hogla Boga country of Nepal, and over the hill of Sandakphu back to Darjeeling. We completed the last lap of the trek, some twenty-six miles from Sandakphu to Darjeeling, from 10,000 feet down to 2000 feet and up again to 8000, in one long day.

I was in Sikkim again in 1956. By this time I had resigned from my tea company and gone into the big game hunting business in India. The life of a tea planter proved less attractive after Indian independence, and the big game hunting safaris in India were in their infancy and just beginning to attract international attention. In the spring of that year, with time to spare between safari bookings, I once again set out for Sikkim. This time I, went up the Sikkim-Nepal border route, a high ridge route that runs south to north and that climbs all the way into the Zemu area. I spent a month searching the frozen dwarf scrub up to 15,000 feet and found nothing more than wolves, snow leopards and bears, the common wildlife of the middle Himalaya. On the return, again with my two faithful Sherpas, I passed through the high moorland of Trejablo, west of Rathong, and one cold and foggy evening, marching over a high ridge and looking for a way down to a lower camp site, we spotted a group of men trekking in single file northwards, about 2000 feet below us. We wondered who they were and set out to cut them off and, if possible, share a camp with them. A month in the high mountains gives one an appetite for company. Some three or four hours later we saw their campfire and walking in out of the gloom we received a warm welcome from some old Sherpa friends, including Ang Tharkey, Tenzing Norgay and Ang Namgyal. After hot mugs of soup and an explanation of what they were doing there—they were part of the new Indian School of Mountaineering from Darjeeling—the talk naturally turned to the Yeti. None of those present had ever seen one but Tenzing told me that his father had encountered one which had crawled on top of his yak herder's hut one night and stayed there until driven off by smoke from the old man's yak dung fire. Tenzing also told me that he had recently talked with an American named Tom Slick, in Darjeeling, who was interested in projecting an expedition to find one of the creatures. Tenzing's wife, back in Darjeeling, had the American's address.

On my return from the second Sikkimese expedition I wrote to Tom Slick in San Antonio, Texas. An exchange of letters took place and six months later, in the spring of 1957, I met Slick in New Delhi and we flew to Kathmandu together. From Kathmandu, after some days of hectic preparation, we flew down to Biratnagar in southeastern Nepal and, accompanied by a Mr. N. D. Bachkheti, an Indian zoologist from New Delhi, we trekked up the Arun River valley and into the ten- to fifteen-thousand-foot ranges of northeastern Nepal. The purpose of the expedition was basically a reconnaissance to determine if a full-scale expedition would be worthwhile. We spent three months in the mountains, during which time I found one set of footprints, in the Chhoyang Khola at 10,000 feet, and Tom, working with a separate party in another area, found a second set. The prints that I discovered were identical with those I had seen in Sikkim years earlier. They were ten inches in length, five-toed, and they were the prints of a bipedal creature of considerable weight. The prints that Tom found were thirteen inches in length and of similar construction. We returned to Kathmandu and immediately started making plans for a full-scale expedition to try and find one of the creatures and photograph it. Some six months of preparation were put into the planning of the new expedition and in early 1958 we again set off for the mountains, this time with a party of five Europeans, ten Sherpa guide companions, and sixty-five porters. Our object, to find the Yeti, once and for all. Our chosen area of search, the deep kholas, or valleys that drain into the upper Arun valley, including the Hongu, the Seeswa, the Iswa, the Barun and the Chhoyang. Sponsors of the expedition were Tom Slick and Kirk Johnson, another wealthy Texan from Fort Worth. Leader in absentia would be Tom, unable to come on this phase of the search because of business and other commitments in the United States. Field leader would be Gerald Russell, a highly respected American naturalist who lived in France and who had already been in the Himalaya with the *Daily Mail* expedition. Expedition photographer would be George Holton, a professional photographer of international note whose subjects were mainly in the field of natural history. Movies were covered by a movie photographer, German-born Norman Dyrhenfurth. Liaison with the government of Nepal, a required appointment in those days, was supplied by a Nepalese gentleman, Captain Pushkar Shumsher Jung Bahadur Rana, late of the Nepalese Army. And I, with my brother Bryan, was to be chief guide and general organizer and logistics expert for the project.

The 1958 expedition was named the Slick-Johnson Himalayan Yeti Expedition and a month after leaving Kathmandu, we established base camps high in the upper Arun. From these bases the party fanned out to cover different areas of interest and searches were combined with inquiries at Sherpa villages on possible areas of habitat. Once every two weeks all of the members of the group came together and compared notes.

After three months only one possible sighting had been made, by a Sherpa who was a member of the guide party, named Da Temba. Gerald Russell was with Da Temba at the time of the sighting but did not see anything. However he believed that the man did see a Yeti and later we spent considerable time in the area of the sighting. Then, one by one, the various members had to leave and before four months had passed all, with the exception of my brother and I, had departed. We stayed on for another five months, making nine months in all and it was not until the snow was deep on the ground that we marched out to Kathmandu, a cold, two-hundred-mile trek that used up the last of our stores and wore out the last of our equipment.

From Kathmandu, in late 1958, we corresponded with Tom Slick. We had sent monthly reports to both him and Kirk Johnson all during the first nine-month expedition and now it was a matter of assessing the value of returning to the Himalaya and continuing the search. In the meantime we were to rest in Kathmandu and this we did at the old, now abandoned, Royal Hotel, a hostelry of comparative comfort for the weary Yeti hunter just down from the mountains. There we stayed for some six weeks, until December, 1958, when we received our second set of orders. They were simple. We were to return to the mountains and continue the search. We were to stay up for as long as it was necessary to find and photograph a Yeti or, failing that, for as long as we could stand the cold, the privation and the various discomforts of living at high altitudes.

We set out again a week before Christmas and if the reader wonders why two young men would leave the delights of a Kathmandu hotel and the fleshpots of an eastern city and its swinging international set a week before Christmas, all that I can answer is that in those days we were very keen young men, dedicated to a task to which we were prepared to devote our lives, to what Tom Slick used to call the Ultimate Quest. It might help to show how keen we were, perhaps, if I were to add that for that first year's work with the San Antonio group we accepted no salary and for the second, for needed personal expenses outside of the expedition proper, we worked for an honorarium of $100 per month each.

For the third expedition—or the second, if the first is to be considered a reconnaissance—we went alone. We took a minimum of equipment with us. No tents, no food. We planned to live off the land and to sleep, as the high mountain shepherds did, in wood shelters when we were below the tree line and in caves when we were above it. This we did, for another nine months, and they were nine very fascinating months during which we believe that we made some contribution to support the theory that there were still a few of the mysterious primates living in the deep, seldom penetrated valleys of

119

northeastern Nepal. Among our finds were the Pangboche temple scalp and the mummified hand of what might have been a Yeti, or a man, a question which has never been satisfactorily determined. The scalp that we unearthed at the Pangboche temple is still there to this day. The scalp that Sir Edmund Hillary's group brought back to the United States and which with much fanfare was subsequently found to be nothing more than a fake, made of the skin of a Serow, a species of Himalayan goat antelope, was simply a copy of the Pangboche scalp, made by a visiting Tibetan taxidermist many years before, to ease an intertemple rivalry that existed in the matter of Yeti scalp possession between the temples and monasteries of Pangboche, Thyangboche and Kumjung. As to the hand, we managed to take part of it out of Pangboche and have it sent back to England for examination. The problem of getting it out of Nepal was simple. One of us took it out across the border in a knapsack. The problem of getting it out of India, through the mails, was more serious. The difficulty was solved by friends of the Kirk Johnsons, who were passing through Calcutta after a visit with an old friend of mine, the Maharaja of Baroda. Baroda arranged for me to meet with them at the Grand Hotel in Calcutta and Jimmie Stewart and his wife Gloria, much amused at the thought of the grisly trophy that they were carrying with them, took it back to London for us.

We carried the search through all of 1959, and we made several interesting discoveries. In one canyon in the upper Arun there was at least one large unknown primate, probably a Yeti, that included frogs in its diet. We trekked and camped for a thousand miles across the high Himalaya, living mostly off the land, enjoying the company, from time to time, of the mountain people both Nepali and Sherpa and generally experiencing a life as adventurous and at times as dangerous as any young man could know.

VI

The Bigfoot Mystery
and Its Shadowy Beginnings

The whole history of scientific advance is full of scientists investigating phenomena that the Establishment did not think were there.
—MARGARET MEAD

THE HUNT FOR BIGFOOT BEGAN, for me, in the winter of 1959. At that time I was winding down the last of three long Himalayan Abominable Snowman expeditions. In these last winter months, with deep snow on the ground and temperatures to 45° below zero, we were living in a cave in the upper Chhoyang Khola, one of the deep gorges that runs down into the headwaters of the mighty Arun river in northeast Nepal. We were tired. Most of our equipment had long since been destroyed, or lost, or simply worn out. Our clothes were in rags and we were subsisting on champa, a Sherpa grain mash not unlike oatmeal, yak's milk, yak milk cheese, and edible ferns and nettles.

One evening as we were sitting at our fire in the cave, a Sherpa runner arrived from Dharan, the British Army Gurkha Recruiting Depot in southern Nepal, 140 miles away. The runner, who had completed the trip in four days, came pounding in out of the dripping gloom of the Himalayan night and handed us a rather crumpled letter from Tom Slick.

The letter contained instructions for us to terminate the three-year hunt for the Snowmen and come out. We were to proceed to Kathmandu, the capital of Nepal, where we would find further instructions awaiting us. In the time that it took us to march down, the letter continued, we were to give consideration to coming to the United States to take over a new expedition that would search for something called the Bigfoot, a giant primate not unlike the Yeti. It, or they, apparently lived in the Pacific Northwest of the United States and their habitat was the thickly wooded coastal ranges of the northern states of Oregon and Washington.

Tom's letter was persuasive, and Bryan and I agreed to give the expedition a try. It took us one day to pack, pay off our local Sherpas, and begin the trek down to Kathmandu.

Three weeks after leaving Kathmandu I found myself installed in a tiny motel in a little town called Willow Creek, in Humboldt County, in northern California. There, a stranger in a strange land, I set about trying to organize the first Bigfoot expedition, a systematic and sensible approach to the problems of finding out, A) if the things really existed, and B) if so, how to go about finding one.

Money, equipment, and men—theoretically on retainer to the expedition—were missing, and it was my first priority to track them down. The first two items proved permanently lost, and most of the "trackers" had also departed. Those who remained I quickly eliminated from the expedition. As an example of the type of Bigfoot hunter associated with the Slick expedition, let me relate the story of Shouter and his friends.

They were three somewhat mysterious figures who were written up in my files as "associates to the expedition." Inquiries showed that they were engaged in the logging and timber trades and that their interest in the expedition seemed to be mainly in the area of supplying evidence which they themselves had unearthed in their own searches. One of them lived in Willow Creek at this time. The others lived in Weed, Oregon, and Drain, Oregon. The Willow Creek individual was the representative of the trio and in due course I made contact with him. As the ensuing farce was something that I can never forget, I feel that it deserves telling in some detail.

I found the leader of the trio to be a tall, angular man with a hard, thin face, a large, bony nose, close-cropped, greying hair and long yellow teeth. Perhaps because of his work amid the constant roar of high-powered logging machinery, he had acquired the habit of shouting. Thus he never spoke, but shouted all the time. Yes! he shouted, ushering me into the

122

house, I had come at exactly the right time. His companions, he roared, his "range and track teams," as he called them, were real woodsmen and at this moment were hot on the trail of a goddam Bigfoot. They expected to capture the bugger at any moment. They were first-class trackers and top woodsmen and they were doing something that none of these yahoos who worked for Slick were able to do. Shit, man, these guys could track a squirrel up a tree and down again. In a few days he would be calling me and I could rest assured that he would have something to show me then. He shouted me to the door and I left with my ears ringing.

Sure enough, three days later, he called. The phone crackled in my ear. We have it, he roared. My range and track team has done it! We've got the bugger! It's only a young one, but it's a real goddam Bigfoot. Why shit, man, it's got hair all over it and the biggest goddam feet you ever did see. You wait until them sciences [scientists] see this bugger, man. When I could get a word in, I asked him when I could see the beast. Why man, he replied, as soon as them sponsors of yours come up with our price, that's when. I gently asked him what the price might be? One million dollars, in cash, and they would hand the beastie over, complete with carrying cage.

I called Slick in San Antonio and told him about the situation. He told me to offer them five thousand and to tell them that we would pay it on sight. At first my bellowing friend would not hear of it. Then he said that he would confer with his partners. He would call me in a couple of days. Two days later he called and said that they would accept the five thousand but that they would have to have it in advance. Nothing doing, I told him and so we went into two weeks of phone calls and argument back and forth, while we bargained for a look at the creature and they bargained for cash on the nail, sight unseen. Then came an urgent call from Shouter. They were getting into difficulties. The only thing that the young Bigfoot would eat was Kellog's Frosted Flakes and it ate them by the hundred-pound bag. It was, in fact, running them dry financially and I would have to do something quickly. There was only so much money available for Frosted Flakes.

I called Slick again and told him about the Frosted Flake problem. He told me to offer them $500 for a look at the creature and to take a camera along. I did this; they said no. Then, as I rather expected, the thing got sick. It weakened. It was near death, and rather than let it die, in the goodness of their hearts, they decided to let it go. You should have seen that bugger run when he got out of the cage, Shouter told me. But I thought you said he was sick? Whereupon he took umbrage at my suspecting his honesty in the matter and did not call me again.

The expedition team finally consisted of my brother Bryan, Steve Matthes, a professional hunter from California, and myself. We were joined from time to time by Tom Slick, always bringing with him interesting people from the United States and other countries. We found a total of twelve sets of footprints during that year (1960). We did not see a Bigfoot. But we worked hard at the problems of finding one, and many good people helped us in our work—honest, dedicated people who were willing to give of their time and their experience for little or no return. The townspeople of Willow Creek and Salyer cooperated wholeheartedly in our efforts and generally tolerated the idiosyncracies of the two foreigners who spent all of their time looking for something which, to many of the townspeople, probably did not even exist. Our efforts were terminated by the death of Tom Slick in an air crash. Tom and his pilot died in a small two-seater that broke up in a storm over Dillon, Montana. His body was flown to Texas for burial and with his demise the first Bigfoot expedition came to an end. We looked upon Tom Slick as a man of vision and enterprise, a gentle man, sensitive to the feelings and needs of others. His death was a great loss to us all. Since those first Himalayan days together, he had been my friend.

I returned to Nepal and resumed my big game hunting and guiding career which had been interrupted by the Yeti and Bigfoot expeditions, and I stayed there running Nepal Safaris, my own professional guiding company, until early 1968. In 1968 I gave up hunting and moved to Washington, D.C., where, with four other Washingtonians—Karl Jonas, M.D., Roy Lyman Sexton, M.D., and two attorneys, Leonard A. Fink and Scott C. Whitney—I helped to found The International

Wildlife Conservation Society, Inc. In late 1968 I returned to Nepal and, working with the government of that country, founded and built the Sukla Phanta Tiger Sanctuary, the first tiger sanctuary in Asia, a 50,000-acre preserve that today offers one of the last retreats for the great cats of Asia. I completed this work in late 1970 and returned to the United States, where I found, after ten years, that there was renewed interest in the Bigfoot phenomenon. I made some inquiries and found that some backing was available if I was prepared to put up a fair proportion of the financing myself, and in early January, 1971, I and a few companions started another search. We chose as our base the tiny townlet of Evans, Washington, just south of the Canadian border, and we worked from there for one year. In early 1972 we moved to The Dalles, a township of some 10,000 people, in northern Oregon on the Columbia River. At the time of writing, four years has elapsed of the new search and investigation; it can hardly be called an expedition any more. A permanent base has been established in The Dalles, Oregon, which includes my own home, an equipment storage facility, and an Exhibition and Information Center. The latter is in a 55-foot mobile home and is permanently housed on a site at West Sixth Street in The Dalles.

The Exhibition is self-supporting and also helps to make extra income for the search and investigation project. But its real value is in the form of information. Opened in May of 1974, it filled a need in the Bigfoot field. Once it became established, with the help of The Dalles Chamber of Commerce and the excellent publicity that it obtained in newspapers, radio, and television, people began to come in with information about the phenomenon. Much of it was old or too insubstantial to be of any real value. Some of it was even imaginary. But a great deal of it was very useful, especially where subsequent investigation showed the people who gave it to us to be men and women of character and integrity. This information, on sightings and on footprint findings, has been the base on which we have built most of our search and investigation plans for the past year. It has helped us to begin, at long last, to form the geo-time patterns that are essential to the search and which in time can lead to success. The main reason for this sudden new flow of information is that people have begun to realize that the Information Center is a place where they can tell their stories; a place where they will get a serious reception, no matter what they have to say, no matter how tall sounds their tale; where they will not be laughed at or ridiculed in any way; where their names and their stories will be held in the strictest confidence.

Four years of work in the new search have produced an extraordinary amount of new evidence. At the Information Center the files bulge with information on sightings, footprint findings, migration routes, eating habits, food, coloration, size. Hundreds of letters have been received from people all over the United States, and with the establishment of the monthly newsletter, *The Bigfoot News*, in September 1974, this flow doubled and then tripled. Visitors have come from all over the world and many of them have stayed to work on a volunteer basis, either with me or with my associates.

One of the most often-phrased challenges to the existence of the Bigfoot is, how is it that no one has ever found any bones? How is it there are no skeletons, no skulls, no bits and pieces found lying around?

There are four answers. A) They do not exist. B) They bury their dead and bury them deep. C) Their bones dissolve and disappear. D) Something comes along and eats them.

Let us deal first with A) They do not exist. If we believe this then there is no further argument. No bodies, no bones and that is all there is to it. But if they do exist? That takes us to B) They bury their dead. This is not an unreasonable assumption. Some of the Neanderthal men buried their dead, as we have discovered, and the Neanderthals were a pretty primitive lot. When he was working with Roger Patterson and headquartered at Yakima, Dennis Jenson saw a letter from a man who swore that he had watched three Bigfeet burying a fourth. They dug a deep hole, using only their hands as tools. After placing the body in the hole and covering it with earth they rolled huge boulders, each weighing many hundreds of pounds, onto the grave. The letter, with its extraordinary story, was lost from Patterson's files after he died in January 1972. Jenson, who saw the letter only once, was unable to

126

remember the name and address of the man who wrote it. If the letter was a true account of an actual burying, then the Bigfeet do bury their dead. If they do, this would help to explain why we do not find any skeletons. If they do not then we have to deal with C) Their bones dissolve and disappear. A nice little theory and one that conveniently disposes of the "no bone" problem. Could it be true? The answer is yes. It depends almost entirely on soil conditions.

Fresh bone is composed of organic protein fibers. When a bone begins to fossilize, the protein material disappears. Percolated mineral material, usually from the ground waters in the surrounding soil, takes its place. This is followed by various chemical reactions at the molecular level and the bone, through the course of time, slowly changes to stone. The chemical changes are such that in pure fossilization, the shape and size of the bone remain unchanged. But, as I said, all this depends on soil conditions.

Bones fossilize in wet alkaline soils and in dry alkaline soils. In the latter, light sub-fossils are usually found. In wet soils that are airless, such as the peat bogs of Denmark or the turf fields of Ireland, complete preservation may occur. But in wet acid soils there is no fossilization and the bones disappear. The soil composition of much of the coastal ranges of the Pacific Northwest, the supposed area of habitat of the Bigfoot, is wet acid.

And lastly, D) Something comes along and eats the bones. Another convenient answer? No, for the forested ranges of the Pacific Northwest have a natural disposal system that is as efficient, if not as violent and quick, as the African and Asian systems. It consists of crows and ravens, buzzards and other meat-eating birds, including eagles. The eagle, incidentally, proud predator though he seems to be, will not hesitate to eat carrion when there is a free meal around. Other members of the disposal squad are coyotes, wolves and foxes, various rodents, and of course, porcupines. And the leader of the pack, close behind the first crows and often even ahead of them? Euarctos, the black bear. Led by the black bear with his extremely keen sense of smell, this highly efficient group of garbage disposers works tirelessly at its job of keeping the forest clean. Everything is eaten, and if the particular carcass

127

happens to be a big buck deer with antlers, those are eaten by the ivory-eaters of Africa, the porcupines. Seldom are bones of any kind found in the northwest, and this is one of the reasons. In the course of the I.W.C.S. investigations I have questioned hundreds of people about finding bones. I have never yet met anyone who has found the bones of a cougar or mountain lion, only one man who has found the bones of a dead bear, and perhaps half a dozen who have seen complete deer skeletons. These latter, when found, were usually quite fresh.

The second most common question, again often asked as a challenge, and usually from a fairly skeptical source, is this. If the Bigfeet exist, what do they eat in the wilderness? Surely there is hardly enough to support the dietary needs of a creature as big as it is supposed to be? What would it eat in the winter?

The answer to this one is actually fairly easy. There is, in the wilderness areas of the northwest and also in British Columbia, an abundance of food for the omnivorous creature we would suppose the Bigfoot to be. And I know whereof I speak, for on several occasions I have been forced to fall back on natural foods when my supplies ran out, and I have been able to keep the inner man happy every day without undue effort.

Creatures of the size that the Bigfeet are supposed to be would have to be omnivorous to survive in the northwest. That is to say, they would have to eat everything that was available. Their diet would therefore include, but not be restricted to, small animals and fish, water life of all kinds, including frogs, prawns, crabs, hermit crabs, newts, water lizards, water snakes, various crustaceans, limpits, cockles, mussels and clams. Like the bear, they would eat carrion of all kinds, and it is possible that their sense of smell would be developed to the point where, like the bear, they would be able to scent it from a great distance and then locate it by scent. They would eat birds' eggs and, of course, young birds. In the herbivorous area, the diet would include bark and the underbark of certain trees which is edible even to man, sedges, lake weeds, berries, rose hips, fruit, nuts, shoots of certain edible bushes, many forms of grass, leaves, flowers and many other kinds of wild plants found in the northwest. And in the insectivorous area, all kinds of insects, including moths, butterflies, bees and their honey, worms, ants and their larvae, and beetles.

Like the bears, they might also be cannibalistic and this of course would be another reason why we just do not find any of their carcasses lying around in the woods. (A male bear will eat his own young.)

The third most oft-repeated question concerns habitat and space. The people who ask it are, more often than not, city dwellers, or foreigners from places like Chicago or New York, who have little or no conception of the size of the Pacific Northwest ranges or the extent of the vast reaches of forest that still stand across the mountains. The question is: Where could the things live? Where could they hide? How is it that more of them are not seen with the mountains full of fishermen and hikers and snowmobilers?

In 1972 the media launched upon the startled world the story of a lost tribe found deep in the jungles of the Philippines. The newspapers, their interest in lost tribes and lost men stirred by the finding of the Tasaday, also speculated on the number of Japanese soldiers who might still be hiding in south Pacific island jungles. Over the years, as we know, several Japanese soldiers have come out of hiding. Sure enough, during that year, another Japanese appeared, twenty-five years after the end of hostilities. The Tasaday, of course, were not hiding. They were just there, waiting to be discovered. There were not very many of them, true, and they did live in dense forest in a little-penetrated area. But they really did not mind being discovered and might even have wanted to be found, if they had known that there was anyone to find them. The Japanese soldier, on the other hand, was in hiding, as he thought, from American soldiers, and up to the very last moment he made every effort to hide and remain unseen. The area of the Philippines, where the Tasaday were found, is 115,707 square miles. The total area of Guam, from the jungles of which the valiant and still-fighting Japanese soldier appeared, is 209 square miles. The area where he—and until recently several of his companions—had managed to remain hidden for some twenty-eight years, has a human population of 87,000 people.

What is known as "the area of habitat" of the Bigfoot is that area which shows evidence in the form of history, footprints, and sightings, that supports the existence of the creatures. It comprises part of northern California and part of northern Idaho. It includes all of the coast range and all of the Cascade range of Oregon and Washington and all of the coast range of British Columbia, north to a line drawn east-west just below Prince Rupert, in northern British Columbia. The size of this area, the actual area that has produced and that continues to produce the evidence of which I write, is not less than 125,000 square miles.

This vast area is composed, for the most part, of very rugged country. It contains many high mountains that hold permanent snow on their peaks. Visible from The Dalles, Oregon, for instance, are three peaks, all in excess of 9500 feet.* There are deep valleys and gorges with ice cold streams, high ridges and cliffs and hundreds of miles of dense forest. There are many government-designated wilderness areas, where, even if there are roads, no wheeled transport of any kind is allowed. There are dozens of deep ravines that never hear the voice of man. For the most part the total area is unoccupied by people, for people in the United States and in Canada seem to prefer to live in the lowlands, where life is less harsh and where the amenities of civilization are within reach. British Columbia itself has a total area of 366,255 square miles and a population of only 2,190,000 people. Three-quarters of this population live in one-fifth of the total land area. The remainder of British Columbia is very thinly populated.

The Bigfeet, if they do indeed live in this huge range of forested mountains, are obviously not sitting around waiting to be discovered. Unlike the Tasaday, who lived in a very small area of jungle and made their permanent homes in a series of caves, the Bigfeet, the evidence suggests, are constantly on the move and, like a tribe of Australian aborigines gone "walkabout," are here today and very much gone tomorrow. Again, unlike the Tasaday, and much more like our Japanese soldiers, they do not want to be found and it is

*Mount Saint Helens, 9677 feet; Mount Hood, 11,245 feet; Mount Adams, 12,307 feet.

suggested by the evidence that they assiduously avoid man at all times. With a range as vast as their habitat suggests, this should really not be too difficult. Statistics show, in fact, how well protected they are by the nature of their habitat, its cover, and its size. A quick glance at the Bigfoot search guide should clarify this for anyone who has ideas about finding one, either alone or with a small army of men. The chart statistics are quite serious, even if the idea of a stationary Bigfoot is not.

These questions of fossil bones, food, and habitat cover will, no doubt, be discussed again and again. The skeptics, enraged that I should put forward such puny answers to their challenges, will take my theories and hurl them out of the nearest window. Alas, after five years of hard research on the subject, they are the best that I can do at this time. Perhaps in time I shall be able to do better. With determination and enterprise even a mouse trap can be improved. Or so people tell me.

BIGFOOT SEARCH GUIDE
One square mile / One searcher / One Bigfoot

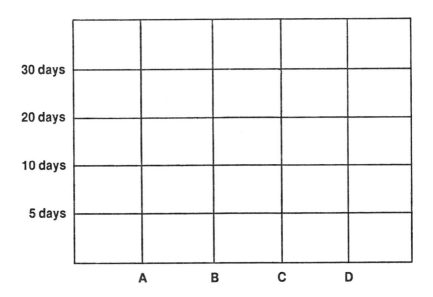

Relative Density of Forest:

A. Light forest with light undergrowth.
B. Thick conifers or other types with light undergrowth.
C. Thick conifer growth or other with medium undergrowth.
D. Thick forest of any type with dense undergrowth.

The above chart is really a simple "How To Catch Your Own Bigfoot" guide. It is not difficult to operate. The first thing to do is to make sure that the Bigfoot, the object of your search, is stationary. Then determine the density of the particular area that you are going to search. Then apply the number of days indicated by the chart. Provided that your Bigfoot does not move and also provided that you have sufficient water and can carry sufficient food for the time involved, success is guaranteed. For larger areas, multiply by the square mileage on your maps. For the total area (of presently indicated evidence) multiply by 125,000. If, of course, there is a possibility that your Bigfoot is moving and is not situated and stationary in one place, the best thing to do is forget the whole idea and stay at home.

VII

The 1967 Film: Big Man in a Fur Coat?
Or the Real McCoy?

If it is a fake then it is a masterpiece and as far as we are concerned the only place in the world where a simulation of that quality could be created would be here, at Disney Studios, and this footage was not made here.
—CHIEF TECHNICIAN at Disney Studios, Burbank, California after an examination of the 1967 Bigfoot footage with Peter Byrne in January 1973

MY SAFARI JOURNAL FOR OCTOBER 20, 1967, tells me that on that day I was deep in the jungles of southwest Nepal, guiding a very difficult, rather gnomelike gentleman from Nashville, Tennessee, on a leopard hunt. Colonel X, as I shall call him, was sixty-five years of age, very rich, addicted to sour mash whiskey and cigarettes. He had a hacking cough, he talked incessantly, and he was one of the worst shots that I have ever encountered. I had refused to allow him to sit in a tree to shoot his leopard. It was simply against my principles and I told him that if he wanted a leopard trophy he would have to shoot it on the ground.

We had been stalking the leopard for two days. Now, October 20, was the morning of the third day and I had a fairly good grip on the big cat's movements. I had carefully instructed the colonel. I had told him that until we got close enough to shoot, all that he had to do was follow me very carefully and very very quietly. When the time came to shoot I would tell him. But in the meantime he was to look only at the ground, at where he was putting his feet, and he was to put his feet where he was looking and with extreme care. Silence, absolute silence, was essential. The slightest noise and the leopard would be gone. The breaking of a tiny twig, the crackling of a dry leaf underfoot, would be enough to have the big cat perform its disappearing trick.

Once that happened we would have to start looking for another leopard.

The morning of October 20 had dawned bright and clear. The winter weather of the southern Nepal jungles cannot be equalled anywhere in the world and it was sometime about seven, after about two hours of stalking, that we began to close in on the cat. We moved very slowly now. Every inch of the ground was carefully studied, the pattern of the pug marks was analyzed and the jungle ahead and on both sides was watched with the greatest of care. Behind me, breathing rather heavily and occasionally making vague choking noises as he tried to smother his smoker's cough, moved the colonel.

Excitement rose as we moved closer, and I could hear the colonel's breathing getting faster. Suddenly a group of rhesus macaques began to chatter over our heads. They had seen the leopard and they were warning the other jungle folk of the danger. Instantly the leopard uttered a deep growl of annoyance and the growl enabled me to pinpoint his position. I moved to the right a few feet and the colonel moved behind me. Ahead of us the jungle opened and for thirty yards or so there was a small glade with short grass and very light undergrowth, dew shining in the morning sun. The colonel, his breath now beginning to sound like a distant express train, moved in behind me.

Then the leopard walked out into the glade and turned and looked directly at us. I remained perfectly still and, keeping my eyes on the big cat, whispered, in the lightest of whispers, to the colonel to shoot. For a few seconds there was silence. The monkeys, sensing a jungle drama about to be enacted, stopped chattering. The colonel stopped breathing. There was no sound and the big dog leopard, his black-rosetted coat of orange magnificent in the morning sun, was frozen in position. It seemed as though time had stopped. Then the colonel made his play. He leaned forward and took a deep breath. He pointed a crooked and shaking forefinger across my shoulder. And in a voice that shattered the jungle silence, set the monkeys to screaming and leaping for their lives, and alerted every animal within a mile, he roared, "That's a leopard!" Needless to say, we never did see that leopard again.

We returned to camp and had breakfast and talked about different tactics and so passed another jungle day, routine, ordinary and, except for the humor of the leopard incident, uneventful. But for two men in the woods of northern California, ten thousand miles away from my safari camp, it was a far from ordinary day. For, if their story is true, in the afternoon of this day, October 20, 1967, they encountered and were able to photograph for the first time, on movie film, a large female Bigfoot.

The film, or rather the footage, which is what it really is, consists of twenty-eight feet of 16mm color movie footage taken with a hand-held camera. The footage is of poor quality and, with the exception of a few frames at the beginning of the sequence, in the middle, and at the end, which are sharp enough to show detail, the footage is blurred and unclear. The subject of the footage is a large, hairy, upright-walking figure. It is seen walking from left to right, turning once to look in the direction of the cameraman and then disappearing into the trees. The site at which the footage was made is the partially dry stream bed of a stream called Bluff Creek, a stream that begins in Del Norte County, flows into Humboldt County and empties into the Klamath River. These counties are in northern California. The photographer and his partner report that the time at which the footage was obtained was somewhere between 1:15 P.M. and 1:30 P.M. and the date, October 20, 1967.

The 1967 Bluff Creek footage has been and is the subject of much controversy. Since the rights were purchased from the original photographer by a commercial company, who then distributed it throughout the United States, very many people have seen it. It has also been released in Europe and Australia and other countries and it has been seen on television as well as in movie theatres by thousands of people. The question is, of course, is it real? Is the subject of the film a real living creature, or is it a man dressed in a fur suit? Here, in this chapter, I am going to set down on paper all that I know about the film and the filmmakers. I will add to this some of the latest findings on the film in reports from groups of expert viewers and examiners in three different countries. I feel competent at least to discuss the footage, for

I have spent many hours with the two men who obtained it, have viewed the footage, for purposes of examination, perhaps a hundred times and have visited and studied the site where it was made in Del Norte County, California.

The two men who obtained the footage were from Washington state. Their names were Bob Gimlin, of Union Gap, and Roger Patterson, of Tampico. Union Gap lies in the Yakima Valley and through time has become almost an extension of the large town of Yakima. Tampico is a scattering of houses and small farms about twenty miles west of Yakima. Bob Gimlin is a horse breeder and cattleman. Roger Patterson, who died in January, 1972, was a horse breeder and rodeo rider. Both became interested in the Bigfoot search in 1963 and from that time conducted, when time out from work allowed, their own private searches in Washington, Oregon, and northern California. Sometime in these years Patterson leased a 16mm movie camera and began carrying it with him. They had agreed that if they could obtain footage of a Bigfoot, they would not attempt to shoot one. As a precaution, however, they both carried rifles.

Being horsemen, their method of hunting was from horseback and when they went out on a search their equipment consisted of two riding horses, one pack horse, and a large horse-carrier truck.

They drove down to Bluff Creek in northern California, the area where we concentrated the 1960 search. It was, even to 1967, an area that consistently produced large, unexplained footprints. They made camp on the west bank of Bluff Creek, just above where it is joined by Notice Creek and from there commenced their search. The bed of Bluff Creek in its upper reaches is mostly dry. The stream, some six inches deep, occupies only a few feet of the bed. The stream bed itself, above Notice Creek, is probably one hundred yards wide. In the afternoon of the day of the incident, the two men were riding north in the bed of the creek. Both men were mounted on their own horses and behind them, trailing on a rope, came a pack horse. The pack horse carried light camping equipment, some food and so on, and was their safeguard against being unable to get back to camp in the same day. It was a fine day, with sunshine and no wind. The hooves of the horses made little or no noise in the soft grey sand of the creek bed.

They approached a large, jumbled pile of logs lying almost in the center of the stream bed. The logs, some of them very large and still carrying their roots, were the result of a sudden flood the previous year that had washed them out of the higher reaches of the creek and piled them up at this point. The pile, or logjam as it might be called, was probably one hundred feet in width and fifteen feet high. It effectively hid the approach of the horsemen from anything that might lie behind it to the north.

Both horsemen came around the log pile together and, according to their story, found a large female Bigfoot squatting on the bank of the watercourse ahead and to their left. She immediately stood up and walked away.

Things seem to have happened very quickly after that. All three horses panicked and both men were, again according to their story, shocked and alarmed at the sight of the huge creature. The pack horse reared, broke its trailing rope and bolted southwards. Gimlin's horse began to panic and he was forced to dismount in a hurry. He slid out of the saddle and took a firm grip on the reins and managed to hold the horse. Patterson had less luck. His horse reared and then fell over sideways, coming down on his right leg, crushing the metal stirrup on his foot and pinning him temporarily to the ground.

While Patterson was struggling to get up, the Bigfoot was walking rapidly away. Then Patterson's horse was up and he rose with it, pulling the camera out of the saddle bag and shouting to Gimlin to cover him with a rifle as he ran after the Bigfoot.

Patterson aimed his camera at the creature and kept his finger pressed on the trigger while he changed position three times and until he ran out of film. There was, according to him, only twenty-eight feet of film in the camera. The remainder had been used earlier to shoot other subjects that were to be part of a general film on the Bigfoot. Then the camera was empty, the Bigfoot was gone, and it was all over. The two men rejoined each other and, after a brief discussion, decided that it was more important to go back and look for the horses—both the pack horse and Patterson's horse, which had also bolted as soon as he left it—than to pursue the Bigfoot. This they did, finding the two horses grazing quietly a mile to the south. They retrieved the horses, returned to the scene of the photography, tied up the horses and set out to try and track the Bigfoot. They were unable to track it and after some searching they came back again to the photography site, made plaster casts of the footprints that the creature had left in the soft sand and then, with the horses, returned to their base camp near Notice Creek. They closed up the camp, loaded the horses in the horse truck and drove out to Eureka, on the coast, to mail the film to a relative in Yakima for processing. They drove out via the Bluff Creek store on the main Hoopa Road to Orleans Road, then through Weitchpec, Hoopa, Willow Creek, and Arcata to Eureka. They stopped at one place, in Willow Creek, to talk with the owner of the Willow Creek Variety Store, a friend. From Eureka, according to Patterson, they mailed the film by registered airmail to Yakima, Washington.

The film was received the following morning, October twenty-first, by Patterson's relative in Yakima. It was taken by this man to Seattle where, on the evening of the twenty-first, it was processed. It was returned to Yakima on the night of the twenty-first and then shown to various people, in Yakima and at Tampico, next day, October twenty-second.

The 1967 footage, as I mentioned before, caused a great deal of controversy. Opinion, among those who have seen it, is much divided. The burning question, of course, is the reality of the subject of the film.

American scientific opinion on the film is, for the most part, fairly blunt. As far as American scientists are concerned, the film is a hoax. The subject of the film is a man in a rather cleverly made fur suit and that is all there is to it. But the trouble with scientific opinion is that with only two exceptions that I know of, not one single scientist in this country has taken the time to inspect the film, make a careful examination of it and/or subject it to expert analysis. The film has been seen by primatologists, mammologists, biologists and zoologists at the Smithsonian, the Natural History Museum of New York, the Primate Institute at Emory University

138

and the Primate Institute at Beaverton, Oregon, the latter probably the foremost institute of its kind in the country. The "examination" in each case was usually limited to one viewing, after which the film was simply declared a fake. I myself have been present at some of these viewings and the reader may be interested in seeing some of the weighty scientific opinions that were directed at the film. I will quote three of them, as follows:

1. Nothing walks like that. Therefore it is a fake.
2. The subject in the film has breasts that are hairy. Apes do not have breasts and humans do not have hairy breasts. Therefore it is a hoax.
3. If they were there, we would have known about them by now.

Two men, both eminent in their respective fields, have had a closer look at the film. One is Dr. Hobart van Deusen of the New York Museum of Natural History. Dr. van Deusen, who is president of the prestigious Explorers Club of New York, made a guarded statement to the effect that it could be real. In conversation with me at his offices in New York he added that as far as he was concerned it was real enough at least to warrant investigation.

The second scientist who has taken the time to examine the footage and also to help have it submitted for further examination, is Dr. John Napier, one-time Director of the Primate Biology Program at the Smithsonian Institution, presently Visiting Professor of Primate Biology at Birkbeck College, University of London. Dr. Napier has not only examined the film, he has written about it and made some very definite statements about it. As we shall see, they are not all positive statements concerning the authenticity of the film. But at least they are statements in written form backed by the weight and authority of Dr. Napier's studies and experience. We shall discuss them to some extent in this chapter. But before we do let us go back to Bluff Creek again for a few moments and have another look at the subject of the '67 footage, its possible size, weight, footprint size, and stride.

The only measurement that we seem to be able to determine with any degree of accuracy is the length of the Bluff Creek creature's feet. According to Gimlin and Patterson and, later, others who found and measured the footprints on or near the film site and who also made plaster casts of them, the feet were fourteen and one-half inches in length. The stride was also measured at the site and although we cannot be sure of the accuracy of that measurement, it appears to have been close to forty-two inches.

As to height and weight, there has been a lot of wild guessing in this area. Patterson estimated the height at seven feet, four inches. Gimlin believes that the creature was very much smaller than this and probably closer to six feet, one or two inches. As to weight, the estimates vary from 350 pounds (Gimlin) to 800 pounds (Patterson).

In an attempt to determine properly the weight of the creature of the 1967 footage, two groups of people have examined the site and made series of measurements of the trees that it contains, the tree stumps, logs, et cetera. Both groups have used human models as a standard of measurement and have shot extra footage of these models, at the site, for comparison purposes. Part of the examination procedure of both groups consisted of superimposing the model used in their footage on the subject of the 1967 footage.

The first group worked with Jim McClarin, of Sacramento, California. His conclusions were that the creature measured six feet, eight inches in height.

The second group consisted of myself and one companion as a model. My model was just six feet in height and using him in superimposition of slides on the '67 footage and taking very careful measurements at the site itself, I came to the conclusion that the subject of the '67 footage stood a maximum of six feet, five inches.

The problem—and perhaps the reason for the inconsistency of measurement between the two groups—is that the first group used as their basic measurement guide a frame from the 1967 film that does not show the actual position of the feet of the figure in the film. The second group—my examination—used another frame that does show the creature's feet, but used it in calculations at the site that were made five years later, when it was not possible to determine accurately the precise position of the figure. Again, it was not possible to be absolutely sure of the position of the cameraman in relation to the frames that were used in the examination. Accurate determination of both these positions would be essential to a definite and conclusive measurement.

When I went to California to carry out my examination at the 1967 footage site I tried to borrow a theodolite, or transit, for use in the calculations. But I was unable to obtain one in the time available. The use of a theodolite would greatly have assisted my work and would definitely have added accuracy to the measurements that I took. However, I did use a measuring pole in conjunction with a large number of background measurements. The result was a mathematical computation that went toward establishing a mean height for the subject of the footage. The result was a figure that is, in effect, a happy medium between Jim McClarin's height estimate of eighty inches and mine of seventy-seven inches. This would give the figure in the footage a height of six feet, six-and-a-half inches. This is the maximum that I would allow.

I did not try to determine weight nor did I come to any exact conclusion about bulk, other than that the figure is very large in comparison with, say, a human figure. The bulk is not out of proportion to the height. Again, the height is in line with human proportions. There are many men in northern California of this height, or even taller, just as there are in the United States now many basketball players of seven feet or even more.

Napier, in his writings on the general subject of the Bigfoot, gives a great deal of attention to the 1967 footage. He discusses, at some length, the analysis done of the footage by a Dr. Don Grieve, a British anatomist specializing in the human gait. Dr. Grieve wrote a detailed scientific report of his findings after a careful examination of the footage. The figure at which he arrives, for the height of the subject of the footage, is six feet, five inches. Napier accepts the Grieve findings in this respect but points out that if this is the correct height, then there is something very wrong with the size of the figure's feet. The foot measurement given by Patterson, and afterwards confirmed by others who examined the footprints or actually measured the plaster casts that Gimlin and Patterson made of the prints at the site, is fourteen-and-a-half inches. According to Napier in his book, this measurement is not in correct proportion to the given height. He feels that a figure with fourteen-and-a-half-inch feet should have a minimum height of seven feet, eight inches. He bases this on the formula, height = maximum foot length x 6.6. He concludes that either the footprints are fake, or the film is, or both are.

The conjecture and discussion aroused by the 1967 footage is endless. A year from now, perhaps even ten years from now, the subject will be hurled back and forth between the skeptics and nonskeptics. Did Gimlin and Patterson have a partner? Was there a third man with them, a big man who climbed into a fur coat and then paraded up and down while they photographed him? Who was the third man, if he exists? Where did he come from? Where is he so successfully hiding now?

Again, did Patterson and associates unknown arrange for this third man without Gimlin's knowledge? Was the third man placed up there in the woods, waiting until he got the signal to move into the creek and then show himself for those few brief moments of frantic surprise that panicked the horses and were over so quickly that Gimlin was bamboozled into belief in a real creature?

There is no doubt in my mind, in the minds of most of the serious Bigfoot "investigators" and, I believe, in Napier's mind, that the 1967 footage is a vital link in the chain of evidence, both hard and soft, that supports the existence of the Bigfoot. Dr. van Deusen, of the New York Museum of Natural History, will agree with me on this. If the footage was faked, it is of course worthless. But if it is real—and we must face the fact that it is possible, it is feasible—then it proves without a doubt that in 1967, in Bluff Creek, Del Norte County, California, at least one female Bigfoot was alive and well and happily striding through the mountain forests.

I was visiting with my brother Bryan in Lake Tahoe in late 1972. We talked about the 1967 film footage and its value as evidence and Bryan pointed out that no one had ever done a really thorough study of the footage with the end in view of definitely establishing the height of the subject of the footage. He suggested that I visit the Bluff Creek area on my return to Oregon, spend some time there, and endeavor to do this. I agreed and called Ernie Alameda, one of my associates from 1960, who lived near Bluff Creek, suggesting that he meet me and accompany me to the film site.

Hoopa, where Ernie and his wife Dorothy live, is in the Hoopa Indian Reservation. Ernie owns and manages the Oaks Cafe, in the Hoopa Valley. At least I think that is what his profession is. I am not sure, for I have never yet arrived at the Oaks Cafe and actually found Ernie working there. Ernie was a salmon fisherman and invariably he was "gone fishing" somewhere down the river. Dorothy is a Yurok Indian and is one of the most gracious and gentle women that I have ever met. She told me, many years ago, of how her father had encountered a Bigfoot in one of the little streams that comes down out of the hills and flows into the Trinity River, in the Hoopa reservation. The point of her father's story that Dorothy particularly remembered, she told me, was that her father said the Bigfoot seemed to sense him rather than see him. It was standing in the stream, up to its waist in water and with its back to her father's line of approach. Because the noise of the stream would have covered any sound that he made as he came around the corner from where he saw the Bigfoot, he believed that it could not have heard him. But it looked around and, seeing the man watching it, leapt out of the stream and with a bound or two disappeared into the forest.

Ernie was unable to accompany me to Bluff Creek and so after visiting with him and Dorothy I loaded my camping gear in the Scout and drove north to Onion Mountain, a peak in the Bluff Creek area. There was an old cabin on top of the mountain and I moved in and made it my base, driving from there on the Onion Mountain to Lonesome Ridge Road every day, to the film footage site, to take my measurements and do my studies. I had with me some tapes of interviews made with Patterson not long after the event of the filming in which he described the incident and the aftermath. These were useful to me in my studies and each evening when I came in after a day down in the creek bed at the film site I played these on my tape recorder and listened carefully to what Patterson had to say. From the top of Onion Mountain one can see the Pacific and the Californian coastline, a splendid sight on a clear day. There is a lot of fog on this coast, even in the summer but during the day it generally stays out to sea. In the evening it moves inland and each evening that I was on the mountain I watched it, a solid wave of ivory-colored cream, pouring in across the coastline and through the trees of the lower slopes. At night, when the wind died, there was no sound other than the crackling of the fire in the cabin stove. Footprints were found on Onion Mountain in the late sixties and I could not help thinking, as I lay in my sleeping bag in the silent night, of how many places there were like Onion Mountain, where a Bigfoot could spend all its life without being discovered by man. In a week I had finished my studies. I loaded up the faithful Scout and in one long day drove right through to base at The Dalles.

Through personal contact with Patterson and Gimlin, contact that included many hours of face to face interviews and conversations, I was able to apply to my investigation of the 1967 footage a more than average knowledge, what might even be called an intimate knowledge. With my knowledge of the backgrounds of both men I was able to ask myself if Gimlin and Patterson were actually capable of creating and perpetrating a hoax of the magnitude of the '67 incident. Were they, for instance, intellectually, emotionally, physically and economically capable of the work involved: the construction of the fur suit that is, as seen in the footage, so perfect that it has, after five years, defied the examination of "where is the zipper" seekers all over the world; the costs involved in its construction, whether it was made privately or by a commercial firm; the problems of maintaining secrecy with the firm that made the suit, I might add, there being only one or two such companies in the United States; the problems of keeping the "third man" quiet, for the rest of all of his life and their lives. Looking at the footage in this light one might phrase the vital question, *how* did they hoax it, rather than *did* they hoax it. In my book both men lacked, primarily, the intellectual capacity essential to the production of a hoax which several examining experts have termed a masterpiece. This is a point which I believe strongly supports the authenticity of the footage.

144

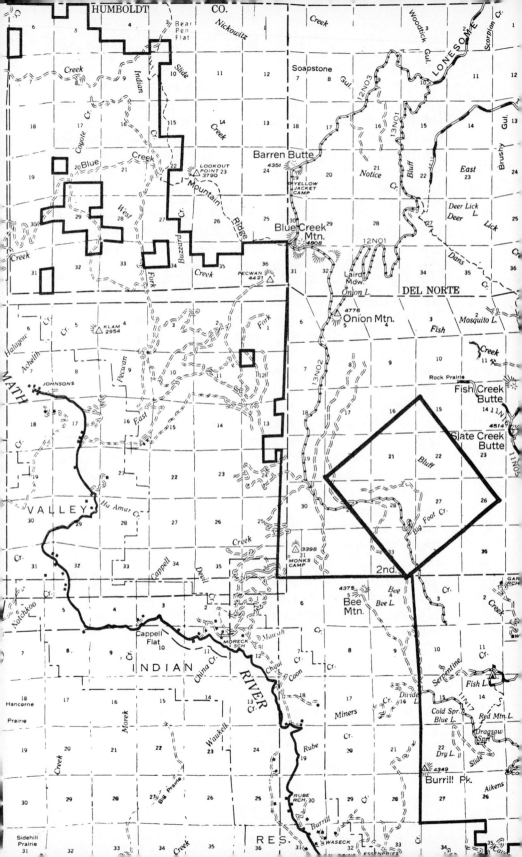

There are other points that help to support the reality of the footage and that came to light as a result of my Onion Mountain research period. Two of them that bear serious examination—when the question of a hoax is being considered—are the actual position of the site in relation to its immediate surroundings and the actual day on which the footage was obtained.

The site of the filming (see map) was an open, dry, creek bed of approximately one hundred yards in width and with high steep sides, partially covered with timber, partially bare. Just north of the site, the stream bed bends to the left (looking upstream) or northwest. To the south it runs straight for a matter of two or three hundred yards and then curves gently to the southeast. From this curve it continues southeast and south, down to the junction of Notice Creek and the site of Louse Camp, scene of many a 1960 campfire for me and my companions of those years. The bed of the stream is bare except for scattered logs here and there and two piles of dead falls that lie just to the south of the site of the filming. One of these was the pile around which Gimlin and Patterson rode when they said they encountered the Bigfoot. In 1967 a road ran along the east side of the stream, close to the stream bed and at places almost in it. It was a dirt and gravel road that had been cut by a caterpillar tractor for use in a log removal program. This road was used, at the time, by the occasional fisherman or hunter and it was negotiable with a four-wheel-drive vehicle. On the west side of the stream, also running parallel to the stream but set in the bank about a thousand feet above it, was another road. This was originally a logging road but in recent years had been converted to an all-weather road with a bitumen surface. This road was negotiable by vehicles of all kinds and could be driven at moderate speed. From this road the site of the footage could be seen.

This, then, is a description of the actual site of the '67 footage. Open to the south, partially open to the north, visible from the approach road that lay in and along the stream bed and visible from the road that came up from the south and ran across the hillside a thousand feet above it. It was, generally, speaking, an open area. A highly visible area

146

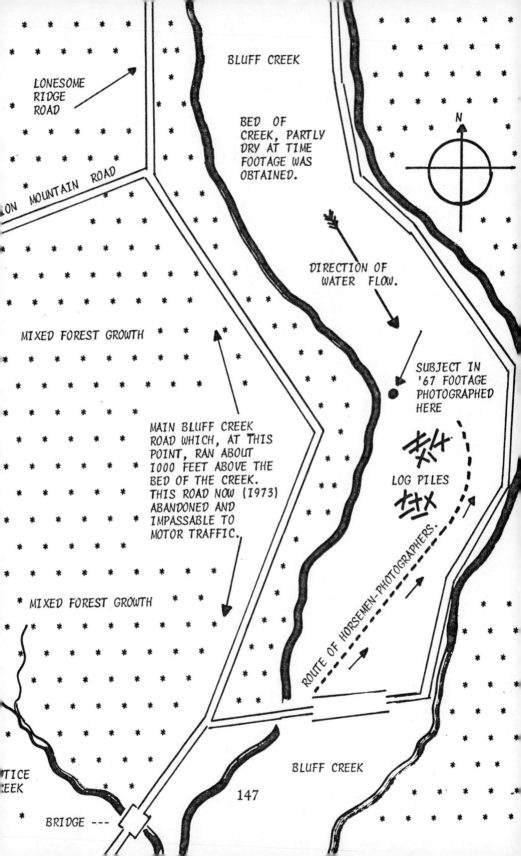

LONESOME
RIDGE
ROAD

BLUFF CREEK

BED OF
CREEK, PARTLY
DRY AT TIME
FOOTAGE WAS
OBTAINED.

N

ON MOUNTAIN ROAD

DIRECTION OF
WATER FLOW.

MIXED FOREST GROWTH

SUBJECT IN
'67 FOOTAGE
PHOTOGRAPHED
HERE

MAIN BLUFF CREEK
ROAD WHICH, AT THIS
POINT, RAN ABOUT
1000 FEET ABOVE THE
BED OF THE CREEK.
THIS ROAD NOW (1973)
ABANDONED AND
IMPASSABLE TO
MOTOR TRAFFIC.

LOG PILES

ROUTE OF HORSEMEN-PHOTOGRAPHERS.

MIXED FOREST GROWTH

TICE
REEK

BLUFF CREEK

BRIDGE ---

and, for a hoaxer making a fake film, a highly vulnerable area.

During my research from the lonely little cabin on Onion Mountain, I put myself in the position of a pair of hoaxers intent on making a fake film. Would I choose Bluff Creek? Probably, because Bluff Creek and the general mountain area of upper Del Norte County had, in the 1960s, produced a considerable amount of Bigfoot evidence. The finds dated back to those made by myself and Bryan and Steve Matthes in 1960, and they included at least one sighting and also an incident in which some heavy road-building machinery had been damaged by "something" which, according to at least one of the men who were there at the time, Thomas Sourwine, of Lyle, Washington, picked up a 300-pound stone and hurled it several times against the sides of the machinery. In other words, Bluff Creek and its watershed area was known as Bigfoot country to many people, country that had produced evidence and where searchers might find more, if they looked.

Again, would I choose the general area between the confluence of Bluff Creek and Notice Creek and the northern course of Bluff Creek? Yes, probably, because it was in this particular area, in 1960 and also prior to that time, that most of the footprints were found.

But, in having to decide on an actual site for the hoax within this area, would I choose the place where Gimlin and Patterson made their footage? The answer was no, definitely not, and for the reasons that lie in my description of the general area: the open visibility of the area from the south, the north, and the west. In 1967, when the footage was made, Bluff Creek was still a favorite area for Bigfoot searchers and any weekend one was liable to encounter small groups of people from Hoopa, or from Willow Creek, or even further, driving in there in their cars, camping overnight, and hoping to get a quick look at a Bigfoot. It was also an area where some deer hunters came and even the odd fisherman. All of these people coming into the Bluff Creek area used the main Bluff Creek road. The road has long since collapsed, but in 1967 it was the main route into the area. Cars, pickups, jeeps, and other four-wheel-drive vehicles came all the way up into the North Creek area using this road and from Notice Creek they would drive still further north on this road, or, if their vehicles were equipped for it, branch off into the bed of Bluff Creek, just above Notice Creek, and take the lower road that runs in and alongside the bed of Bluff Creek. A hoax party could too easily be surprised by a car coming up this creek bed road and no one in his right mind would choose the actual site of the '67 footage for time-consuming and elaborate preparations that would have to precede the actual shooting of the footage, or the actual shooting itself. From the upper road, the one that runs on the west hillside a thousand feet above the creek, not only could people arriving by car see down into the site of the filming, but a hoax party, working in this area, might not see the onlookers. They would not see them, in fact, unless they were actually watching for them and would certainly not hear their approach above the noise of the water in the shallow stream that flowed down one side of the dry creekbed. Again, there were other possible sites further up the stream that were much safer and where a hoax party would stand much less chance of being surprised. A dozen small streams flow into Bluff Creek in its upper reaches and several of these offered heavier cover, good film sites, and closed surroundings that would give adequate protection for the hoaxers against surprise. One of these, for instance, is Scorpion Creek, a deep, densely forested ravine that I examined during my Onion Mountain research program.

As to the day and the time that the footage was made, these are two more points that seem to stand in favor of the footage being real and as such they should be mentioned. In separate statements and in tapes both men state that the time was between 1:20 and 1:30 P.M. Now the actual time is not important. What is important is that it was afternoon and, also, that the afternoon in question was a Friday.

Friday is the first day of the weekend, the day when people like to get off from work early and out for the weekend. It is the day that campers and hikers, hunters and fishermen and, yes, Bigfoot searchers of the weekend type, pack their rucksacks and fishing and hunting gear and set off for the woods. It would be, for a hoax party, the most dangerous day of the week in which to try and make fake Bigfoot footage and of this most dangerous day of the week the very worst time would be the early afternoon.

Gimlin and Patterson spent four years doing their part-time searching for a Bigfoot. I somehow think that if the '67 footage was faked that it must have been something that they planned for a long time and not something that they dreamed up in a few afternoons of riding through the forest. The making of the fur suit alone would have occupied many hours and days of tedious and painstaking work. Surely, when it came to choosing a site for their elaborate and carefully planned fake film, they could have done better than that open creek bed between two roads, where, with the arrival of just one car and the sighting of their activities by one man, all of their carefully laid plans would have gone down the drain. And surely they could have picked a better day than a Friday and a better time within that day than the early afternoon. As I stated before, I will not credit either man with the intellect necessary for the making of the '67 footage and the near-perfect story that goes with it. But I will credit them with intelligence enough to know the seemingly unjustifiable risks involved in the use of that place, at that time, for the perpetration of a hoax.

I am inclined to give the 1967 footage a 95% chance of being genuine and the subject of the footage a 95% chance of being a real living creature. I base this belief on my own examination of the evidence that the footage supplies, of the footage itself, which I have viewed probably a hundred times, and of the site. I am inclined to disregard statements such as "nothing walks like that, therefore it is a fake," in spite of their learned scientific origin. I am equally inclined to refute Dr. Napier's statement (much as I respect his qualifications), about the size of the feet being totally out of proportion to the size of the creature. I believe the very basis of this statement, Napier's formula, height of figure equals length of foot times 6.6, to be totally inappropriate to the particular subject. How can one apply a known formula to an unknown quantity? Why should a totally unknown, unclassified, never-examined creature of six feet, five inches not have fourteen-and-a-half-inch feet? Or ten-inch feet? Or twenty-inch feet? Where is the rule by which we measure the unknown in this case? To my mind there is none. Applying this formula is exactly the same as saying that because it has hairy breasts, and apes do not have breasts, and humans do not have hairy breasts, it must have been a fake. Why should it not have hairy breasts, if it is a creature that is totally new to science?

I would be a lot happier about scientific opinion on the '67 footage if it were based on thorough scientific examination of the footage under controlled laboratory conditions. But it is not and much as I respect the opinion of men like Dr. Napier, I feel strongly that, where the subject of the 1967 footage is concerned, scientists in this country should be talking less about fakery and working more toward some solution of the enormous question that this unique strip of film poses. The question of the existence of a giant primate of unknown origin, alive and well—at least, in the forests of northern California in 1967—and, presumably, as the evidence tells us, equally alive and well in other parts of the Northwest today.

DR D. W. GRIEVE'S REPORT ON THE FILM OF A SUPPOSED SASQUATCH

The following report is based on a copy of a 16 mm. film taken by Roger Patterson on October 20th, 1967, at Bluff Creek, Northern California, which was made available to me by Rene Dahinden in December 1971. In addition to Patterson's footage, the film includes a sequence showing a human being (height 6 ft. $5\frac{1}{2}$ in.) walking over the same terrain.

The main purpose in analysing the Patterson film was to establish the extent to which the creature's gait resembled or differed from human gait. The bases for comparison were measurements of stride length, time of leg swing, speed of walking and the angular movements of the lower limb, parameters that are known for man at particular speeds of walking. Published data refer to humans, with light footwear or none, walking on hard level ground. In part of the film the creature is seen walking at a steady speed through a clearing of level ground, and it is data from this sequence that has been used for purposes of comparison with the human pattern. Later parts of the film show an almost full posterior view, which permits some comparisons to be made between its body breadth and that of humans.

The film has several drawbacks for purposes of quantitative analysis. The unstable hand-held camera gave rise to intermittent frame blurring. Lighting conditions and the foliage in the background make it difficult to establish accurate outlines of the trunk and limbs even in un-blurred frames. The subject is walking obliquely across the field of view in that part of the film in which it is most clearly visible. The feet are not sufficiently visible to make useful statements about the ankle movements. Most importantly of all, no information is available as to framing speed used.

Body shape and size

Careful matching and superposition of images of the so-called Sasquatch and human film sequences yield an estimated standing height for the subject of not more than 6 ft. 5 in. (196 cm.). This specimen lies therefore within the human range, although at its upper limits. Accurate measurements are impossible regarding features that fall within the body outline. Examination of several frames leads to the conclusion that the height of the hip joint, the gluteal fold and the finger tips are in similar proportions to the standing height as those found in humans. The shoulder height at the acromion appears slightly greater relative to the standing height (0·87:1) than in humans (0·82:1). Both the shoulder width and the hip width appear proportionately greater in the subject creature than in man (0·34:1 instead of 0·26:1; and 0·23:1 instead of 0·19:1, respectively).

If we argue that the subject has similar vertical proportions to man (ignoring the higher shoulders) and has breadths and circumferences about 25 per cent greater proportionally, then the weight is likely to be 50–60 per cent greater in the subject than in a man of the same height. The additional shoulder height and the unknown correction that should be allowed for the presence of hair will have opposite effects upon an estimate of weight. Earlier comments that this specimen was 'just under 7 ft. in height and extremely heavy' seem rather extravagant. The present analysis suggests that Sasquatch was 6 ft. 5 in. in height, with a weight of about 280 lb (127 kg.) and a foot length (mean of 4 observations) of about 13·3 in. (34 cm.).

Timing of the gait

Because the framing speed is unknown, the timing of the various phases of the gait was done in terms of the numbers of frames. Five independent estimates of the complete cycle time were made, from 'R. toe-off', 'L. toe-off', 'R. foot passing L.', 'L. foot passing R.' and 'L. heel strike' respectively giving:

Complete cycle time = 22·5 frames (range 21·5–23·5). Four independent estimates of the swing phase, or single support phase for the contra-lateral limb, from toe-off to heel strike, gave:

Swing phase, or single support = 8·5 frames (same in each case). The above therefore indicates a total period of support of 14 frames and periods of double support (both feet on the ground) of 2·75 frames. A minimum uncertainty of ± 0·5 frames may be assumed.

Stride length

The film provides an oblique view and no clues exist that can lead to an accurate measurement of the obliquity of the direction of walk which was judged to be not less than 20° and not more than 35° to the image plane of the camera. The obliquity gives rise to an apparent grouping of left and right foot placements which could in reality have been symmetrical with respect to distance in the line of progression. The distance on the film between successive placements of the left foot was 1·20 × the standing height. If an obliquity of 27° is assumed, a stride length of 1·34 × the standing height is obtained. The corresponding values in modern man for 20° and 35° obliquity are 1·27 and 1·46 respectively.

A complete set of tracings of the subject were made, and in every case when the limb outlines were sufficiently clear a construction of the axes of the thigh and shank were made. The angles of the segments to the vertical were measured as they appeared on the film. Because of the obliquity of the walk to the image plane of the camera (assumed to be 27°), the actual angles of the limb segments to the vertical in the sagittal plane were computed by dividing the tangent of the apparent angles by the cosine of 27°. This gave the tangent of the desired angle in each case, from which the actual thigh and shank angles were obtained. The knee-angle was obtained as the difference between the thigh and shank angles. A summary of the observations is given in the following table.

FRAME NO.	EVENT OR COMMENT	ANGLES MEASURED ON LEFT LIMB					
		Apparent on film			Corrected for 27° obliquity		
		Thigh	Knee	Shank	Thigh	Knee	Shank
3	R. toe-off	+ 7	14	— 7	+ 8	16	— 3
4		+ 1	19	— 18	+ 1	21	— 20
5		— 7	10	— 17	— 8	11	— 19
6	blurred	— 18	3	— 21	— 20	3	— 23
7	R. foot pass L.	UNCERTAIN					
8		OF					
9		LIMB					
10		OUTLINES					
11 }	R. heel strike	HERE					
12		— 27	13	— 40	— 30	13	— 43
13	L. toe-off	— 25	22	— 47	— 28	22	— 50
14		0	61	— 61	0	64	— 64
15		+ 10	63	— 53	+ 11	67	— 56
16	L. foot pass R.	+ 10	64	— 54	+ 11	68	— 57
17		+ 13	62	— 49	+ 14	66	— 52
18		+ 17	45	— 28	+ 19	50	— 31
19		+ 23	38	— 15	+ 25	41	— 16
20		+ 28	29	— 1	+ 31	32	— 1
21 }	L. heel strike	+ 17	6	+ 11	+ 19	7	+ 12
22		+ 20	10	+ 10	+ 22	11	+ 11
23		+ 19	16	+ 3	+ 21	18	+ 3
24 }	R. toe-off	+ 17	18	— 1	+ 19	20	— 1
25		+ 19	33	— 14	+ 21	36	— 15
26		+ 8	15	— 7	+ 9	16	— 7
27		+ 2	19	— 17	+ 2	21	— 19
28 }	R. foot pass L.	+ 4	28	— 24	+ 4	30	— 26
29		NO MEASUREMENT					

The pattern of movement, notably the 30° of knee flexion following heel strike, the hip extension during support that produces a thigh angle of 30° behind the vertical, the large total thigh excursion of 61°, and the considerable (46°) knee flexion following toe-off, are features very similar to those for humans walking at high speed. Under these conditions, humans would have a stride length of 1·2 × stature or more, a time of swing of about 0·35 sec. and a speed of swing of about 1·5 × stature per second.

Conclusions

The unknown framing speed is crucial to the interpretation of the data. It is likely that the filming was done at either 16, 18 or 24 frames per second and each possibility is considered below.

	16 fps	18 fps	24 fps
Stride length approx.	262 cm.	262 cm.	262 cm.
Stride/Stature	1·27–1·46	1·27–1·46	1·27–1·46
Speed approx.	6·7 km./hr	7·5 km./hr	10·0 km./hr
Speed/Stature	0·9–1·04 sec.	1·02–1·17	1·35–1·56
Time for complete cycle	1·41 sec.	1·25 sec.	0·94 sec.
Time of swing	0·53 sec.	0·47 sec.	0·35 sec.
Total time of support	0·88 sec.	0·78 sec.	0·58 sec.
One period double support	0·17 sec.	0·15 sec.	0·11 sec.

If 16 fps is assumed, the cycle time and the time of swing are in a typical human combination but much longer in duration than one would expect for the stride and the pattern of limb movement. It is as if a human were executing a high speed pattern in slow motion. It is very unlikely that more massive limbs would account for such a combination of variables. If the framing speed was indeed 16 fps it would be reasonable to conclude that the metabolic cost of locomotion was unnecessarily high per unit distance or that the neuromuscular system was very different to that in humans. With these considerations in mind it seems unlikely that the film was taken at 16 frames per second.

Similar conclusions apply to the combination of variables if we assume 18 fps. In both cases, a human would exhibit very little knee flexion following heel strike and little further knee flexion following toe-off at these times of cycle and swing. It is pertinent that subject has similar linear proportions to man and therefore would be unlikely to exhibit a totally different pattern of gait unless the intrinsic properties of the limb muscles or the nervous system were greatly different to that in man.

If the film was taken at 24 fps, Sasquatch walked with a gait pattern very similar in most respects to a man, walking at high speed. The cycle time is slightly greater than expected and the hip joint appears to be more flexible in extension than one would expect in man. If the framing speed were higher than 24 fps the similarity to man's gait is even more striking.

My subjective impressions have oscillated between total acceptance of the Sasquatch on the grounds that the film would be difficult to fake, to one of irrational rejection based on an emotional response to the possibility that the Sasquatch actually exists. This seems worth stating because others have reacted similarly to the film. The possibility of a very clever fake cannot be ruled out on the evidence of the film. A man could have sufficient height and suitable proportions to mimic the longitudinal dimensions of the Sasquatch. The shoulder breadth however would be difficult to achieve without giving an un-- natural appearance to the arm swing and shoulder contours. The possibility of fakery is ruled out if the speed of the film was 16 or 18 fps. In these conditions a normal human being could not duplicate the observed pattern, which would suggest that the Sasquatch must possess a very different locomotor system to that of man.

D. W. GRIEVE, M.SC., PH.D.,
Reader in Biomechanics
Royal Free Hospital School of Medicine
London

THE FIRST RUSSIAN REPORT ON THE 1967 BIGFOOT FILM FOOTAGE, BY DOCTORS DMITRI BAYANOV AND IGOR BOURTSEV OF THE ACADEMY OF SCIENCES, MOSCOW

Preliminary Notes on the Materials of American Hominologists: The 1967 Footage—Filmstrip, Photographs and Plaster Casts of Footprints, Professor Krantz's (Paper on) the Anatomy of the Bigfoot

GENERAL REMARKS ON THE FILM — Roger Patterson's filmstrip shows a hairy man-like creature, walking erect, having well-developed breasts and buttocks. The last three points, if we accept for a time the authenticity of the creature, indicate its belonging in the Hominid, not the Pongid (anthropoid), line of evolution of higher primates.

Morphology of the head shows a very outstanding brow ridge, a low bridge of the nose, very pronounced prognatism, a cone-shaped back of the head.

Judging by the well-developed breasts the creature is female. However, the muscles of the back, arms and legs are so much in relief that they call for comparison with those of a heavy weightlifter.

The creature "has no neck," or at least the neck is not to be detected at first sight. Looking back the creature turns its upper torso along with the head to a much greater extent than would normally a human being. This might indicate a somewhat different attachment of the skull to the spine than in man, and a strong development of the neck muscles which conceal a short, sort of simian, neck.

In the initial frames, where the creature is standing and then walking in a stooped posture, one is struck by the great flexibility of its spine, which is suprising in so bulky a body. This quality may be of an adaptive nature: picking berries, digging roots and rodents' holes, the relict hominoid must be a habitual "stooper." One reason for the large size of the creature's thigh muscles as seen in the film may well be the necessity for the hominoid to squat frequently and move in that position while feeding, as attested by some sighting reports.

LOCOMOTION AS SEEN IN THE FILM — It seems smooth and resilient like that of a big quadrupedal animal. One gets the impression that the creature steps on slightly bent legs. If that is the case the impact on the heels should be less manifest than in man's walk, and the hominoid tracks, usually rather even in depth, seem to corroborate this conclusion. While walking the creature swings its arms intensely using them as walking beams as it were.

COMPARISON TO SUPPOSED GAIT OF NEANDER-THALER — Prof. Boris Porshnev, who put forward the Neanderthal hypothesis ot the relict hominoid origin, in his monograph (1963), page 288, refers to the opinions of anthropologists V.P. Yakimov, G.A. Bonch-Osmolovsky and V.V. Bounak concerning the walk of Neanderthalers as construed by analysts of fossil material. We find it very significant that the two characteristics mentioned above—i.e. less impact on the heels and arms swinging—are listed by anthropologists as supposed traits of Neanderthal locomotion, while slightly bent legs are ascribed to Neanderthalers even in a standing position.

THE HOMINOID FOOT — The main features standing out in both the American and Soviet material: 1. Tracks show flat feet (without an arch). 2. The width of the foot in proportion to the length is much greater than in man's foot. 3. The hominoid foot is generally much bigger than man's.

Besides, as has been often noted by Pyotr Smolin, chairman of the Hominoid Problem Seminar at the Darwin Museum in Moscow, the hominoid foot is distinguished by a great mobility of its toes which can bend very much or fully extend or spread very widely.

One more peculiarity: the so-called double ball at the back of the big toe as evidenced in many North American tracks (Green, 1968; Krantz, 1972). We find Grover Krantz's explanation of this feature very interesting, and we especially value at this stage the conclusion drawn by him concerning the size of the creature's calcaneus (heel bone). (We'll give our reason further on.)

As for the double ball itself we would like to make here the following remark. The double ball is made up not only of two bulges of tissue but also of a furrow between them which is like a kind of fold on the sole. Hence the question can also be put this way: Why is a fold formed at this spot on the hominoid sole?

The answer, probably, can be like this: because the hominoid foot is not so rigid as man's foot, it still retains a certain measure of mobility inherited from the hand-like foot of the ape, and therefore has a furrow somewhat analogous to lines on man's palm.

Grover Krantz finds the correlation between the great weight of the creatures in question (as evidence, among other things, by the depth of footprints) and the anatomy of the foot, as it is revealed in the very same footprints, so natural and binding that he makes the following conclusion: "Even if none of the hundreds of sightings had ever occurred, we would still be forced to conclude that a giant bipedal primate does indeed inhabit the forests of the Pacific Northwest."

It's the first time such an unambiguous statement is made by a professional anthropologist regarding the problem of relict hominoids, a statement made even more welcome by the fact that it came about as a result of study of material evidence which is the plastercasts and photographs of footprints.

COMPARISON TO THE NEANDERTHAL FOOT — As far as we know, none of the American researchers has compared the hominoid foot, as revealed in footprints, to the Neanderthal foot, reconstructed on the basis of fossil material.

In the Soviet Union this job has been done by Prof. B.F. Porshnev who noted a similarity in such features as lack of an arch, the width to length ratio, great mobility of toes (Porshnev, 1963).

It seems that a new and very important development in this direction of research is a comparison made by us between the calcaneus (heel bone) of the Neanderthal foot and that of North American Hominoids as shown in the materials of American hominologists.

As the enclosed photos show, the heel bone of Neanderthal is much bigger than that of man. Grover Krantz, on his part, concludes that the Bigfoot has "enlarged heels," "the heel

160

section must be correspondingly longer." He also writes that the creature's "ankle joint must be set relatively farther forward along the length of the foot," its length is expected to be "set relatively farther forward on the foot than in man."

Thus, this is also true of the Neanderthal foot, as can be seen at a glance in the enclosed photos which graphically and, shall we say, dramatically illustrate the above point.

To make things even more fascinating, the very same features show on the foot of the creature in Roger Patterson's filmstrip (see enclosed photo of a corresponding frame). To our knowledge, this fact has not been mentioned before by analysts of the film.

It follows that analysing a possible anatomy of the hominoid foot we find agreement in three, apparently, independent sources: 1. Roger Patterson's film; 2. Photographs and plastercasts of footprints obtained by Rene Dahinden and others, and analyzed by Grover Krantz; 3. Morphology of the Neanderthal foot.

NEANDERTHAL OR PITHECANTHROPUS? — This, on the one hand, says a lot for the authenticity of the film and footprints, and, on the other, gives more weight and substance to the Porshnev theory. As for the giant size of North American Hominoids, we think this cannot be a sufficient argument against Porshnev's standpoint since big variations in size are also true of the species Homo sapiens.

Yet, there is, in our opinion, one serious obstacle to identifying the Patterson film creature with a relic of the Neanderthal stage of evolution, which is that the creature's head is too much ape-like. An ape-like head on a man-like body is rather the formula for Pithecanthropus as follows from anthropological studies of fossil material (Urisson M.I., 1966).

It was the opinion of the late Prof. Alexander Mashkovtsev that relic hominoids are survivors of the Pithecanthropus stage of evolution of bipedal primate. Unfortunately, for lack of fossil material the Pithecanthropus foot has not been yet reconstructed, but it can be expected that the features of the Neanderthal foot mentioned above, were more or less present in the Pithecanthropus foot as well.

Still, the worth of the Porshnev theory, as we understand it, is not in its offering a clue to exact classification of relict

161

hominoids, which it doesn't, but its shedding new light on, and, in fact, revolutionizing the entire approach to the problem of evolution of bipedal primates.

According to the theory such terms as Neanderthal Man or Java Man are a misnomer. The creatures were not men but animals, since man begins where speech begins, while both their morphology and artifacts tend to show that Pithecanthropus and Neanderthalers (with maybe just few exceptions for the latter) had no speech, no abstract thinking.

If that is so, we can expect that in certain areas of the earth there remain relict "Neanderthal beasts," in other areas—"Pithecanthropus beasts," still in third—mixed forms of the former two or even other forms. For the evolution of the family Hominidae (or Troglodytidae, in Porshnev's classification) proceeded at such a fast pace (in terms of evolution) that the forms it created were, so to speak, on the move and genetically open, not set and sealed like species created in a very long and slow evolutionary process.

(In our analysis we did not refer to Gigantopithecus because virtually nothing is known about that form of primates except their giant size. As for what is known of the foot of Australopithecus and "Home habilis," it does not seem to fit the pattern of the hominoid foot we are dealing with.)

NOT MAN-MADE — So our conclusion at this stage is the following: though it is not yet clear in what relation North American hominoids stand to the making of man, it is pretty clear now they themselves are not man-made.

Moscow   October, 1972   Dmitri Bayanov   Igor Bourtsev

References:

Porshnev, Boris

1963 Sovremennoe sostoyanie voprosa o relictovykh gominoidaks (Present state of the problem of relict hominoids), Moscow, V.I.N.T.I.

1969 Troglodytidy i gominidy v sistematike i evolutsii vysshikh primatov (The Troglodytidae and the Hominidae in the Taxonomy and evolution of higher primates) in Doklady Akademii Nauk SSSR, volume 188, issue 1.

Krantz, Grover
1972 Anatomy of the Sasquatch Foot, Northwest Anthropological Research Notes, Vol. 6., No. 1.

Urisson, Makhail
1966 Pithecanthropus, Sinanthropus and the related hominid forms, in the Collection of articles Iskopaemye Gominidy i Proiskhozhdenie Cheloveka (Fossil Hominids and Man's Origin), Moscow, Nauka publishing house.

We would like to add the following: Some of the points Grover Krantz makes about the Sasquatch foot are graphically illustrated and quite dramatically leaped to the eye here.

About the frame from Patterson's film: The creature's foot seen in this picture has an unnaturally protruding heel. To a casual observer this may seem a sticking out edge of an artificial sole, but to those who know better this is an omen of the creature's reality.

THE SECOND RUSSIAN REPORT ON THE 1967 BIGFOOT FILM FOOTAGE BY DR. DMITRI D. DONSKOY, CHIEF OF THE CHAIR OF BIOMECHANICS AT THE USSR CENTRAL INSTITUTE OF PHYSICAL CULTURE IN MOSCOW, USSR

A Scientific Report on the 1967 Bigfoot Footage, Made by Dr. Dmitri D. Donskoy, Chief of the Chair of Biomechanics at the USSR Central Institute of Physical Culture in Moscow, USSR and Entitled "A Qualitative Biomechanical Analysis of the Locomotive Movement of the Subject of the 1967 Film Footage"

As a result of repeated viewings of the walk of a two-footed creature in the 1967 "Bigfoot" footage and detailed examination of the successive stills from the footage one is given the impression of a fully spontaneous and highly efficient pattern of locomotion shown therein, with all of the particular movements combined in an integral whole, suggesting a smoothly operating and coherent system.

In all of the strides the movements of the arms, or upper limbs, and of the legs, or lower limbs, are well coordinated. A forward swing of the right arm, for example, is accompanied by a movement of the left leg. This is called cross-limb coordination and is essential for man as well as being quite natural for many patterns of locomotion in quadrupeds, such as in walking or trotting movements.

The strides are energetic and strong, with the leg swinging far forward. When a man extends his leg in this manner he walks at a rapid pace and overcomes by momentum the breaking effect of the angled hurdle provided by the outstretched leg. Momentum is proportional to mass and speed so the more massive the biped the less speed is needed to overcome the breaking effect of an outthrust striding leg.

The arms have swinging motion which suggests that the muscles are exerted at the commencement of each cycle, after which they relax, allowing the movements to continue by momentum. The character of the arm movements indicates that the arms are massive and the muscles strong.

After each heel strike the leg of the creature bends, absorbing the full weight of the body and smoothing over the impact of the step. During this movement certain muscles of the leg are extended and become tense in preparation for the next toe-off thrust of the foot. In normal human walk the considerable knee flexion as demonstrated by the creature of the footage is not so noticeable. (It would be noticeable in the movements required by some sports, such as cross country skiing.) This particular characteristic suggests that the creature is very heavy and that its toe-off thrust, contributing as it does to rapid progression, is powerful.

In the swinging movement of the legs considerable flexion is observed in the joints. Different parts of the limb lag behind each other. The movement of the foot follows the movement of the shank which in turn follows the movement of the hip. This kind of movement is peculiar to massive limbs with well relaxing muscles. In this case the movements of the limbs appear fluid and smooth, with no breaking or erratic movement at the completion of each cycle. The creature appears to use to considerable advantage the effect of muscle resilience. This effect is seldom practised by modern man under normal patterns of locomotion.

The walk of the creature is confident, with regular strides and with no indication of any loss of balance or any unnecessary or unbalanced movement. When the creature makes a turn to the right, to look towards the cameraman, the movement is accomplished by a swinging turn of the body. This suggests alertness and probably a limited mobility of the head and neck. In some situations of, say, surprise, man also turns the whole body in this manner. During the turn the creature spreads the arms widely to increase its body stability.

In one toe-off movement the sole of the creature's foot is visible. By human standards it is large when compared with the height of the creature. There is no longitudinal arch typical of the human foot. The rear end of the foot formed by the calcaneus (heel bone) protrudes considerably. Such proportions and anatomy, in a foot structure, facilitate the work of those muscles which allow for upright posture and increase the propulsive forces of locomotion. Absence of an arch may be the result of great weight.

The general movement of the creature is harmonious. The movements are repeated uniformly from step to step. This harmony is the result of synergy, i.e., the combined operation of a whole group of muscles.

Since the creature is manlike in appearance as well as bipedal, its gait resembles in principle the gait of modern man. But all of its movements indicate a much greater weight than is normally found in modern man. Its muscles appear to be much stronger and the walk swifter than that of the normal walk of a man.

There are certain characteristics of the creature's walk which are difficult to explain in words. They might be called "expressiveness of movement." In modern man this is some- times seen in a sporting or labour activity where economy and accuracy of movement is vital and essential to the activity. In study this particular characteristic can be seen by an experi- enced observer. In "expressiveness of movement" the motor systems upon which the particular quality is dependent are perfectly adapted to the tasks which they are called upon to perform. In other words, in the case of this creature, the movements have a neat perfection which through regular use have become habitual and automatic.

On the whole the most important thing in the study is the consistency of all of the above-mentioned characteristics. They not only complement each other but also interact in many ways.

All of these factors together allow us to evaluate the gait of the creature of the footage as a natural movement without any sign of the artfulness that one would see in an imitation. At the same time, with all of the diversity of locomotion illustrated by the creature of the footage, its gait as seen is absolutely non-typical of man.

VIII

Conclusions:

And the Scientific Support for the Probability of Bigfoot's Existence

The only kind of conclusion that a man should indulge in is the oral conclusion. You see, it's so easy to deny it later. Now to indulge in a written conclusion is something else. In fact it can be fatal, especially if you are wrong.
    —BRENDAN BEHAN, in conversation at Davy Byrne's Tavern, Dublin, Ireland, 1961

AND SO WE COME TO the last chapter and, as its title says something about conclusions, it looks as though the author is going to have to make a few. He will try and wriggle out of it of course. He will beat around the bush, make excuses and generally try to confuse the reader with literary parallelograms and other deviousness. But in the end the title of the chapter will pin him down and he will be forced to put in writing, for all to see and for the skeptics to play merry hell with—for a time at least—his own conclusions on the reality of the Bigfeet and on what should be done about them. The skeptics apart, he is going to have to do this out of respect for the reading public, the—no doubt very many—members of which have paid good money for his book. (If they have got as far as this last chapter then they must have bought the thing, he thinks. Let's avoid irritating them any further by at least bringing it to a decent ending.)

So, let us summarize and conclude and let us start by looking back at the four areas of evidence that seemingly support the existence of the ubiquitous Bigfeet. They are: the history, the footprints, the sightings, and the 1967 Bigfoot footage.

To start with, in the history, I think that we might be stretching a point if we allow the Norsemen's encounter with creatures they described as "horribly ugly, hairy, swarthy and

167

with great black eyes" to be put forward as evidence. But Leif Erikson's story has a colorful ring to it and so we shall leave it with the ages and comment on it no further. The remainder of the history, the accounts of the various incidents that took place through the 1800s, the Yale, British Columbia, capture of what might well have been a young Bigfoot, the 1924 Ape Canyon incident, and the many other stories that my associates and I have examined and checked for authenticity, all seem strongly to support the actuality of a group of large, hairy primates. Where authentication is concerned there is, of course, a problem with many of the older stories. The people concerned with them have passed on and in many cases there is only the briefest of records. With the Yale, British Columbia, story for instance, there is just the one newspaper article. After that there is nothing, and to this day no one knows what became of "poor Jacko," whether he was shipped to England, as the owner talked of doing, or whether he succumbed in his cage to the no doubt unmerciful attentions of a gang of north woods railwaymen. Thus, all that we can say of these early stories is that most of them—and certainly the ones that have been described in detail here—do seem actually to refer to the creatures that we know in the present day as Bigfoot.

The second area of evidence is the footprints. Before this examination, let us take a look for a moment at what is meant by the word "footprints," where we refer to it as evidence. It means, in this context, large, five-toed, humanoid prints of unknown origin, usually found on mountain roads in the coast ranges, in isolated areas, on surfaces that include sand, mud, dust, shingle, snow, or grass. The prints usually contain a heavy impression suggesting great weight and they are separated by a stride that is longer than a normal human stride.

Prints seem to average from fourteen to seventeen inches. I have heard of larger prints, but I have never seen one. I have heard of twenty-four-inch prints, but I personally do not believe in prints of that size being real.* The stride seems to

*It is my opinion that twenty-four-inch supposed Bigfoot prints that have been reported in snow are the result of melting. Footprints in snow will melt out from two inches (e.g., deer) to ten inches or more within a few days. Again, odd conditions of air movement and temperature may cause the opposite effect and ten-inch prints will shrink to four inches or less. It is important to remember, however, that there is never, ever, perfect and continuing uniformity of size and shape to prints that are the result of melting.

average from forty to sixty inches. For the guidance of the reader, the author is six feet in height and has a normal stride of thirty-three inches. The prints, when found, seem to indicate a huge weight, and although it is nearly impossible to determine this weight with any degree of exactness, some of the prints that I have personally seen were impacted in mud and in snow with a great weight behind them, a weight that I believe was in excess of 400 pounds.

I have seen sixteen sets of large unidentified footprints in the course of my own searching. Bigfoot prints? Possibly. I have also seen a half-dozen or so sets of footprints made by Piltdowners,* several large, bare, human footprints that people would have me believe were Bigfoot tracks, and several sets of bear paw prints that were given to me in honest ignorance as being Bigfoot tracks.

There is no doubt that many of the footprints that people find in the wilderness and that are taken to be Bigfoot prints are made by bear. Because of this, I think that we should have a look at the bears for a moment. There are a lot of bears in the Pacific Northwest, thousands in fact, and every time a bear moves more than a yard or two he lays down at least four paw prints. Euarctos, the common American Black Bear, comes in different colors and different sizes. Some are brown, some are cinnamon, some are black. Regardless of color, however, the one bear common to the United States and parts of southern Canada is the Black Bear. There is no other species of bear as numerous, as prolific and, with his different colors, as confusing to the public as the Black Bear. When cinnamon he is often confused with the grizzly and when brown with the Brown. The Black stands about two to three feet at the shoulder, weighs in at 200 to 450 pounds and has rear paws—the ones with which we are concerned here—that seldom exceed six inches in length. (The grizzly, on the other hand, is a very much larger bear, stands three-and-a-half feet at the shoulder and weighs up to 1100 pounds. The Brown, the largest bear in the world and the largest meat-eating animal on the face of the earth, can be four to four-and-a-half feet in height and can weigh up to 1600 pounds.)

*The term Piltdowner—meaning a charlatan or faker—has its origin in the famous Piltdown Hoax of fifty years ago. (See the *Bigfoot News,* July 1975.)

The front feet and the rear feet (of all bears) are quite different in shape. The front is shorter, has a rounded pad, and its imprint is a pear-shaped mark outlined with the pad prints of five toes. Its rear foot is almost twice as long and is very human in shape. There is a narrow heel and an instep, and when the print is capped off with five toe marks, the result is often mistaken for a human footprint. And, when the person who finds it has the Bigfoot "bug" and is far out in the mountains, with the wind moaning in the pines and the nearest human habitation far away and a Bigfoot lurking behind every other tree, the print is invariably taken to be that of a Bigfoot.

Reports of sightings and footprints come in regularly to the Information Center in The Dalles. About 75% of the prints that are found and that are reported to the Center as genuine Bigfoot footprints are Black Bear paw prints. They are usually found by people who honestly believe them to be Bigfoot prints and who call the Information Center in good faith. People calling or writing the Information Center with information on the phenomenon are always thanked, and as far as is possible the information is always acted on by the Center. For the public is the main source of information from which the Center draws its investigative material. An experienced woodsman would not confuse a bear paw print for a Bigfoot print, or, for that matter, with a human footprint. But the average person may well do so, and in the excitement of a find the inexperienced finder is apt to forget that 95% of all the Bigfoot prints ever found have been more then ten inches in length, while the Black Bear seldom has a rear foot that exceeds six inches. Thus, while the Black Bear does make a Bigfoot-like print, I do not think that the American species can be blamed for what are normally believed to be real Bigfoot prints. (At the same time I do think that they can be blamed for making what have been mistakenly called Bigfoot beds. The female Black, when about to have cubs, often makes a most elaborate "nest." This can be up to six feet in diameter and will be constructed of carefully laid, almost woven, sticks, moss, leaves and grass. The result looks for all the world like a huge bird's nest and several of these have been found by Bigfoot hunters who believed them to be Bigfoot beds, or lairs.)

The grizzly bear has a hind foot that is similar in shape to that of the Black Bear of the United States, but of course his paw print is very much larger. Could the grizzly be blamed for some of the huge humanoid footprints that have been found in the United States and that have been believed to be Bigfoot prints? Yes, if there were grizzly in the United States and in the places where the prints have been found. There are still grizzly in some parts of the United States, in Wyoming, possibly in northern Idaho, and just possibly, occasionally, in northern Washington. But there are none, any more, in Oregon or in northern California. The grizzly, a big, short-tempered, easily provoked bruin, is, like the American Indian, a creature that barely survived the white invasions of the nineteenth century. Hunted and shot, harried out of existence, he disappeared from nine-tenths of his former United States range and is today, in this country, an endangered species. Again, the grizzly has a set of thick and powerful nails set in the toes of each foot. It *is* possible for the animal to walk without showing any nail impression, for the nails are raised above the level of the foot pads. But this is only when its walking surface is very hard soil or rock. In mud, sand, snow, or heavy dust, the claw mark will always show and no claw marks have ever been found in what have been regarded as genuine Bigfoot footprints. The grizzly, like the Black, is thus ruled out as the villain behind the scenes where Bigfoot footprints are concerned. Which leaves us with the question, who or what makes the footprints?

There is no doubt in my mind that some of the footprints that I have seen, which others regarded as real Bigfoot footprints, were faked. This includes some of the footprints that we found in California in 1960. The falsity of some of those latter findings was confirmed by Steve Matthes, an expert with tracks—and expert is a word that I use with care—who declared them fake and showed how and why he thought so. There is equally little doubt that some of the footprints that others, less expert, have found in more domesticated areas, have also been faked. Some are made with a care and attention to detail that convinced many people that they are real.

Others, made with crude wooden feet, or with thick, rubber-soled shoes, the soles of which have been cut to the shape of large human feet, would not fool a five-year-old child. But not everyone realizes this. At a recent meeting with the Anthropological Department of Portland University, where I spoke on the subject of the phenomenon, a medical doctor, supposedly an associate of mine for a while, produced a pair of stiff-soled, crudely carved wooden feet and proffered these as evidence to prove that *all* Bigfoot prints were faked! Prints, made from the set that he so proudly popped out of his little bag, would have been quite ludicrous in appearance and good for nothing but a laugh or two.

But a few sets of footprints have been found in what I will call "credible" areas. These few sets, that looked real, that had deep impression and long stride, were found in places where a hoaxer would hardly have placed them and expected them to be found. The particular areas were isolated, far from human habitation and, more important, seldom visited by people. One such set was found by my brother and me in northern California. One day in the winter of 1960 we drove the Scout some twenty-five miles into the mountains. We used an old logging road and when this came to an end, left it and drove on hard snow up an access road to an old logged area. The snow was hard but the crust kept breaking and only the Scout's four-wheel-drive and low-ratio gears got us through. At the end of this second road we left the Scout and walked up onto a ridge, a distance of about one mile. On top of the ridge was a trail of fifteen-inch, five-toed, humanoid footprints, fresh, imprinted half an inch into the snow crust and running in a north-to-south direction.* They looked very real to us and their location, on top of this isolated ridge, some twenty-six miles back in the mountains, added to their authenticity. For not only had we told no one where we were going that day—we never did, if only to try and keep one jump ahead of the Piltdowners—but when we set out that morning we had not had any particular destination in mind. We arrived on that ridge merely by chance and it was then, as

*We used bloodhounds to follow those prints for several miles until heavy brush stopped the dogs and their handler would take them no further. We then followed them on foot until we lost them in the valley floor, on hard ground where there was no snow, some seven miles further on.

172

it is now, extremely doubtful ·to me that a hoaxer would have made prints out there in the winter cold, so far from human habitation, in an area so isolated, just in the hope that someone would find them. We judged the footprints to be genuine and to have been made by a Bigfoot. The prints showed great weight impression and the stride was an average of fifty-two to fifty-six inches. Today, many years later, I feel much the same about many of the footprints that have been found in the mountains in the last ten years. A few have been faked, but for others there is no other explanation than that they were made by a long-striding, big-footed biped of great weight, something with a humanoid foot that was not a man.

Next, the sightings. How many of them are real? How many faked? How many of them imagination? How many of them are concocted stories created to boost the sorry egos of Piltdowners and pseudo-woodsmen? Let us first examine the probability of fakery in this area. Briefly, there has been "sighting fakery" where films are concerned. The I.W.C.S. teams conclusively proved that the 1970 "Bigfoot" film made in northern Washington was faked, and the scientific examiners at Yerkes Primate Institute, Emory University, Atlanta, say that a second one, made by the same person, was also probably faked. (This latter film showed a stumbling white figure in a baggy fur suit that at one time, I was told, waved at the cameraman!) This means that there are, to use the term, "gorilla suits" being made and being used by at least two hoaxers. The suits have been used in films and will in all probability be used again. But to use a fur suit in a fake film where one is being photographed by one's wife, or one's partner, under reasonably secure circumstances and surroundings, is one thing. To put on the same suit and go capering up and down some lonely road in the middle of the night, or across someone's meadow or farmland, or up on a high, open ridge, is another kettle of fish altogether, because the Pacific Northwest, whatever else it is, is gun country. I do not know how many guns there are in the hands of private owners in the northwest, but the number probably runs into several millions. It is not unusual for a Pacific Northwest rancher to have a dozen guns in his house.

It is also not unusual to see people carrying guns, both pistols and rifles, in their cars when they are out on the roads. The "easy rider" type pickup, with the rear-window gun rack, is a common sight in the back country of the northwest and when the rifles are not visible on the gun rack, they are usually behind the seat or underneath it. If there is no rifle there is generally a pistol lurking somewhere, either on the seat, or under the seat, or in the dashboard compartment. The given reason for all of this armament is usually protection. But in actual fact it is something else. It is a carryover of the great Western gun cult that sprang to life in the roaring days of the first miners and settlers and that today has developed into a syndrome that is an accepted part of life in the northwest.

When I first came to the Pacific Northwest, to commence my investigation of the Bigfoot phenomenon, many people asked me if I intended to shoot one. I said no. That was, and still is, my intention, and part of my work here and the work of my associates has been strenuously to oppose the "shoot it to prove it" gunmen who would kill one to serve their own ends. There is undoubtedly a protective feeling among many people in the northwest concerning the Bigfeet. We have encountered it again and again in the concern of people that harm or injury might come to one of the creatures, creatures that in their knowledge have never harmed anyone. At the same time there is an unfortunate movement among a few of the gun-toting community to have one shot, if this is possible. The movement is propagated by the promise of some vague reward from some equally vague institution and among some people this ethereal promise has now become fact. There are no details of the amount of the reward. The institution that will buy a Bigfoot carcass and then happily hand over a million dollars or so is not named. It is not named because it does not exist. But this promise of huge monetary reward, strengthened by a recent newspaper article about a Texas millionaire who would pay half a million dollars for the body of one of the creatures—there is no such person—has in some uneducated quarters grown to the point where it is firmly believed. The result is several gun-carrying Bigfoot hunters who have openly stated their intention of shooting one should they get the chance. (Their excuse is that it would not be fair to expect them to turn down the chance of a million dollars.)

The hoaxers that we have encountered in our Bigfoot research have been people who were generally aware of what activity was taking place in the Bigfoot field. They knew of the stated intention of the few gunmen who hunt the Bigfoot with rifles and they were well aware of the number of guns carried by people in the northwest, the ability of those people to use them, and the risks involved in walking around in the woods in a fur "gorilla" suit. They knew that the hoaxer who is going to do this, pretending that he is a Bigfoot, is not only asking to be shot but very probably is going to be shot, particularly if he persists. Any man who does this and who is aware of the risks involved is either a fool or a madman. There are, no doubt, hoaxers living in the northwest or in Canada today who will do almost anything to satisfy their peculiar cravings for notice. But I know of none who will knowingly and continuously face the probably fatal risks involved in fakery at this level.

How many of the sightings are imagination? How many people see things on lonely roads at night, in the flashing lights of a car, or far ahead where their car lights barely reach, that they think are Bigfoot? Tree stumps, clumps of bushes, telephone poles? The answer: quite a few. One man called us to say that he had very definitely seen a Bigfoot, standing with its back to him, streaked grey and black, huge, bent over, broad-shouldered, head down, unmoving. He had stopped his car, backed up, and it was gone. Investigation revealed a big roadside stump. The man, who honestly thought that he had seen a Bigfoot, was quite astounded when we showed him the stump and his tire marks, where he backed almost, but not quite, up to its base. One woman called us late last summer. Her son had seen a Bigfoot crossing a road near The Dalles. We investigated and found small bear paw prints arriving at one side of the road, crossing the road and then leaving from the other side, at the precise place where the boy said that he had seen a "large hairy figure." When we showed him the bear tracks he refused to accept them, suggesting that we were wrong and that they were Bigfoot prints. But imagination in an individual is, I believe, in direct proportion to the individual's measure of intelligence, level-headedness, and plain common sense. Some of the sightings reported to us have been the result of pure imagination. But not all of them, and certainly not, to my way of thinking, those that I describe in the preceding chapters.

How many of the sightings are simply fabricated stories, concocted by the ego-hungry individual as a means of supplying something missing in his life? Answer: not a few. But the fabricated story is often fairly easy to expose especially if, like the members of The Dalles Information Center team, one has a background of experience and knowledge that can be used in the questioning of a "suspect." A knowledge of the country, for example, is very useful when questioning someone about a particular area where they may say they had a sighting. One man told us that he had once seen a Bigfoot about half a mile down a canyon in the central Cascades. He was riding a horse at the time, he said. The expression, "down the canyon," struck us as odd in his story and I asked him which way he had entered the canyon. He told us, after a slight hesitation, that he had entered the canyon from its upper end and that he was riding downstream when he saw the Bigfoot. Unfortunately for the credibility of his story, we had been in that canyon only a few months previously and we knew that its upper end was enclosed by a sheer rock wall several hundred feet high.

Another man told us that his sighting took place high on a mountain ridge and the Bigfoot that he saw was moving at a distance of 350 to 400 yards. It was never closer than 350 yards and he saw it without binoculars or rifle scope. But he was able to tell us the color of the creature's eyes (dark blue, he thought) and also to notice that its fingernails were thick and broad and flat. Fingernails, like eyes, could not be distinguished for color or shape by the human eye, unassisted by binocular magnification, at a distance of 350 yards. A story of a sighting at this distance, that included these details, could only be construed as being a fabrication. This kind of story, like the canyon story, simply goes into the files and we waste no more time on it.

176

I think that most people will agree that there are some fabricated sightings, stories of Bigfoot seen in the forest, that have no basis in truth. At the same time I do not believe that this detracts to any great extent from the accounts given of sightings by men of character and integrity like Bill Taylor and the Welch brothers of British Columbia and others of their standing and character.

This brings us, in conclusion of our examination of the Bigfoot supporting evidence, to the 1967 footage. We have already discussed this to some extent, so let us recap the pros and the cons on the filming.

The skeptics, who say that the 1967 footage is a hoax, put forward a very unconvincing argument. The basis of this argument is that the Bigfoot does not exist and that therefore the footage must have been hoaxed. Among the skeptics, as I have mentioned previously in these pages, are many scientists, and their reasoning why the footage must be faked is summed up in the only three statements that I have been able personally to hear on the subject. These are 1) "They do not exist because if they did exist we would have known about them by now." Personally I think that it would be very interesting to apply this statement to the Tasaday, of the Philippines. "The Tasaday do not exist because if they did we would have known about them by now." Or to the coelacanth, the fossil fish that was discovered, alive and well, off the coast of Africa just a few years ago. "The coelacanth does not exist because if it did we would have known about it by now." 2) "Nothing walks like that and therefore something walking like that must be faked." A fascinating statement and all that I can say about it is that I am glad that I do not have the mentality that went into the creation of that utterance. For surely a halfwit can see that if the Bigfeet do exist, and if they are indeed a totally new and unknown species of giant primate, that they probably do walk quite differently from anything known to science.

Surely any scientist can see that if the Bigfeet do exist, they are entitled to have a neuromuscular system different from the human system. That being different, they are not obliged to walk in the same manner as any other primate, including man, regardless of what the rules of the anthropological and biological game say. To me it does not matter if the subject of the 1967 footage does not straighten its leg in stride, as the footage seems to suggest. It does not matter if it has a forty-two-inch stride which is scientifically believed to be wrong for its height. It does not matter if its feet are too big or too small, in proportion to the size of its body. It is obvious, if the thing in the 1967 footage is real, that it is something completely different from anything ever known to science. Something that is totally new and unknown and thus, by its very newness, is entitled to look different, entitled to move differently, entitled to be different in all of its physical behavior, from any other animal on the face of the earth.

The 1967 footage is further discussed in the appendix of this book. For myself, I am inclined to give it a 95% chance of being real. I allow it this because of the reasons which I have already discussed. They are not scientific reasons. They are a layman's reasons and they are based on personal contact with the people who made the footage and my knowledge of how they made it, of their intellectual limitations, and of the circumstances surrounding the production of the footage. If the 1967 footage is a fake, then it is a masterpiece, and I think that I can sum up on my belief in the validity of the footage by saying that it is mainly based on my inability to understand how the two men concerned could have created that masterpiece. I give it 95% credibility and I reserve 5% to apply to the possibility that I could be wrong. But it would not take too much to have me drop that 5%.

Toward the end of his book about the Bigfoot and Yeti phenomena, Dr. Napier, having gathered all of the evidence and analyzed it in an intelligent and scientific fashion, arrives at the point where he feels that he must come to some conclusions and, as a writer, put them down on paper. He does this in an ambiguous statement which, I believe, leaves his readers very much up in the air as to what he really means. He writes that he is convinced that the creatures exist but thinks that they are not all that they are cracked up to be. I find this statement confusing. For me it clouds an otherwise—with the exception of his 1967 film examination and his views on the dearth of food in the northwest for a

178

primate as large as the Bigfoot—reasonable analysis of the phenomenon. A statement of conclusion should be more definite than this.

The evidence that has been examined in these chapters is not all of the evidence extant in support of the Bigfeet. There is a great deal more, in fact. What has been presented in these pages is the more solid evidence that I and my team of associates have been able to uncover and examine and analyze in our five years of investigation. It is not, and I shall be the first to admit this, what the scientists call hard evidence. But nevertheless it is evidence and I feel that all of it together presents us with supportive material that is well worth the time and money that was spent on its finding. Because it has allowed us to make some very definite conclusions on the phenomena as a whole.

How have we gone about collecting this evidence? In all the ways I have discussed: examining footprints, investigating reports of sightings, and continuing full time research, one example of which is the surveillance we conducted of a potential area in 1972 and 1973. This was done with the assistance of the Academy of Applied Science of Boston, and an account of the surveillance and how we conducted it seems worthwhile here.

It was through the good offices of my friend Tim Dinsdale that I first met Robert Rines and, through him, the fascinating group of people who were associated with or actually taking part in the Loch Ness project. Tim took a lively interest in the Bigfoot phenomenon, and urged me to fly to Boston to see if the Academy of Applied Science—his own part-sponsors—could become involved in my search.

Bob Rines, who was later to become a personal friend of mine, is a Boston patent attorney. He is also Dean of the Franklin Pierce Law School in Concord, New Hampshire, and President of the Academy of Applied Science, chartered in March, 1963, as a nonprofit, scientific and educational corporation, under the laws of the Commonwealth of Massachusetts. It is an institution that is concerned with fostering cooperation among the creative individual, industry, education, law, and government. What is called the historical purpose of the Academy was outlined in one of its first monographs, published in 1972. It reads:

> To bridge the gap in communications, understanding, and cooperative effort (particularly to attach problems requiring simultaneous interdisciplinary inputs and approaches) between the engineering, technological, innovative and applied scientific community on one hand and industry, university and legal and government institutions, on the other.

Since 1963 the Academy has been engaged in programs in very many areas within the United States and also in Taiwan, New Zealand, and westward through Asia, the Middle East, Europe, and the United Kingdom. The activities of members of the Academy throughout the world have been widely diversified. One of these has been the investigation of the Loch Ness Monster mystery.

In Boston, on that first visit, I was honored by being asked to speak to members of the Academy at the Academy offices in Belmont, a suburb of Boston, and further honored, later, by being made a member of the Academy. Robert Rines introduced me and I talked for about thirty minutes on the subject of the Bigfoot. The talk was well received and afterwards Bob told me that he believed that he could persuade the Academy directors to start taking an interest in my project and give it some support. The result of this was a visit to The Dalles, soon afterwards, from him and Tim Dinsdale. They came to make a personal evaluation of the phenomenon and to see what action I was taking in my search/investigation and how they could assist me with planning and with equipment. They were particularly interested in The Dalles, and together with Dennis Jenson, we walked out most of the area where the sightings had taken place over the years and where we had our observation post. They stayed in The Dalles with me for several days, working on plans for the May/June surveillance from the observation post. Tim thought that we might try to get nearer to the hill of Crate's Point, the hill down which we believed the Bigfoot came in his periodic visits to Hidden Valley. He suggested a route up the back of the cliff above what is called Tuli Terraces, a trailer court area that lies north of the hill itself and skirts the old Dalles to Hood River Highway. We thoroughly discussed the problems of concealment, and with Tim's experience at Loch Ness and my own experience with the problems of getting close to large dangerous animals, we worked out some new plans for the observation of the Hidden Valley meadows and the hill face of Crate's Point. Bob Rines, who as well as being an attorney is also an MIT physics graduate, explored the problems of actual surveillance. I hoped, for this season, to have enough people working with me, volunteers and local helpers, to keep a watch on the area by both day and night. Diurnal surveillance posed no problems, but night watching was another matter. With powerful binoculars—and we had those—we could see, over the five to six days of the full moon, distances up to 500 yards. Without the moon, this visibility was reduced to one hundred yards or even less, depending on clear skies and starlight. Bob thought that the answer could lie in electronic night vision equipment, and he promised to give some thought to obtaining some, through the Academy of Applied Science and possibly from the Army.

To round off their visit to The Dalles, Dennis and I took our visitors out for a short camping trip. A study of our charts showed that one area, in the mountains south of the Clackamus River, had a potential for sightings at this time. We loaded up the Scout and drove down there and made camp. It was still fairly early in the year and we had to lend our guests some woolen underwear.* The forest was cold and dark in the high mountains and I remember on our first night how Tim looked around him, out to the gloom beyond the campfire where, for the uninitiated, there is often a Bigfoot behind every tree. Later he admitted to being a trifle nervous and I recall that we found this amusing. But I wondered how we would have felt taking part in some of his lonely watches on the Ness, floating on the silent lake in that grey Scottish fog, the nearest help several miles away, and underneath, separated from one's feet by only half an inch of fiberglass, a thousand feet of black water. For us, I feel, there might well have been a monster behind every fog wraith, a huge serpentine beast just waiting to seize us and drag us down into the depth.

Bob Rines returned to Boston and Tim went back to England to continue his search. In Boston, Bob started making inquiries into the possibility of obtaining some night

*Dinsdale never did return my long johns. I think he still uses them at Loch Ness.

181

vision equipment, and early in 1973 he found what he was looking for and called me. I had been honored by an invitation from the Explorers Club to be a guest speaker at their annual dinner at the Waldorf Astoria. My subject, of course, was the hunt for the Bigfoot and for the occasion I had put together a short 16mm movie that included the footage from Bluff Creek, California, and scenes from the search activity in The Dalles and elsewhere. The Explorers dinner was a grand affair and I gave my talk before an audience of one thousand members from all over the world. A few days later I flew to Boston for talks with Bob Rines. There, at the Academy offices, he told me that he had been able to obtain the loan of some very high-powered night vision equipment and that it would be ours for a full month. In addition, there would be some medium-powered viewers, smaller apparatus that could be used in the hand. All of this would be available through the May-June period that we considered crucial in The Dalles area, for the full period.

This was great news. He added, in his telephone call, that two men would be accompanying the equipment. One would be a technician from the Institute, whose job it would be to provide maintenance and also, should we wish it, to take part in the watch. The other was an Army sergeant, whose duty it would be to guard the equipment against theft or loss.

The equipment duly arrived and with it the two men. The technician was one Warren Robinson, a genial fifty-year-old whose knowledge of night vision equipment of all kinds was the result of years of work and experience. Mr. Robinson quickly became "Robbie," and on his arrival he indicated his willingness to take a full part in the watch from the observation post and in any other work in connection with the project. The Army sergeant was John W. Cannady, a night vision expert, a southerner, and a career soldier of serious mien.

The equipment consisted of two hand-held Starlight Scopes, each with a range of about 500 yards, depending on light sources. For short-range work there was a hand-held Thermal Device. And for installation in the observation post there was a massive Night Observation Device, with a 40mm tube and, as we discovered, almost unlimited range.

We started out our surveillance of what we called the area of potential a few days after Robbie and John arrived. Our plans were to include them in the watch from the hill and so, without delay, we installed them in a comfortable motel in the city and briefed them on their duties.

As their actual working equipment was for night use, I planned to have them accompany us only on the night watch. This meant going on duty at six in the evening, 1800 hours to our Army man, and staying in the observation post until nine the following morning. During the day they could rest and have the daylight hours free. This plan worked well. With the help of a volunteer group that included my part-time assistant, Lyle O'Connor of The Dalles, Jim Day and Darrell Buckles of The Dalles, Celia Killeen of Dufur, Oregon, and Nick Bielemeier of Hood River, we managed to break the night watch down to actual work periods of no more than three hours maximum. Daylight watches were somewhat longer. We found it easier to stay awake during the day.

The principal piece of equipment and the one that was in constant use for over a month, without a break, was of course the 40mm NOD. We tore down and rebuilt the front of the observation post to allow full vision with the big scanner. When we had, with some difficulty, eventually seated it on its heavy metal tripod, the whole area could be covered with a 160-degree angle of view.* Previous to building the observation post on Table Mountain, we had charted all of the area of surveillance. From our chart we knew the distances to all of the principal landmarks, and on the first night in the post Robbie demonstrated to us the extraordinary capability of the big NOD. There was no moon, only starlight, and this reduced the limits of ordinary vision down to about a hundred yards. There was a tall poplar tree directly in front of and below the post, standing at a distance of over a thousand yards. Through the NOD, with nothing but starlight for power, we were able to see this tree quite clearly.** We found that we could also see all the way up the face of Crate's Point Hill, distances of

*With the tripod this whole piece of equipment weighed close to 100 pounds. Volunteers for the daily task of carrying this juggernaut up and down the 600-foot face of Table Mountain were conspicuous by their absence!

**Later, after some experimentation, we were able to photograph this tree, clearly, at night, in color. Its actual distance from the observation post was 1600 yards.

183

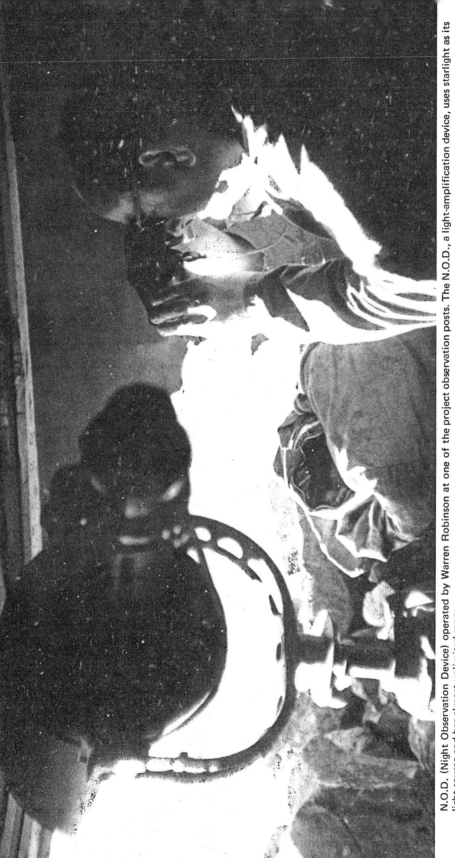

N.O.D. (Night Observation Device) operated by Warren Robinson at one of the project observation posts. The N.O.D., a light-amplification device, uses starlight as its light source and has almost unlimited range.

from two to three thousand yards and even beyond that to the highest point of the hill, the 2020-foot ridge, at a distance of five thousand yards. True, at that distance a man, or a manlike figure, could not be seen on the screen. But larger objects would show clearly and in the meantime we were satisfied to be able to pierce the darkness all the way across our surveillance area.

One night we watched a large bull elk come down the face of Crate's Point Hill. It stayed out in the open at the north end of Hidden Valley, grazing, and later, in the cold hours before the dawn, climbed up the hill and disappeared into the ridge oak forest. Another time a group of seven deer came out into the meadows below the post and commenced browsing. We watched them on the scanner and then switched to the Thermal Device. On the sensor, they showed up as small green mushrooms, their pattern slowly changing shape as they moved around.

Late one night, as we kept our silent vigil from the hilltop, a car drove into the quarry that lies at the base of the hill. The vehicle moved slowly and parked, lights off, at the edge of the Hidden Valley meadows. The quarry owners, who lived nearby saw the headlights as the car came in and suspecting a prowler, called the Sheriff's Office. The car left before the Sheriff's patrol could arrive and we watched it on the scanner as it drove off in the direction of Hood River. Next day, through the local grapevine, we learned the driver's identity. He was a gun-toting Bigfoot hunter from Canada, one of the mindless clique who openly state their intention of getting a Bigfoot by the simple method of shooting one on sight.

Next night he was back. Again it was very late. We watched as the car slid quietly into the darkened quarry and as the driver switched off his lights and parked, we turned both the NOD scanner and the Thermal Device on him. We were not too worried about his disturbing our area of potential, an area which at that time of night was otherwise dark and very quiet. What perturbed us was the high-powered rifle that he was known to carry should he see "man-like" figures on the hilltop, and the probability of his shooting in our direction. We watched him for about five minutes. The Thermal Device showed, on its flickering green screen, the car's engine and lights and also a curious point of heat that seemed to lie within the driving compartment. Then the Sheriff's Department patrol car, driven by Deputy Sheriff Bob Hazelett, came racing into the quarry and pulled up behind the prowler. Hazelett came forward and ordered the driver to step out. His license was examined. He was advised that he was trespassing and ordered to leave at once. Later I asked Bob Hazelett what the other heat spot within the car could have been. Our gun-toting prowler, he told us, had been smoking a pipe.

In the months of May and June, 1973, to his old stamping grounds in The Dalles the Bigfoot came not. Why? We do not know. We know why he did not come in 1972. In that year, during all of the days of the season when he normally appeared, another group of Bigfoot hunters from Eugene, all armed to the teeth and with at least one large German Shepherd, made a camp right on the Crate's Point ridge, the most likely Bigfoot trail into The Dalles. Each night they burned a huge fire and generally made so much disturbance that no Bigfoot in his right senses would have come within a mile of them. During the day the dog ran free and at least two of the seekers—I refuse even to give them the name of hunters—wore brightly colored shirts which on one occasion were detected by myself and Lyle O'Connor at a distance of 3000 yards!

But in 1973 we saw nothing of our giant visitor. We did our night watches and our day watches and tenaciously peered through our instruments from the observation post on the top of Table Mountain. The weather in late May and June was cold and then hot and then cold again. Our real enemy was not prowling gunmen but the wind. The lookout post faced almost due north and toward the mouth of the Columbia gorge. Every night the wind rose, and at times the post seemed to rock on its very foundations.

The instruments, particularly the big scanner, had to be held against the constant gusts that hit the post. When it rained, which it did a couple of times, the drops came like bullets through the front opening. Constant repairs were necessary as the wind tore at covers and fittings. One night a gust took the back door off its hinges and blew it five hundred yards, down into Jack Bryant's quarry, on the west side of the hill. There was one violent storm during the period of the surveillance. That night I was on the hill with Celia Killeen and young Mike Kuhn, our youngest volunteer. We watched black clouds racing up the Columbia River and listened to the wind beginning to howl. Then vivid lightning began to crackle across the gorge on the Washington side, and when the first bolts were reaching for the top of Table Mountain we decided that discretion might be the better part of valor and departed. Next morning with the dawn we were back.*

During the watch we made frequent reports to Bob Rines in Boston. Then we came to the end of it. Robbie and John returned to Fort Belvoir. Our volunteers dispersed. Lyle O'Connor left to join the Air Force, and about the same time Jim Day flew to San Diego and joined the Navy. It was a disappointment to all of us that our determined and prolonged effort had produced no results. It was a particular disappointment for Bob Rines and the members of the Academy of Applied Science. After the considerable effort they had made on our behalf and the support that they had given us it was disappointing to all concerned that there were no new findings.

At the present time, the Academy is taking an increasingly active interest in the search for the Bigfoot. Their activities at Loch Ness continue and so for the present—and until Bob and his friend Tim Dinsdale get the clear, color, 16mm footage or equally clear 35mm stills that they want of one of the Ness creatures—the energy of the Academy and its members is divided between Loch Ness and the Pacific Northwest.

Both Rines and Dinsdale intend to visit the Pacific Northwest again and, when time from their present activities becomes available, to take part in the continuing and widening search that is centered in The Dalles. Neither Rines nor Dinsdale will contribute to the "no place to hide" theory. They have both seen the northwest, have flown over it, and have camped out in its vast forests. They have studied the maps on which we have charted the footprints and sightings. They have examined the evidence and talked with eye-

---

*In February, 1974, a gale partially destroyed the Table Mountain Observation Post. We repaired it. In late June, 1974, a series of 80 mph gusts out of the Columbia gorge completely destroyed it, blowing the roof—which weighed several hundred pounds—a distance of 200 yards.

witnesses. They have looked closely at the progress made in our investigations over the last three years and they are satisfied that a successful conclusion to our slow, methodical search is not too far away.

After those first talks and meetings in Boston in 1971, before Bob and Tim had visited the Pacific Northwest and seen at first hand the magnitude of the vast forests of the coast ranges, their attitude toward the phenomenon of the Bigfoot was one of sensible open-mindedness. Nowadays their points of view have changed considerably. They are still tolerant, but only just so, of people who base their skepticism on the "no place to hide, nothing to eat" theory. But when the nonbeliever steps forward and drags out the time-worn "Well, what about the Loch Ness monsters? No one has ever found one of them," rather than gently chide the unread person for not keeping up with what is going on in the world, they are inclined to smile, turn away, and switch the conversation to other subjects.

One conclusion is that the skeptics are quite wrong. But then, I feel that they deserve to be wrong, for in all cases where their views are adamant—and at times even virulent—they are the views of people who have not and will not examine the evidence.

Another conclusion is, quite simply, that the evidence that I and my teams have produced does indeed support the existence of the Bigfoot and that there is a small surviving group of them living in the mountains of the Pacific Northwest and British Columbia.

Having come to this conclusion—regardless of how acceptable it may be to many people—there really remains only one more point to discuss. This is the question of what is to be done with them, what is to be done about them, now and in the future? The answer to this important question can be divided into four parts.

1) Leave them alone. This is undoubtedly the best approach. The record shows, without any doubt, that they are perfectly harmless, that they assiduously avoid man at all times, and that they are totally nonaggressive, shy, gentle creatures that ask only to be left to themselves in the forests. In the history we have studied there is no authentic account

of violence toward man and, with the exception of the two extraordinary stories of kidnapping—Albert Ostman and Much-alat Harry—there is not even any indication of any interest in man in the northwest. Every year thousands of hikers go into the coastal mountains. They include hundreds of children and very many families that take advantage of the better mountain roads for picnics or overnight camping trips. I think that it is safe to say that people, with their children, have been camping in the northwest forests for probably a hundred years. No child has ever been hurt. No child has ever been kidnapped, or chased or threatened in any way and, as is obvious to any intelligent person, if the Bigfeet are living in the woods there must have been many times when they have seen children or have been close to them, close enough to capture or even kidnap one had they wished. Perhaps it is their shyness that has prevented them from doing this? Perhaps it is their gentleness? Perhaps disinterest? Whatever it is, the record stands. The Bigfeet are not a threat to man in any way and in the long run, if they could be left alone, if people could just accept them and let it go at that, the best policy would be to leave them alone. But alas, man in his curiosity has to know more and more about his surroundings and is never satisfied until he feels that he knows all. And with the Bigfoot there is left—until he finds one and can see or touch it for himself—that indefinable aura of mystery that, instead of satisfying man with its intrinsic beauty, seems only to whet his appetite for more knowledge of the subject. Thus we face the fact that man is not going to leave the Bigfeet alone. He is not going to be content with having them living peacefully in his forests and not bothering anyone. He is going to go after them, seek them out, find out all that he can about them and then, maybe, leave them alone. How is he going to do this? By *finding* one: by shooting it, by capturing it, or by photographing it.

2) Let's shoot one. It seems incredible in this day and age that there are people who would want to shoot something like a Bigfoot. But there are, and I have met them. Not only will they shoot one if they get the chance—heaven hope that they never do—but they even go so far as to propagate this philosophy on the grounds of its justification to science! One

individual who actively pursues this murderous approach is basically an example of the other few who follow his footsteps. His proposed modus operandi, should the opportunity arise, is to shoot one, cut off its head and then bury the remainder. He would then, he states, show the head as evidence and, having established the actuality of the creature, sell the remainder of the carcass to the highest bidder. To me, wanting to shoot a Bigfoot is cruel and unjustified thinking. I would not condone it, not even for so-called scientific reasons. As to wanting to shoot one for monetary gain, this is mindless cretinism of the lowest form. The gunmen who follow this path are few and I and my associates keep a careful watch for them in all of our research work. To us they are kin to the people who wound and leave deer in the forest, who shoot coyote and porcupine and badgers for the "fun" of it, who snag salmon and trout at waterfall pools where they lie in wait for their upstream runs, who shoot out of season when young animals and birds need the protection of their parents, who dump old car bodies in the streams and throw rusting beer cans in the rivers and who generally by their intent or their negligence make malignant contribution to the slow but creeping destruction of the wildlife and the environment of one of the most beautiful countries on the earth. Thinking as we do that the creatures are hominid and that they are probably in actual fact a form of sub-man, or undeveloped man, rather than ape, and knowing the feelings of the very many people who now take an interest in the Bigfoot, a protective and almost parental interest, personally I would hate to be the man responsible for the death of one.

3) Capture one. Capture has to be defined. Is it to be permanent capture or temporary capture? Five years of research and many hours of intense discussion on this subject have given me some insights into it. Permanent capture means just that. It means that the creature or creatures would be incarcerated in a cage and held until it or they died, of disease, of old age, or simply of the psychological effects of captivity. If one is to consider permanent capture one has to consider this side of it. For scientific reasons a permanently held creature would no doubt be of great study value. That its normal life patterns would completely change under

captivity would hardly matter in the light of the amount of material that could be obtained from observation and study, or so it would be believed. The only eventuality that might save it and allow it ever to leave a cage would be if some form of communication were developed between it and its captors that would allow it to promise them that, A) it would behave itself in public, B) make proper use of the toilet, and, C) wear clothes. Either way, in a cage or in a suite at the Hilton, I feel that the Bigfoot would be as out of place as a wretched zoo-held gorilla. I would vote against permanent capture and it is not presently, or in the foreseeable future, a part of my planning.

As to temporary capture, it poses many problems. One supposes that one of the creatures would be taken in the forest and then held for a short period during which a team of scientists would be able to examine it, photograph it, et cetera. The problems that would arise here would be the length of time involved in an examination, the means that were used to hold the creature and the temptations that would arise—and that they would there is no doubt—among the examiners not to let it go. For the scientist it would be like allowing a priceless specimen, on which he had worked hard for many years, walk out the door, never to be seen again. And for the laymen present there would be the nagging questions, are we getting all that we can out of this, have we used it for all of its worth? Would it not be worth more to hold it? Or even to kill it and then keep the body? It was George Haas, of Oakland, who summed up what might happen in the case of a temporary capture and who put into words what many of us had thought about over the years when considering this possibility. What would happen, he said, if while you have the creature in hand, either drugged or in a cage, healthy and well, some powerful organization like Disney Studios walks up and offers a check for half a million for the body? Are you then going to let the thing go?

As to actual capture, there are many problems in this area also. In modern terms this means shooting one with a hypodermic containing a serum or drug that will knock it out for time enough to allow a team to get to it, truss it up and get it into a cage. Or further drug it and thus tranquilize it for transportation or for study. The trouble is that nothing is known about the creature's blood, its metabolism, its reaction to drugs or anything else. What drug does one use? The common suggestion has been to use one of the serums that have been tried and tested with other primates, and there are two or three of these that are obtainable today with a veterinary prescription. But will they work? Or worse still, will they overwork and kill the target? In the course of our studies we have examined two. One seemed excellent. It was tested on primates and had also been used safely on other animals. It had a fast reaction time and was guaranteed to knock out an elephant, provided that the right dosage was used. To determine the dosage was easy. One simply estimated the weight of the target and regulated the serum accordingly. But how to estimate the weight of something like a Bigfoot, seldom seen and often varying in size from sighting to sighting? The answer was to use not this drug, but one that had more latitude, a wider safety margin that would allow for error in weight estimate. We found another drug that had these requirements. We could overdose with almost perfect safety. We could dart a 300-pound Bigfoot with a load meant for a 500-pounder and the only difference would be that the creature would stay immobilized longer. But there was a snag.

The first drug, the one that required an exact dosage, had a fast reaction time. With large animals it was something close to two minutes and this would be effective as long as the dart was properly placed for an intramuscular injection. This meant that the creature, once hit, would not be able to go very far. The darters would be able to close in at once and get to the creature immediately as it went down. But with the second drug, the reaction time was something close to nine minutes, and this posed very many problems. One was the problem of keeping up with the creature, should it decide to try eluding its pursuers. On top of this was the danger to the creature itself, should it try and scale up or down a cliff, or try to swim a river, or even cross a highway. An agile, fast-moving Bigfoot could go a long way in nine minutes and this possibility presented definite hazards to a potential target.

Leave it alone, shoot one, capture one. Three parts to the question of approach on the problem that the things exist, or on the problem of assuaging man's insatiable curiosity about the creatures. There is a fourth part and that simply consists of photographing one, or more than one, of the creatures and proffering the pictures as evidence. If the pictures were accepted as evidence then little more would be needed as proof of the creature's existence. If they were not then we would be back to square one. If the pictures were not of good quality and if the photographer were not of unquestionably good character, then they would most probably not be believed. For there is no doubt that one can work wonders in a modern studio these days and a clever photographer, with the right props and a certain amount of time and money, could produce stills and possibly even movies of half a dozen Bigfeet flying over the top of Mt. Rainier if he wished.

Where pictures are concerned, their acceptance will depend entirely on the credibility of the photographer and on the quality of the pictures. Processing under bond would be essential and the photographer would probably have to swear, before ever even seeing his own pictures, that their subject was a genuine Bigfoot, as he saw it in his lens and as he believed it to be, and that he would stake his own amateur or professional reputation as a photographer—and incidentally his own personal reputation, his business reputation, and his social standing and integrity—that the subject was as he stated or at least as he believed it to be. Then, and only then, would he begin to move toward that acceptance that would be essential to using the photographs as positive proof of the Bigfoot reality.

If we include the one year that I spent in full-time investigation of the Bigfoot mystery in 1960, the total time spent to date is over five years. Moving into the sixth year of the long-drawn-out search, I find myself repeatedly faced with the question, is not six years a rather long time to be spending looking for your hairy friends? Do you not think that you should have been able to find one of them by now? Or that someone else would have photographed one, or shot one, or hit one with a car? Or that some kind of definite proof should have been forthcoming that would have put people's minds at rest about the positive existence of the things?

There are days, truly, when the search seems long. But when I am looking out the window of my office in The Dalles, watching the evening sun gold the distance hills, or sitting by a campfire deep in the forests of the Cascades with the night birds calling and the stars marching down the sky, I am reminded of men like Dr. Otto Schoetensack, a German paleontologist. In 1887 Dr. Schoetensack became interested in a large sand pit near Mauer, Germany. The pit was close to an area that had yielded much fossil material from the Pleistocene Age, and he felt that it would be worth digging there. He felt this so strongly that he started digging at the pit and did so almost every day for twenty years. The result, in 1907, was the famous Heidelberg mandible, one of the great finds of the paleontological fraternity. There are many other examples: the decades that it took Louis Leakey of Kenya to find the first real fossil skull, the Zinjanthropus skull, in Olduvai Gorge; the years that it took to have the gorilla accepted as a real living creature. First mentioned in European literature in the fifteenth century, the lowland gorilla was not known to science until the late 1800s. The mountain gorilla, a subspecies, was not officially recognized until 1902.

It is obvious to me, as it is to all who have searched for the Bigfeet, that these, the most elusive and man-wary creatures on the face of the earth, are not going to be found within a year or two. This is my opinion and the opinion of the scientists with whom I work, and of my associates at the Bigfoot Information Center in Oregon. But two things could change this rather pessimistic outlook. One would be what is presently the basic need of the search that is run from the Information Center—new and sufficient funding. For in spite of what some of the glossier magazines have had to report over the last few years, the funding of the project has been extremely limited. (One magazine recently reported that the Information Center received in 1974 a grant of $50,000! We wish that it were true.) Insufficient funding has been the bugbear of The Dalles project, and lack of funds has prevented me and my researchers from putting into action many of the very high potential plans that we have designed over the years, plans that are the end result of thousands of man-hours of study of the phenomenon and of how to get to the bottom of it. Both the International Wildlife

194

Conservation Society and the Academy of Applied Science have been generous in both financial and moral support, as have many private sponsors. But I.W.C.S. funds have mostly been applied to conservation projects and, as has already been mentioned, the efforts and funding of the Academy of Applied Science have mainly been used to project the Loch Ness investigations. Full funding of a proper search project has never been available to the present teams and, as a result, the work that has been executed, all of the planning that has taken place, all of the searching that has been done in northern California, Oregon, Washington, and British Columbia, has been restricted and contained to the point where much of it had often to be left unfinished or even, at times of severe financial drought, unstarted.

With enough money to start a full-bodied search and investigation, using the plans that at this time are ready to go into operation, I would predict a definite find, possibly within two years, and certainly within five. The "find" would probably be in the form of first class photographs or 16mm movie film, evidence that in the eyes of some would not be sufficient proof of Bigfoot's existence. But the impeccable credentials of the two institutions now associated with the project would make it acceptable scientific evidence.

What would the new funding do to the present project and how would it be expanded into a full-scale search? What equipment would be added to the search team's present equipment and what other changes would take place? Briefly, the whole project would be reorganized and expanded. The expansion would include the recruitment of new personnel, among whom would be qualified people in the fields of anthropology, zoology and biology. They would have to be energetic people, active, dedicated to long hours and hard work and prepared to spend months in the field at a time. Part of their task would be comparative ecological studies in the different areas of evidence, with an eye to determining factors common to each area. These factors could be food, or certain types of tree cover, or even minerals of the type that wild creatures like to eat, such as salt or sulphur veins.

New equipment would include long range two-way radios with a range of several hundred miles and base station in The

195

Dalles at the Information Center. Each vehicle would be equipped with a two-way set for constant communication with base and there would of course be set-calling hours for all personnel. New vehicles would be purchased and this new fleet would be an extension of the present two-vehicle fleet of 1975 International Scouts, vehicles that have proved their worth in our operations over thousands of miles of very rugged terrain.

Dogs would be used as part of the search team and at this time one of our associates, David Hasinger, of Philadelphia, is exploring this possibility. The plan with dogs would be to train a certain species of dog, possibly a bloodhound or something close to a bloodhound, to follow distinctive scents. Part of the experimentation that is presently being conducted with dogs includes research on scent and as of this year an internationally known laboratory has produced two distinctive scents that contain the glandular secretions of female gorilla and orang, woman, and so forth.

The Bigfoot News would be expanded through advertising and a target of 100,000 monthly issues would be aimed at within two years. Its purpose would be what its main purpose is now, to draw information to the Information Center from the thousands of people who live in the Pacific Northwest, who work in the forests and the mountains or who go into the mountains to hike, fish, or camp. Through this huge public relations campaign the eyes and ears of virtually thousands of people would be used by the Center, people who at present are finding footprints or making sightings and are not reporting them to the Center because, A) they do not know that it exists, B) they do not know that their reports will receive serious attention and immediate investigation, or, C) they are not aware of the policy of confidentiality that protects them from the public and from any possible ridicule.

The present $1000 reward* that is offered for information leading to a find by Center investigators would be increased to, probably, $5000 and through the pages of *The Bigfoot News* this would be made known to the public. With the

*The terms under which this reward is offered are as follows: $1,000 will be paid for information leading to a find by information investigators that is deemed of value to the continuing research program of the Center.

reward offer would be a description of the policy and aims of the Center towards the Bigfeet: the total disinterest in a capture and in imprisonment, the care that is constantly taken and that is an integral part of the hunting methods of the center that one of the creatures is not harmed in any way, and the end result of the proof of existence—protective legislation for them both in this country and in Canada.

Many other changes would take place and there would in essence be total overhaul of the present search methods that are so restricted by lack of funds and large-scale expansion into new fields of research and investigation. Lastly, we would begin to move on what we call our geo-time patterns. These GTPs, as they are called, are basically geographic areas where, at certain times, evidence has appeared in the shape of a definite time pattern. For example, Area X. In this area footprints were found in 1953, in 1962, and in 1970. The area also shows four sightings, in 1953, 1967, 1970, and 1971. And the pattern? A study of the calendar shows that all of the footprints were found in the fall months of the year and all of the sightings took place in the same months. This gives us what is called a geo-time pattern for a single area and the result is an area with very high potential for a find. The pattern suggests that in these months one or more of the creatures comes into this particular area. The reasons, as yet, we may not know. Probably food, probably as part of a migration route. Whatever the reason, the evidence shows some movement and the presence of at least one Bigfoot, for one area, within certain months. This is very valuable information for our searchers, pointing as it does to a single contained area.

But searching one of these areas, or even concentrating searchers in one, can often be a time-consuming and consequently an expensive task. The area may be hundreds of miles from base, and nowadays the expense of reaching into such an area, with men and supplies and all of the logistics involved, can be considerable. To date we have not had the funds necessary to explore thoroughly and take advantage of a single one of the several geo-time patterns that our research has built over the years. When we can, when we start to put into operation the full-scale searching of a fully funded team, then I feel that we will at last come to grips with the Bigfeet and with our efforts pierce the shadows of one of the most extraordinary mysteries of our time.

Introduction
to
Appendix A

The following scientific report, by Dr. Ivan T. Sanderson, describes the discovery and examination, in December, 1968, of the corpse of what appeared to be a hominid type of anthropoid and what might well have been a Bigfoot.

The corpse in question was examined by Dr. Sanderson and Dr. Bernard Heuvelmans, F.Z.S. (Lon) and shortly after the examination both scientists wrote reports of what they had seen. Both men admitted that they were hampered by the fact that the corpse was enclosed in ice and also covered with a layer of glass. The owner of the corpse would not allow them to remove this. However, they were able to see enough of their subject to describe fully the external morphology. They also believed that what they examined was a complete corpse of a once living creature and not a composite. They judged it to be a primate and an anthropoid. But they did not reach a definite conclusion as to whether it was hominid or pongid.

The origin of the corpse is rather vague. At first the owner stated that he had obtained it in Hong Kong and that it had been preserved there after being found floating in a huge block of ice in the northern Sea of Japan. In July, 1970, many months after this report was written, he changed his story. In a statement to the press he gave a long and detailed account of how he had personally encountered and shot the creature while on a hunting trip in northern Minnesota, not far from the Canadian province of Manitoba. He claimed that while on a deer hunting trip he had shot and wounded a deer. He was following a blood trail that the wounded animal had left when he suddenly came across three of the creatures in question. They were, he said, grouped around the fallen deer and were pulling out its entrails and eating them. One of the creatures, the young male, immediately charged him, he said. The man fired, hitting it in the left eye. At the sound of the shot the others fled and the man walked up to the creature and shot it again, in the chest. (Sanderson's examination showed what appeared to be bullet holes in the left eye and in the chest.) He left the creature where it lay and went home, telling no one of what he had done. Later, he returned and picked up the body. The shooting took place in December and the body, he said, had been frozen solid—and preserved—by the extreme cold of the northern winter.

Early in 1972 I went to New Jersey to visit Dr. Sanderson. I stayed at his S.I.T.U. Headquarters near Columbia, N.J., and we were joined by Gerald Russell, visiting from his home in France. Gerald had been with me in Nepal on the '57 Yeti Expedition and also with Ralph Izzard on the '53 Daily Mail Expedition. Thus the main subjects of our several days of conversations were Yeti in Nepal and Bigfeet in the Pacific Northwest. I was able to bring Dr. Sanderson up to date on certain findings in connection with the Bigfoot phenomenon and he was able to provide me with new information concerning the "Ice Man" and its strange disappearance and possible whereabouts. He had heard about the new story concerning its origin and after we had studied some topographic maps of northern Minnesota and southern Manitoba and found, in his files and mine, some history of Bigfeet in the area, he agreed with me that the creature known as the "Ice Man," which he and Dr. Heuvelmans had examined, could indeed have been a young Bigfoot. I personally believe that it was.

Appendix A

IVAN T. SANDERSON

Preliminary Description of the External Morphology of What Appeared to be the Fresh Corpse of a Hitherto Unknown Form of Living Hominid

The possibility of the continued existence of one or more kinds of ultraprimitive hominids in various parts of Eurasia, Orientalia, Africa, and North and South America, has been mooted for several decades. The suggestion has never, it appears, been questioned in Mongolia, China, Thibet, and surrounding provinces, but it was not until the early years of this century that Professor, now Academician, V. A. Kakhlov introduced the matter to the western scientific world in Russia. Starting in 1920 a complication arose in the misnaming of another reported creature in the eastern Himalayas, called in colloquial Nepali the *Meh-Teh*, which appellation has since been converted and contracted to *Yeti* and become synonymous with the false moniker « The Abominable Snowman ». This latter is clearly a tradition of — if not a series of factual records of — some form

201

of highly advanced, mountain-climbing pongid; and it is the consensus of educated opinion that, if such a creature does still exist, it will most probably prove to be a descendant of or related to *Gigantopithecus* known from fossil remains in adjacent southern China. Concurrently, several reports of as yet undiscovered pongids emanated also from Africa. However, all reports of bipedal, fully-haired anthropoids from the other four continents named above, without exception concur in describing the creatures as being hominid, and leaving uniquely human-like footprints with an *apposed* great toe. Apart from this feature, there would appear to be considerable variation both in the size and form, and the behaviour of these hominids. These characters and characteristics spread the possibility of their identification all the way from neanderthaloid types of *H. sapiens* to the earliest Australopithecines. This paper describes the external morphology of what appeared to us to be a fresh corpse of one type of such large, fully-haired, bipedal primate that was preserved in ice, in a refrigerated coffin, in the United States of America, and which was examined by the writer in collaboration with Dr. Bernard Heuvelmans of Paris.

INTRODUCTION

On the 12th December, 1968, the Society (*) of which the writer is Administrative Director received a telephone call from a Mr. Terry Cullen of Milwaukee, Wisconsin, to inform us that he had inspected a corpse of what appeared to be a fully-haired hominid preserved in partially clear ice in a side-show at the International Livestock Exposition's annual fair in Chicago during the period 28th November to the 7th of December. Mr. Cullen who was then unknown to us is a zoologist maintaining a commercial enterprise specializing in herpetology, and is the discoverer of several new species of iguanid lizards in the Caribbean area.

Mr. Cullen's report included some details of this corpse's appearance that, taken together, prompted us seriously to consider the possibility of its being a real body, and not just a model

---

(*) *The Society for the Investigation of the Unexplained*, of New Jersey, U.S.A.

or composite constructed by oriental artists, long noted for faking « mermaids », as the exhibit was billed. Mr. Cullen further repeated to us a story of the origin of this specimen allegedly related to him by the man in charge of the exhibit, a Mr. Frank D. Hansen. According to his account at that time, it had been found floating in a six-thousand-pound block of ice in the sea somewhere off the east Siberian coast by a Russian sealing vessel ; was then confiscated by the mainland Chinese authorities, but had finally turned up in Hong Kong. This story was subsequently changed several times, and first to the original discoverers having been a Japanese whaling vessel, but all accounts coincided with Mr. Hansen's final explanation, given directly to us, that he found it in an enormous plastic bag in a deepfreeze plant owned by a Chinese gentleman of British nationality in Hong Kong., In view of the intelligence received from Mr. Cullen, and after having the existence of the specimen confirmed by two of our Society's members from Chicago, Messrs. Richard Crowe and Richard Grybos, I traced Mr. Hansen on the phone and decided to drive out to his home which is near Winona, Minnesota, and where he had the specimen stored for the winter.

It so happened that one of our members, Dr. Bernard Heuvelmans, Fellow of the *Comitato Italiano per lo Studio dei Problemi della Popolazione*, and of the Zoological Society of London, and a *Collaborateur scientifique 'a l'Institut Royal des Sciences Naturelles de Belgique*, was staying at our Society's headquarters on his first visit to the United States en route to Central and South America to study mammals threatened with extinction. Dr. Heuvelmans, as is known to the *Comitato*, and as is also universally appreciated, has devoted many years to the investigation of reports of ultra-primitive hominids said still to be living. The writer therefore invited Dr. Heuvelmans to accompany him on this investigative trip.

We left on the 14th of December and examined the specimen on the 16th, 17th, and 18th days of that month Heuvelmans took a large number of photographs of the specimen in both color and black-and-white. The writer made detailed technical drawings, employing prescribed methods that are outlined in fig. II. We first examined the specimen together, and then during the next two days we did so separately. Our subsequent reports were written without reference to each other until completed, when the results were compared and a list of divergencies in detail — but not in opinions — was composed. These original reports were not altered and are on file. Subsequently, new and fuller papers were prepared by both of us while resident in different places. These were not compared. Heuvelmans submitted his (in a French version) to the *Institut Royal des Sciences Naturelles de Belgique*, and it has been published in their Bulletin, No. 45, 4, Bruxelle, 10 February, 1969. This paper is the writer's — Ivan T. Sanderson's — final summation, brought up to date as of the 8th June, 1969.

THE SPECIMEN

This is «preserved» in clear ice, in a rectangular block 6'11" long by 2'8" wide and (said to be) 3'6" in depth. This block is said to have been cut from a much larger piece of (allegedly) drift-ice, found floating in the sea. This original block is said to have weighed 6000 American pounds. This was first trimmed around the sides to its present dimensions and then about two feet were taken off the bottom to a point where the under, or back side, of the contained specimen could be seen. Then, the owner states, he had a professional « ice-carver » — a technician and artist who creates large decorative pieces for banquets in clear ice by chiselling and ablating — shave down the upper surface as far as possible to the upper contours of the corpse. This resulted in a « mountainous » surface in low relief, the upward bulges doming all protuberances such as the feet, knees, abdomen with a hand on top of the same, the chest, the face, and the left arm that is thrown back over the head. The whole block was then lowered into an insulated coffin, measuring internally exactly 36" x 7'4", with two large nylon straps passed under either end of the block about a foot in from the ends. The two-inch space all around it was then filled with tap-water and frozen solid with a refrigeration unit attached to the coffin.

The corpse is only partially visible (see illustration, Fig. 1) for two reasons. First, considerable sections of the ice have recrystallized in tabular plastrons of opaque constitution. Second, there has been considerable exudation of gases from the corpse forced outward from all orifices and from skin pores through the hair-fine tubules that penetrate even clear, amorphous, palaeocrystic, and other forms of ice. These have created « bursts » of flowerlike, tridimensional « crops » of semi-opaque « twigs » of crystalline ice. These two features of the matrix in which the corpse is encased make it exceedingly difficult to inspect its details. However, with strong floodlights directed from the lowest angle possible above the glass top of the coffin, many details are brought out when the surface of the corpse is viewed from directly above. It was by this means that the drawn reconstruction was made.

The corpse or whatever it is, is rotting. This could be detected by a strong stench — typical of rotting mammalian flesh — exuding from one of the corners of the insulation of the coffin. Whatever this corpse may be, it would seem to include flesh of some kind ; and such cannot be preserved permanently in mere ice, although the temperature within the coffin is in this case kept at a maximum of 5-degrees F.

GROSS MORPHOLOGY

Any conclusions that follow amount, frankly, to little more than speculation because the specimen could not be handled and had to be viewed from no closer than a foot at best, through four sheets of plate glass and a varying amount of clear, frosted, or totally opaque ice. This whole exercise is therefore equivalent to describing an unknown form of any animal fixed in a solid block of plastic — such as is used to encase demonstration specimens — but with more than half the exposed surfaces identifiable only as a shadow under opacity.

1. *Overall Impression.*

Our first impression on viewing this specimen was its great bulk, and this grows on continually the longer one inspects it, and especially with the use of side lighting. Above all, it is the hands that are most startling because of their excessive bulk — not mere dimensions — and which look out of all proportion to the body and even to the immense arms.

The other notable impression was, from the outset, that the thing was some kind of human, hominid, or humanoid — and this, despite several extremely pongid features. This could be what is called a psychological effect, but is probably due most to the length of the legs and the « stance » of the creature on its back in such a typical human position.

2. Bulk and Weight.

There is no way of estimating its weight, since only two-dimensional measurements can be taken and one is thus unable to estimate its gross mass. Mammals as a whole average about the density of salt water, but bulk is no real criterion. The writer, who is exactly six feet tall but weighs only 160 pounds, cannot sink even in fresh water, while he can name two men of the same height but quite fat who, although almost professional swimmers (as far as body actions) sink at really extraordinary speed even in salt water the moment they cease to swim. Estimates of the weight of animals other than man are more than hazardous, except by such specialized experts as the breeders of domestic animals. Nevertheless, assuming the legs are as bulky as we assume, we would suggest somewhere in the neighbourhood of 250 pounds for the weight of this specimen. The author happened to obtain the record Lowland Gorilla —- a specimen of *Gorilla gorilla matschei* — in the Assumbo Mountains of the Cameroon, and this when stretched out, measured just six feet from crown to plantar surface and had a 9'2" armspan, but weighed more than 600 pounds.

3. Measurements.

All measurements were first taken directly from the corpse using a straightedge rule from the center of the head-end of the coffin to the central point at the foot-end. A large metal set-square was moved along this, first down one side and then down the other of this fixed central rule. The front edge of the set-square was extended by another metal ruler so that it reached the sides of the coffin. Points of reference were fixed from directly above by lying on top of the glass of the coffin. Drawings were later made from these measurements on the scale of 1/2" to 3", and a 1/2" grid was then ruled on a clear plastic sheet, overlaid on the completed drawings, and the measurements checked thereby. The reference points had necessarily to be arbitrary in that the ideal points — such as convergence of the legs behind the scrotum in the groin, tip of the elbow, etc. — were not always visible at all, while those points that were clearly visible had to again be judged through the thick hair covering.

From these measurements it would at first appear that the arms are excessively long, without taking into account the hands. This, however, is not necessarily so, as will be seen below. Further, a very strong word of caution should be put on record here; namely, that while the right leg (to the left in the drawing, of course) is definitely raised considerably at the knee-joint while the other, (the left) appears to be fully extended with the foot turned downward, there is — in this author's estimation, at least a very distinct possibility that both legs are elevated from the groin. Thus, their length could be several inches greater in the overall than as shown in the photographs and sketches.

The measurements of the « face », eye-sockets and nares (orifices), the hands, the penis, and the right foot as seen are of considerably greater precision than the other measurements because of the absence of hair. The mouth, however, is indeterminate since two-thirds of it are invisible under opaque ice.

4. *Proportions.*

These we consider to be of much greater significance, especially in regard to identification and classification, but numerous words of caution are here required. On detailed and somewhat prolonged analysis, the proportions — apart from the bulk as opposed to the linear measurements of the hands — are not as outrageous or exceptional as first impressions would indicate. Further, as the whole corpse cannot be seen from directly above (nor photographed in this way) due to the low truck ceiling, far too great a notion of length of everything is gained. The unaided human eye is very deceptive in judging measurements from an angle of 45 degrees, as was abundantly proved in this case when the scale drawing composed from actual measurements taken from directly above at each point, as described above, was compared with our rough estimates made before these drawings were completed and gridded, and with the final photographs.

The feature that at first throws one off is the excessive size of the torso, and the fact that the chest flows into the abdominal mass and continues — as in apes, incidentally — down to the *hips*, as opposed to a «waist». (Unfortunately, the navel cannot be seen, so no measurement between it and even the scrotum can be obtained.) This ultra-massive « body » gives the impression of great length. Further, what would seem to be the clavicles actually arch up under the chin, and this adds to the impression.

At the same time, the legs at first appear to be long, if not very long. This is most odd (again probably « psychological ») and could be due to preconceived notions — to a zoologist, at least — that pongids have short legs and hominids long ones. The truth is that, as can now be seen in the appended technical drawings, the legs are short and, judging by the combined lengths of both, just about match the torso from clavicles to scrotum.

The width of the chest is great in proportion to the torso length but again, not excessively so for a hominid. Be it noted that it is enormous compared to that of a chimpanzee or orang, but not compared to that of a male gorilla. Then again, a very high proportion of human beings have just these dimensions and proportions, and these do not have to be hod-carriers or wrestlers. The shoulders also are (were) unexpectedly wide, though by no means excessively so for either man or gorilla, while there is a type of very large, very hirsute chimpanzee that has even broader shoulders. (This type, of which we have seen only two specimens, one in the Rochester Zoo fifteen years ago, and the other in a primate collection in Florida in 1959, is in our opinion a distinct species and not necessarily even of the genus *Pan*)

The proportion of « face » to body generally is not actually excessive for a hominid and is definitely small for a pongid, but as the head is thrown back, nothing above or behind the low forehead — and there *is* a « forehead » above the very slight brow-ridges with their line of scant eyebrow hairs — can be seen. The face is exceedingly wide, but the eye-sockets and the nares are disproportionately large even for such an (apparently) brachycephalic type of face.

It just so happened that while this paper was in preparation a young man, seventeen years of age, and a keen athlete notable for his record in his school basketball team, was introduced to us. A mutual friend arranged the meeting when we were discussing the proportionate length of the arms and hands to the body of this specimen, and as a result of mentioning that the young athlete's hands reached more than halfway down his thighs. The attached photographs were taken with the author as a check since both are exactly six feet tall and weigh about the same — 160 pounds. The author has to buy the longest standard arm-length for shirts for his size, yet, as will be noted, his wrists are almost three inches above those of Mr. Richard Lambert (the athlete), as may be calculated from the black lines drawn across both right wrists; while, further, the hands of the latter extend almost six inches lower than those of the author.

We were also able to take comparative photographs, to scale, of this young man's hands and feet compared with those of the author. (These are reproduced as Figs. 4, 5, 6 and 7) From these it will be seen that while Mr. Lambert's hands are in perfect proportion for the normal white Caucasoid, they have a span and length considerably exceeding those of the author (with ring for identification). This gentleman's feet lead us into quite another matter due to the extraordinary length of his toes — a matter that is not pertinent to the present discussion.

From these comparisons — with a person, we should stress, picked at random and quite by chance — it is manifest that, disregarding the bulk of the specimen under review, neither its hands nor its arms are excessively long, while their proportions fall well within the range of human beings.

The feet of the specimen, however, do display a remarkable proportion, being (proportionately) more than twice as wide as those of Mr. Lambert, and nearly twice as wide as those of the author.

However, it is in the width and overall bulk of the individual fingers and toes that this specimen diverges most strongly from the typical human proportions. This matter is further discussed below.

Finally, the length of the penis in the specimen is not great for a hominid — and it is not known if it is erected or semi-erected — but would be very large for the average pongid, if flaccid. It is not well seen, being in clear ice but under a top film of opaque ice. The scrotum is small and wrinkled and the testicles small, but this detail is even harder to see.

DETAILED MORPHOLOGY

To see and record the details of the specimen's morphology called for special side lighting and prolonged peering from several angles before the true conformation of the parts could be reconstructed. All the following is thus derived from mere conjectures. There is a great deal else that both of us « feel » or « believe » we saw, but these details are not stated herein. Only those points upon which both of us agreed subsequently — and we made our detailed examinations separately and compared notes only later — are herewith discussed. Further, there is of course *no proof*, of a proper scientific nature, that this specimen was the corpse of anything recently alive.

1. *The Face.*

This is deliberately not referred to as the head because, as stated above, none of the latter, other than the face, can be seen. This is of a yellowish — i.e. Caucasoid «white» or pinkish — color and naked but for two most remarkable hair tracks. The first runs up the septum between the nares from the top of the upper lip (there is no moustache but some scant, almost feline-like whiskers) to the frontal point of the very «pug» nose. The other is a mere scattering of bristly, short hairs on the brow ridges but not joining across the (non-existent) bridge of the nose. There are virtually no brow ridges, and the forehead slopes only slightly backward, as far as can be seen. The malars are wide and prominent and the chin is wide. But, most notable to this author, were a series of folds and wrinkles around the mouth.
The eye sockets are unexpectedly round and rather large. Both eyeballs are out and, in the opinion of this author, are miss-

ing. However, both the caretaker and Heuvelmans assert that they can see one of them on the left cheek. There is considerable outflow of red blood from the left eye socket which streams off into clear ice to the right (i.e. to the right side as seen from above) of the face.

The nose is by far the most unusual feature of the face. This is pronouncedly what is called «pugged», being turned upwards just like that of a Pekinese dog, and having the large, exactly round nares pointing straight forward to the general plane of the face. The nostrils are fleshy and rather heavy, but flow into the upper lip without a noticeable crease. To some extent the whole nasal structure may be likened to that of a young gorilla, but there is more actual « nose » and this is turned upwards rather than being flattened, while it is not, as a whole, very wide in comparison, proportionately, to the width of the face, as in many human beings.

2. The Torso.

This, as has already been said, is very bulky, with wide shoulders, and it tapers only slightly down to the hips — not to a waist. There are no visible pectoral muscles and the nipples are rather far to the sides. There is virtually no neck in front — only about an inch, which is covered with dense hair — despite the fact that the head is thrown back. It is impossible to see how the head is attached to the shoulders on either side because of opaque ice. The most outstanding feature of the torso is the position, conformation, and alignment of the clavicles. Unlike humans, these bow upwards, meeting high over the neck so that, seen from the feet-end, the upper torso looks just like a plump. plucked and stuffed goose. I have seen such a structure in human dwarfs in whom it is a gross abnormality. The conformation on this specimen, however, looks absolutely natural.

3. The Arms.

These, while appearing very massive, are probably rather slender but are clothed in the longest hair on the whole body, or at least those parts of it that can be seen. The upper arm gives rather definite evidence of being much more slender than the forearm which, despite the heavy hair covering, has an extremely wide wrist. It should be noted that the only arm visible is the left (to the right side of the corpse as now viewed) and that this has a very visible break, from which blood exudes and in which the ends of the radius and ulna may be seen on the distal side. This is what gives the whole arm, as thrown up and back, the first appearance of being a sort of flaccid «tentacle» more like that of an octopus.

4. *The Hands.*

These are, as has been said, by far the most noticeable and outstanding morphological structures visible. They can only be described as enormous but this, as has also already been noted, is due more to their great bulk than to their actual linear measurements. They are slightly more pink than the rest of the skin, and they are *not* what is commonly called « gnarled ». To the contrary, they look more like those of a huge man who has had his hands in very hot dishwashing water for some hours. That this effect is not due to post mortem bloat would seem to be indicated by the fact that the sub-digital pads are not swollen nor the folds between them obliterated. In fact, the latter are rather prominent. The back of the right hand is very heavily haired, but the individual follicles are far apart and the stiff hairs curve gently over the sides and the tips of the fingers above the nails. The latter are «cropped» just as if they had been neatly manicured ; are rather flat and yellow in color ; and are almost square. There is no evidence of post mortem growth.

Of the hands, the most remarkable feature is the thumb. This appears to be as fully opposed as is ours, but it is remarkably slender and appears to reach almost to the terminal joint of the first or index finger. It also tapers, rather than expanding like the average man's. The nail on the thumb is not visible on either hand. The knuckles are neither prominent nor even well-defined. A most notable feature of the palmar surface of the hands is one that puzzles us. This is that there is an enormous and prominent pad on the « heel », at the *outer* side, behind or « above » the fifth digit back. This far exceeds the sub-pollex pad in dimensions and protuberance. From this one is forced to speculate whether this creature may indeed spend time «on all fours» with the hands applied to the ground in a plantigrade manner as are those of the baboons. The conformation of this pad is brought out in the sketch (Fig. I).

5. *The Genitalia.*

The penis is very hard to see even with strong light at various low angles, and it has been somewhat over-emphasized in the drawing compared to the other visible surface. This was done deliberately to record the compendium of observations we made upon it from various angles. It is slightly curved or bowed to the right (left, as seen from above), is rather slender, and tapers to a point, from which this author felt he saw a small floral-shaped emission of pinker flesh some four millimeters in width. It is pale yellow. The scrotum is very hard to see and this author is somewhat dubious of what is herein stated. It appears to be wrinkled, is brownish, and shaped as if containing two small testicles. There is no hair on the penis but there appears to be on the scrotum.

6. *The Legs.*

Actually, it is impossible to determine the real length or bulk of these, and for several reasons. First, as noted above, both may be elevated at the groin from the supine position of the body as a whole.Second, the right leg is more elevated at the knee than is the left, while both ankles are hidden below opaque ice. Third, the thighs and shanks are deeply buried in the ice, but they are very heavily clothed in long, stiff, straight hairs that mask their outlines. The knees are, however, very prominent and readily seen, bearing only very sparse short hairs. They are pink and the patella is *typically human.* This we consider to be of the greatest significance as pongids just do not have «knees» constructed like this.

7. *The Feet.*

These are, of course, the key point in this whole case. As we noted in our introductory remarks, the only remaining criterion for separating the hominids from the pongids — on purely morphological grounds, that is — is whether the hallux is apposed or opposed. We would stress the morphological as against the anatomical criteria here. In this case, the feet are definitely hominid. That they are apparently excessively wide and, it would seem by prognosis, rather short, and due to the size and «pudginess» of the toes, would seem to indicate that they have the proportions of whatever left the allegedly « neanderthaloid » tracks and imprints in the cave clay of Toirano in Italy (see bibliography).

The forward projecting foot is pink in colour, has bulbous terminal pads, and horny yellowish nails that are also « cropped » in that they do not curl over the ends of the toes as do ours if left untrimmed and as those of the *Guli-avans* are said to do — see reference in Russian works to these under the heading of the *Jelmoguz-Jez-Tyrmak* or « *Copper Nails* » of the Tien Shan. The hair on the top of this foot is very long and curves over the toes and is very profuse to either side, curving over the main plantar mass. The toes are astonishingly equal in size, the little toe being large and the great-toe rather small in proportion. All form an almost straight « front » which would seem to be the ideal conformation for steady forward progress in snow or loose soils. (Square-fronted snow-shoes have at last been found to be much more efficient and less tiring to wear than the standard spindle-shaped form).

There is finally one point about the feet that the writer cannot confirm nor absolutely assert. This is that, as reconstructed (through a very long and repeated inspection through the ice) there would seem to be *two* post-hallux plantar pads such as form such a prominent feature of the *Sasquatch-Ohmah-Hungerussu-Dzuteh*, giant type of primitive hominid.

TRICHOLOGY

There is little that can be said about the true dimensions, conformation or even coloring of the hairs at the present stage of investigation, except to note that the body is generally very fully haired. The caretaker told us that when they were shaving

214

down the ice, samples of hair were taken and sent to « the greatest experts ». When asked who these were, he could not « remember » but stated that they had gone to « Somebody somewhere in New Jersey ». When asked if there were any reports made on these samples, Mr. Hansen told us that there had been, but that they were « In our California office », adding that he would get us copies. These have not eventuated.

No overall description of the pelage of this specimen is possible on two counts. First, only about a third of it can be seen clearly, though fortunately these portions do represent most of the front, or ventral side of the creature. Second, the hair-tracks are very elaborate. The latter problem has, however, been fully overcome by combining the sketches of both authors and rendering the agreed-upon composite on the accompanying drawing. — Fig. I.

A number of points of great interest to mammalogists are herein brought out. Starting at the hands, we find first that their backs are covered with sparse but long, curved hairs that drape over the whole hand. These emerge right down to the top of the ultimate joints of all digits. The hair on the under or inner side of the wrist is visible; but this on the left wrist alone, which is held above the head, palm upwards. This narrow band of hair stands straight up but curves one way towards the hand at one side, and backwards up the inner side of the arm on the other. All the hair visible on the upper arm flows evenly to the elbow, as it does in the chimpanzee particularly. That on the upper arm, however, flows downwards from the shoulder to that point, so that the two flows form a « drip-tip » on the outside of the elbow. The arrangement of the hair in the armpits must be examined in the accompanying drawing. The amazing thing to us is that the axilla is filled with the same type of hair as the surrounding areas. There is no sign of true axillary hair such as that of humans. Further, neither of us could find any evidence of pubic hair either, though there is undoubtedly fairly thick, fine hair all over the pubic region. This absence of these types of hair is typically pongid ; even *simioid*.

Apart from the sparse bristles on the brow ridges mentioned above and the curious stubbly line up the front of the septum between the nares, the face is naked. However, there appears to be hair above the brow, and flowing backwards on the side of the head. (No ears are visible as the head is thrown back into opaque ice.) Under the chin there is a dense forward-pointing mass of short hairs filling in the inch to two-inch « neck » between the immense arched clavicular torso top and the wide chin.

The most striking features of the trichology of the torso are twofold. First, there is a sort of fringe of what is obviously a long-haired cape covering the dorsum which just emerges around the sides of the torso and forms a sort of continuous incurved eaves (as on a house). The rest of the chest is almost naked but for widely scattered long, lank, straight hairs. These are concentrated as shown in the drawing down the midline of the sternum, being slightly parted in the median line and then flowing on downwards into the sparse pelage of the belly region. The contrast between the « eaves » of the back cape and this sparsely-haired chest and front is very striking and is, it should be noted, completely in accord with pongid trichological arrangement rather than with that of hominids. Human beings with developed hypertrichosis invariably manifest excessive growth first on the chest and front of the belly, and this hair is almost invariably oval in section and thus curly or even kinky.

The pelage in the inguinal region is not visible. The legs from the uppermost point visible on the thighs to the bottom of the shanks, where they disappear below opaque ice, are well-haired. These hairs are perfectly straight, on an average over two inches long, widely separated — their follicles being well over an eighth of an inch apart — and all flow straight downward.

Finally, the tops of the feet are very heavily haired, and right down to the ends of the terminal joints of the digits. These hairs look wiry, are fairly widely spaced, and curve gently over the feet in all directions.

The Hairs.

It is, of course, impossible to supply or even suggest any concrete facts about these apart from mere visual observation. From this, nonetheless, and as seen through the clearest ice covering, it would appear that they are extremely coarse or thick, average about two to three inches in length more or less all over the body, and are mostly quite straight. Those that curve have been mentioned above. An interesting fact is the very wide separation of their follicles. We tried to measure these distances but the distortion caused by the ice made it almost impossible ; but we would estimate that it is on an average nearly as much as a quarter of an inch — say three to four millimeters. On the chest and upper belly they are even more widely spaced, and despite the extremely « hairy » appearance of the arm, we have reason to believe that the follicles are no closer together there, the effect being due simply to the much longer length of the individual hairs.

The « cape », as far as it can be seen, is definitely darker and denser and appears to be jet black. The rest of the pelage is dark brown, but one most important point stands out. Would that we could give absolute proof of this observation but, without having examined so much as one hair we cannot ; yet, all the long, straight hairs would seem to this observer to be definitely but dully banded in what is known to mammalogists as the typical « agouti » manner. This is to say, each hair has lighter bands, starting wide at the base and decreasing in width towards the tip. If this be a valid observation, we have here a most unique item in that no hominid or pongid hair is known with this type of coloration. Not until we come to the so-called « monkeys » —· Cynopithecoids, Coloboids, Cercopithecoids, etc. — do we encounter this condition.

CONCLUSION

This paper describes, in somewhat general terms, the results of a preliminary inspection of the corpse of what appeared to be some form of large primate of hominid form. The notion that it is a « composite », manufactured from parts of human corpses and/or other animals, must, of course, still be considered, since the body has not yet actually been examined ; should it be, the « artist » who put it together, insering several million hairs in a skin before it rotted or was preserved, would have to have had some concept to work from, and there is no such extant. This for the following reason. This body is not that of any known hominid or pongid and, what is much more significant, it does not conform to any reconstruction or artist's conception of any fossil man or ape or other anthropoid. Its general features and particular characters as detailed above display an extraordinary mixture of what have until now been assigned either to men or apes, but it also shows others that have never been assigned or attributed to any of either.

However, two separate companies specializing in model-making for waxwork museums, exhibits, and film companies in Hollywood California, have been traced, and individual model-makers working for both have stated that they made copies with wax or latex and using hair from bears. Mr. Hansen, the caretaker, informed us in January of this year that such a model had been made in April of 1967 because the owner of the original was worried about its safety. An object such as this *could* possibily be constructed, starting with the skin of a large male, pale-skinned chimpanzee, using a human skull, glovemakers wood racks for the hands, and so forth. The *original* could have been of this nature, and then a copy, or copies, made from it.

Just in case this might not be the origin of the specimen, we should consider the alternative ; namely, that it is a genuine corpse of a comparatively recently killed specimen — not « fossilized » in any way -- of some form of parahominid. This is the considered opinion of Heuvelmans and is based on as thorough an examination as he was able to make considering that the specimen is encased in ice that is more than half opaque, and sunk about two feet below the glass cover of its container. And, if this is the correct interpretation, we would opine that it would more probably be on the hominid rather than the pongid stem of anthropoid evolution. Just where it should be placed on that stem can not, of course, be said until it has been properly examined out of its ice envelopment. Further, and much more important, will be any analysis of its blood, plasma and other body fluids, if they are still sufficiently preserved for typing. Even then, we may well be confounded because this specimen displays such a combination of characters attributed to the two presently thought quite widely separated *families* of anthropoid primates. And this constrains us to add a note of added caution.

In view of the fact that pongids and hominids have now been shown to fall into several groups, *together — vide* the Caucasoid and Congoid hominids with the gorillas and chimpanzees on the one hand; and the Mias, Siamangs, and Gibbons among the pongids with the Mongoloid hominids on the other, is it not possible that not only the hominids but the pongids have a grid-like genetic origin. If this be the case, could the concept not be further extended to include all the anthropoids so that there may have been — and, in this case may still be truly « manlike apes » and « apelike men » ?   This specimen is by several criteria a hominid, noticeably by its feet, but it has many pongid characters.   Are the diagnostic features we are currently employing to separate the apes from men valid ?   If not, are both our « families » invalid, and could both groups form but one complex ?   If so, we will have to add the « Hairy Man » to Desmond Morris' « Naked Ape ».   Anything of this nature will absolutely demand an overall revision of our ideas of both physical and social anthropology, and will present a somewhat alarming problem to scientists and religionists alike.

This author's personal opinion as to the precise identity of this specimen is at the moment not formulated.   As a trained zoologist and one who spent many years collecting mammalian and particularly primate specimens for examination, dissection and preservation in the field and while fresh, we would not presume to make any definite pronouncement upon anything other than a purely generalised, overall description of its external appearance.   The corpus must be freed from its ice encasement and properly examined first.   However, some speculation as to the taxonomic status of this creature, if it finally proves to be real, is perhaps permissible, since we do have detailed measurements and photographs to back it up.

It is Heuvelmans' opinion, which he states categorically in his paper (*op. cit.*), that this body represents the fresh remains of a neanderthaloid human.   Such hominids are currently classed as a sub-species of *Homo sapiens*, yet Heuvelmans has named this item *Homo pongoides*, and thus of full specific rank.   Though we suggested that appellation (*pongoides*) in the first place, we envisaged it either as a subspecific to *H. sapiens* — since we have no idea as to the external morphology of the fossil neanderthaloids — or merely as a possible specific for some other genus of anthropoid. However, this suggestion was purely tentative in that, despite the existence of this specimen, we have no more idea of its anatomy, histology, or physiology than we do of the external morphology of the neanderthalers. I am therefore officially disassociating my name from that given in Heuvelmans' paper.

We are constrained to do this not only because we are personally averse to naming any specimen before it has been physically obtained and properly examined, but also more precisely because we are not convinced that this specimen is neanderthaloid or even a member of the genus *Homo* as presently constituted. Further still, it might not even be an Anthropoid, but rather a survivor of a line divergent from, and possibly lying between, the hominid and the pongid branches, but derived from a common ancestor to all three. In the absence of the corpus itself, as of the time of writing, and in view of our total lack of knowledge of the external morphology of any anthropoids other than the living hominids and pongids, we consider it to be most incautious to attempt to identify this specimen as of now, and more especially to confine it whithin a subspecific title. And anent this ; one essential feature of this specimen seems to have been overlooked.

What can be seen of the conformation of the face, meaning the front of the head, in no way conforms to *any* known fossil hominid — apart from the juvenile australopithecoids — and particularly to that of any neanderthaler of comparable size. There is no prognathicism; virtually no brow-ridges ; the forehead does not slope acutely ; the two teeth that can be seen are infantile. In fact, from what can be assessed of the anatomical structure of the fore part of the skull, this creature is almost as far removed from the standard neanderthaloid construction as is possible. In these same respects, it shows no more affinity with *Homo erectus*, *H. habilis* (what is known of same), or more especially such ‹lower› types as were once called pithecanthropines, australopithecines, or suchlike. In fact, if it does prove to be a hominid, by whatever criteria may be decided upon to define that family when and if it is examined, it might well be called *Homo pongoides ;* but it most certainly should not be assigned to the neanderthal race or complex.

Our final conclusion, therefore, is that the specimen we inspected was that of a genuine corpse — as opposed to a composite or a construction — and that it is some form of primate We would categorize it, as of now, as an anthropoid, but whether it is a hominid, a pongid, or a representative of some other previously unsuspected branch of that super-family we are not prepared either ot say or even to speculate. There are certain firm indications that the specimen examined by Heuvelmans and this writer — though it has been removed from the place where we saw it, and hidden, while a substitute model has been installed — has not been destroyed and may therefore eventually become available for proper scientific examination. Until such time as this is achieved we advise that it serve only as a pointer to the possible continued existence of at least one kind of fully-haired, ultra-primitive, anthropoid-like primate, and be used only as a lever to pry open the hitherto hidebound notion that any such thing is impossible.

TECHNICAL NOTES ON THE ILLUSTRATIONS

The illustrations accompanying this paper fall clearly into three distinct categories of origin. Each of these requires some technical explanation since each in its own way is of very consi derable importance to a proper appreciation of the subject matter in the text. The first two plates — Figs. I and II — are re-scaled reproductions of the author's original technical drawings made from measurements taken, and sketches made, in Minnesota, directly from the specimen, in its container. The next five — Figs. III through VII — were taken by our Society's photographer and Executive Assistant, Miss Marion Fawcett. Fig. VIII is a composite of four colour stills taken by Bernard Heuvelmans of the specimen, through both glass and ice, in Minnesota ; and Fig. IX is a reproduction of a painting made by the professional artist and illustrator, Mr. John Schoenherr, from a tracing of the Heuvelmans composite, and was published in ARGOSY Magazine — May issue of 1969.

The method by which Figs. I and II were made was described above in the section entitled « measurements ». These pictures are herewith submitted since they hold a much greater degree of linear accuracy than the photographs taken at the site because of the vile conditions for photography pertaining there. The specimen is under both glass and ice, and is housed in a low-ceiling trailer-truck so that it was impossible to elevate the cameras sufficiently to obtain even an overall « shot » of the whole, let alone any without distortive parallax.

Figs. III to VII are straightforward shots, but it should be emphasized that those of the hands and feet were taken from a fixed camera position above, so that absolute comparison is possible.

Figures VIII and IX need special comment. Due to the confined space in which the photographer (Heuvelmans) had to work, a considerable amount of distortion was unavoidable in all the pictures and most notably in the four that comprise his composite (Fig. VIII). These four had to be taken from four different angles, which may be described as north, east, south, and west, and all from a somewhat acute angle, the camera being hand-held, after focussing, under the ceiling. The artist, Mr. Schoenherr, had only this composite to work from in preparing his painting, and he worked from a tracing. The photograph is extremely hard to decipher apart from a few prominent, light-coloured, fixed points such as the nose and one big toe. Proportions of the hands and other details had virtually to be guessed at. When, however, we superimposed this artist's conception on the photograph, on television closed circuit, we obtained perfect alignment. Further, the artist, we found, had reproduced details with almost uncanny accuracy, and in exact conformity with other mere sketches that Heuvelmans and the writer had made of such items as the hair tracks. (Note, however, that the gape of the mouth or lips is on the *right* side of the face, not on the right as seen in the coffin).

We feel therefore that Figs. I, II, VIII, and IX, give as accurate a depiction of this specimen as can now be extant. It will be of much interest to see how close this composite of composites coincides with the specimen if and when it is deglaciated, and properly photographed without parallax.

On the 8th of May, 1969, the Smithsonian Institution issued the following release regarding the specimen described in this paper.

« The Smithsonian Institution has withdrawn its interest in the socalled Minnesota Iceman as it is satisfied that the creature is simply a carnival exhibit made of latex rubber and hair. Information has been received from a reliable source, that the Smithsonian is not at liberty to disclose, concerning the ownership of the model as well as the manner, date, and place of its fabrication. This information, combined with some recent suggestions received from Ivan T. Sanderson, the science writer and original « discoverer » of the Iceman, as to the manner in which the creature could have been artificially made, has convinced us beyond reasonable doubt that the « original » model and the present socalled « substitute » are one and the same.

Dr. John Napier, the Director of the Primate Biology Program at the Smithsonian, points out that the Smithsonian's attitude has been one of scepticism combined with open-mindedness throughout, and that their only interest in the affair has been to discover the truth which they are reasonably certain is as stated above.

This procedure was in part initiated by the author, and for three reasons. First, we learned that, just as Mr. Hansen had himself informed the Smithsonian in writing, the specimen that Heuvelmans and the present author had inspected had been permanently withdrawn from public display and a fabricated copy made. Second, we traced a professional model-maker, working for a reputable firm in California who stated that he had made just such a copy. Third, this writer was asked whether he — having spent twenty years collecting and preserving mammals for the British Museum of Natural History — could make anything like the original.

Two of my previous assistants in that work happened to be available and, after consultation, we were able to submit a memorandum describing, in outline, how we would proceed. Simultaneously, the Smithsonian traced another man, also in

California, who stated that he had made a latex model, using bear hair, in April of 1967. As a result of these facts, it was deemed advisable to defray any further expenditure of time and effort in the hope of obtaining the original specimen for proper examination.

This new model went on public exhibit in May of this year. It was photographed with the permission of the caretaker, and the photographs clearly demonstrate that it is not the original specimen examined by us — and in a number of readily discernible details. It is, in fact, a very fair reproduction of Mr. John Schoenherr's « artist's conception » that illustrated a popular article by this authos in ARGOSY Magazine and which had appeared a month previously. These details were not visible in Heuvelmans' photographs but they were quite legitimate embellishments by this fine artist for the purposes of a purely popular article.

Mr. Hansen has throughout adhered to his initial explanation of the discovery of the original specimen, as having been found in Hong Kong, and he has always stated that he never did know what it really was, while the owner refused to disclose the results of alleged hair and blood analysis. Mr. Hansen is a showman, and only employed to exhibit this specimen by its owners. He has told us frankly that what is now on exhibit is a copy and man-made. Comparison of the photographs of what he now has on view with those of the original corpse taken by Dr. Bernard Heuvelmans prove this beyond any doubt.

Fig. 1 Scale drawing of the Iceman prepared by
Ivan T. Sanderson.

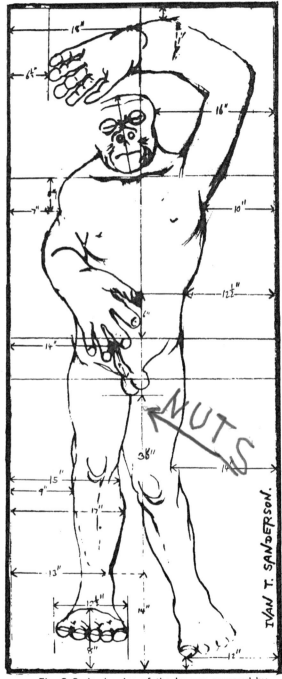

Fig. 2 Scale drawing of the Iceman prepared by Ivan T. Sanderson.

Fig. 3 Two six-foot male caucasoids, showing proportionate length of arms.

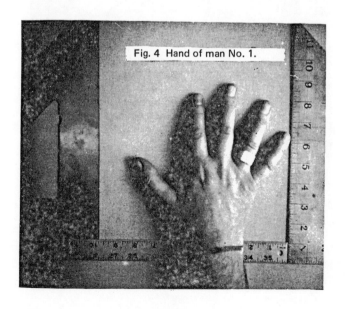

Fig. 4 Hand of man No. 1.

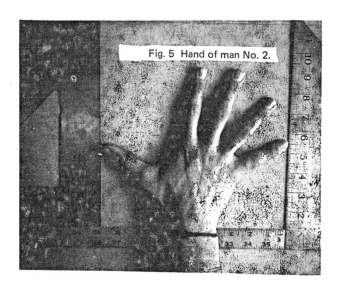

Fig. 5 Hand of man No. 2.

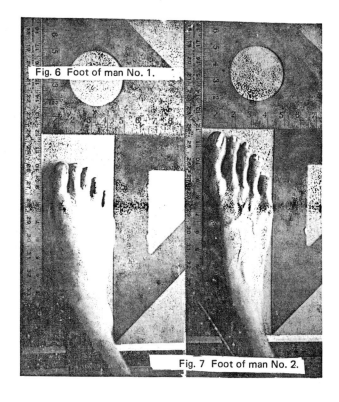

Fig. 6 Foot of man No. 1.

Fig. 7 Foot of man No. 2.

SUMMARY

This paper describes the ◆discovery◆ of the corpse of what appears to be a hominoid type of anthropoid, fully clothed in hair, preserved in ice in a glass-covered coffin that is kept at 5° F. This was housed in a special trailertruck on private property near Winona, Minnesota, U.S.A., by a caretaker who had been responsible for moving it around the United States for two years and exhibiting it at fairs, on midways, and in carnivals. The specimen is said to be owned by a resident of California who, after publication of a detailed description of the specimen by Dr. Bernard Heuvelmans (*op. cit.*), allegedly removed and hid it, substituting a model for next year's exhibit. The specimen is said to have been found in a refrigeration plant in Hong Kong, and to have originated somewhere in northeastern Asia. So far the owner has refused to give any precise details as to its origin or how it was brought to the United States.

The external morphology of this specimen is herein described as far as it could be ascertained visually, and by photography, through four sheets of plate-glass with a layer of ice below that was more than one half opaque. From what could be seen, the specimen is hereby declared to be, in all likelihood, a complete corpus, and not either a composite or a construction. It is judged to be a primate and most probably an anthropoid, but no conclusion or even speculation as to whether it is specifically a hominid, a pongid, or a representative of some other hitherto unknown branch of the anthropoid stock is advanced.

The specimen we inspected, although allegedly removed and hidden, has not — as far as written expressions have so far been made — been destroyed, and the owner refused to make it available for examination by the Smithsonian Institution. Its relative value, as of now is, therefore, pointed out to be essentially and only potential proof of the continued existence of at least one form of human-like anthropoid such as up till now has been flatly denied as being possible by the majority of not only physical and cultural anthropologists but also by primatologists. As such, it is suggested that it might constitute a very valuable contribution to knowledge, and potentially to a better understanding of primate, anthropoid, and possibly hominid ancestry.

Introduction
to
Appendix B and C

The following reports are by Dr. Grover Krantz, physical anthropologist with Washington State University at Pullman, Washington. Dr. Krantz has been intensely interested in the Bigfoot mystery for many years and his interest has carried him all over the northwest. He has personally interviewed many witnesses, has visited The Dalles groups and has seen and made plaster casts of Bigfoot footprints.

As a result of his studies Dr. Krantz believes that there is a small surviving group of the creatures still living in the northwest of the United States and in British Columbia. More than this, he is not afraid to state this belief, both orally and in writing, and these reports of his on his personal study of footprints are unique.

They are unique in that Dr. Krantz is one of the very very few scientists in this country who has had the courage actually to put anything down on paper that is not against the existence of the Bigfeet. He is also one of the very few scientists who has taken the time to study the phenomenon and taken the time to study the 1967 film footage. His studies convince him that the creatures do exist, while other scientists, who have examined neither the 1967 film nor any of the mass of evidence that now exists on the creatures, think that they do not. Perhaps the reader will see the significance of this? The following reports are published here with Dr. Krantz's permission.

Appendix B

Anatomy of
the Sasquatch (Bigfoot) Foot

BY DR. GROVER KRANTZ, LECTURER IN PHYSICAL
ANTHROPOLOGY, WASHINGTON STATE UNIVERSITY,
PULLMAN, WASHINGTON

Reprinted from Northwest Anthropological
Research Notes—Vol. 6, No. 1

Abstract

Many plaster casts and photographs of footprints have been examined in
detail which were reportedly made by a species of bipedal primate, the sasquatch or bigfoot. They prove not to be simply enlarged human footprints
but show several peculiarities. These include flat arches, a double ball,
and enlarged heels. Examination of leverage mechanics of the human foot
indicates that with excessive body weight certain modifications would be
advantageous. The expected modifications are the same as those seen in the
reputed sasquatch footprints.

Within the last century, several hundred people have reported sightings
of gigantic man-like animals in the forests and mountains of the Pacific Northwest. Hundreds more have seen the huge footprints left by these hairy creatures.
Possibly ten times as many people have seen these giant primates and their
tracks without reporting anything to newsmen or law officers for fear of
ridicule.

The animal in question is commonly called sasquatch -- based on one Indian
name for it -- or "bigfoot" for obvious reasons. If this animal really exists,
it would probably be man's closest living relative and a member of the zoological family Hominidae. It is not human, however, in any sense of the word; all
reports agree on its lack of language, artifacts, and social organization.

While a few scientists take these reports seriously, the majority doubt
that any such animal exists. Sightings are usually dismissed as being of
standing bears, hallucinations, or fabrications; footprints are explained
as those of bears or, if they are quite distinct, as deliberately planted hoaxes.
Also, skeptics point out that no specimen, living or dead, is available for
scientific examination -- not even a single bone has been identified as
belonging to this species.

Tangible evidence for this type of primate consists mainly of several
photographs, two short movie strips, handprints (Krantz 1971), and the footprints themselves which have been measured, drawn, photographed, and cast in
plaster. I will not attempt to review here all of the above evidence, but will
confine this analysis primarily to what can be deduced from the recorded footprints. Other evidence will be used only to help establish the approximate
body weight involved, since this is the major factor in understanding the
design of foot suggested here.

There are many sources of information on sasquatch or bigfoot tracks, not all of them equally reliable. I have examined casts made from the footprints of 17 different individuals and photographs of tracks and casts of another 50. On one occasion I saw an actual footprint left in snow. It is possible that some of the photographs are of faked prints -- people are known to have attempted this -- but most of the material upon which my study is based is probably as authentic as any that exists.

Information on sasquatch body weight is more difficult to obtain. Most people who report seeing them are sure they are very heavy. Estimates range from approximately 300 pounts to half a ton or more, but these are usually made under trying circumstances and cannot be taken as very precise.

Equally vague are estimates based on depth of impression of footprints. A sasquatch foot has about three times the surface area of a typical man's foot. One might assume that if the print is as deep as a man makes in the same ground, the sasquatch is three times as heavy. If the print is twice as deep, the body weight of six men is indicated. Normally when people compare their own footprints with those of a sasquatch, it is by daylight and often many days later than the original made at night. Changes in soil softness and compressibility make such conclusions only rough estimates.

There are at least three cases I know of in which more precise information is available. The first is the reported capture of a young specimen in 1884 near Yale, British Columbia, by a railroad crew (Green 1968, 1970; Sanderson 1961). The original newspaper account has recently been confirmed to me by the grandson of one of the men involved. The creature, which soon disappeared, reportedly stood 4 feet 7 inches tall and weighed 127 pounds -- a very stocky body build.

Roger Patterson, who took a short movie of one walking in northern California, estimated its body weight at 500 pounds. Review of this film shows the subject to have been just 7 feet tall. Patterson's estimate can be taken seriously because of his long good look at the animal and on his ability to accurately guess human weights -- he called my own 210 pounds exactly.

The third case is quite unverified but fits well into the series. An experienced hunter and prospector in northeastern Washington claims to have shot and killed one. He told me it measured 8-1/2 feet tall and weighed 850 pounds according to careful examination of the body. (Since he has produced no evidence to back up his story, it is assumed by some to have been fabricated.)

When plotted on a graph, these three height and weight figures closely fit a curve based on theoretical calculations. The volume (and weight) of an object does not increase in direct proportion with its linear dimension or height but with the cube of that dimension. Thus, if an animal's body is made twice as tall, keeping the same shape, it will be eight times as heavy. On a lesser scale, if an animal's height is increased by half, its weight increase will be 1-1/2 cubed (1-1/2 x 1-1/2 x 1-1/2) or 3.375 times as great.

Jim McLarin of Willow Creek, California, was the first to apply this principle to sasquatch dimensions by taking a base figure of 6 feet tall and

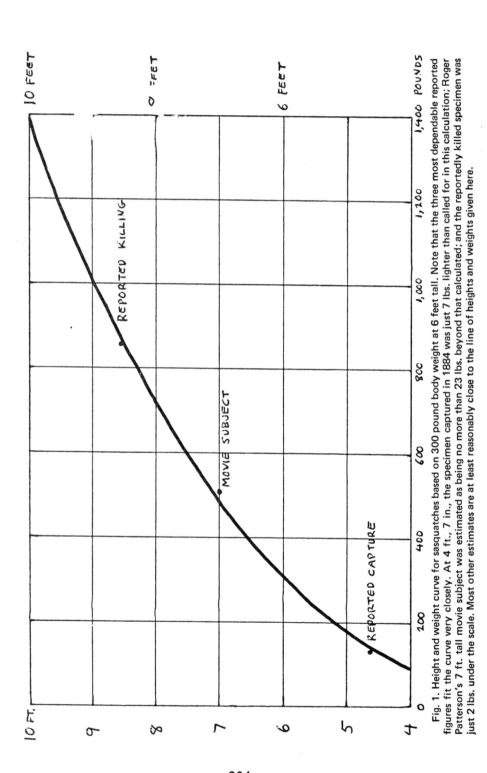

Fig. 1. Height and weight curve for sasquatches based on 300 pound body weight at 6 feet tall. Note that the three most dependable reported figures fit the curve very closely. At 4 ft., 7 in., the specimen captured in 1884 was just 7 lbs. lighter than called for in this calculation; Roger Patterson's 7 ft. tall movie subject was estimated as being no more than 23 lbs. beyond that calculated; and the reportedly killed specimen was just 2 lbs. under the scale. Most other estimates are at least reasonably close to the line of heights and weights given here.

300 pounds body weight, and extending on this. A curve drawn from this base line gives 134 pounds instead of 127 at 4 feet 7 inches, 477 pounds instead of 500 at 7 feet, and 852 pounds instead of 850 at 8 feet 6 inches. All three instances fit the curve very closely (Fig. 1).

The vast majority of sasquatch heights are reported to be in the range of 7 to 9 feet tall. Body weights of 500 to 1,000 pounds are then the most reasonable expectations. Greater heights and weights have been claimed, and extending on this scale gives 1,389 pounds for 10 feet tall and 2,350 pounds for 12 feet tall, etc. I am inclined to set 9 feet and half a ton as the greatest size of bipedal primate that could properly function.

The typical sasquatch footprint looks superficially very much like a man's increased to about 17 inches. Closer examination, however, shows several differences which have aroused some curiosity but little in the way of explanation until now. The key to figuring out the kind of foot involved lies in understanding how the indicated body weight would affect a gigantic, but otherwise normal, human foot. From this, one can go on to predict what kinds of modifications might reasonably be expected in such a foot in order to support a body of 500 to 1,000 pounds.

Increasing body size has an interesting effect on the strength of anatomical structures. The pulling power of muscles and the breaking strength of tendons and ligaments are directly proportional to their cross-sectional areas. Yet their weight, like that of the whole body, increases with volume. Cross-sectional areas increase with the square of a linear dimension, while weight increases with the cube. Thus if a man were doubled in height, keeping all proportions the same, his muscles and supporting tissues would be four times as strong, but his weight would become eight times greater. In relation to the weight he would have to maneuver, his strength would be cut in half. Some changes in body design, especially in lever lengths, would be desirable for such an enlarged man to move about like other people. The large size indicated for sasquatch poses the same kind of problem.

The first peculiarity in these giant footprints is that they are quite flat. The instep or longitudinal arch of the foot is not there. In man this arch is maintained by ligaments and by the muscular pull on tendons. Given 500 pounds or more of body weight, these structures would not have sufficient increased strength and the arch would have to flatten. While adult sasquatch prints are flat, a number of supposed young ones show some arching. It is an interesting question whether the feet flatten with maturity just because of the weight, or if there are genetic mechanisms which would lead to a flat foot regardless of usage. If a number of people were making fake bigfoot prints, it might be expected that many of them would not have thought about this characteristic and would have included arches comparable to their own. None of the evidence I have examined shows a normal human arch.

Many sasquatch prints show what is called a double ball at the base of the big toe. Where the ball occurs in the human foot, there are often two distinct bulges, one behind the other (Fig. 2). The single bulge on the human foot is at the distal or forward end of the first metatarsal bone (see Fig. 3 for the bones of a normal human foot). The question then arises as to which of these two balls corresponds to the one of the human foot and what it is that the other one represents.

In his book, Ivan T. Sanderson (1961) suggested that the posterior ball is at the end of the metatarsal, and that the anterior ball is a pad of flesh under the first segment of a very long toe. Assuming all the toes are similarly long, it follows that they are webbed for a great part of their lengths. If these animals do a great deal of swimming as some people suspect, such toes would appear to make sense. However, this interpretation does not fit well with what is indicated of the creature's weight.

Very long toes cannot be pressed into the ground with great force in walking. They do not directly transmit body weight, but will push down only as a result of the pull of the tendons along their undersides. The muscular strength available to flex or curl such long toes would not be nearly enough to dig them into the ground as deeply as the rest of the foot. Long toes would bend upward with each deeply indented step, yet all footprints show well-indented toe impressions.

Only a relatively short toe could have the proper tendon leverage to press firmly on the ground. Thus, it must be concluded that it is the anterior bulge that corresponds to the ball of the human foot, leaving relatively short, strong, and unwebbed toes. The posterior bulge remains to be explained.

Given a totally flattened foot, all structures that would have constituted the arch will be firmly pressed to the ground. Behind the ball of the foot is the next bony projection, the near or proximal end of the first metatarsal (Fig. 3). If the posterior bulge is formed under the other end of this same bone, the two bulges would be much farther apart than is evident on any sasquatch footprint. The only way for the posterior bulge to be as far forward as it is, by this theory, is to assume that the metatarsal is abnormally short and the bones behind it abnormally long. An examination of the mechanics of walking will show that indeed this should be the case for a gigantic hominid.

The foot can be described as a simple lever at the end of the leg. In taking a step, muscles of the calf (gastrocnemius and soleus) tighten and pull up the projecting heel. With the foot pivoting at the ankle its forepart then presses downward, thus lifting the body in the basic "step-off" action. If the power arm of this lever (heel) is short and the load arm (forefoot) is long, a significant extension is added to each step. This is the normal human condition (Fig. 4).

If the body weight is increased many-fold and the strength of the calf muscles is increased to a much lesser degree, then this action is no longer possible in sustained walking. If his foot were built just like a man's, the sasquatch would not have enough strength in his calf muscles to easily lift his vastly greater bulk with each step.

The simplest way to handle this problem is to change the lengths of the lever arms. If the heel, or power arm, is lengthened, greater force is applied to the step-off; if the forefoot, or load arm, is shortened, less force is required. Put another way, this adjustment means the ankle joint must be set relatively farther forward along the length of the foot.

The metatarsals are the longest bones in the forefoot. If this region is to be relatively shortened, the base of the first metatarsal must be moved far forward. Given a sufficient shortening of this bone, its two ends will be in the proper positions to form the double ball as seen in many sasquatch footprints.

236

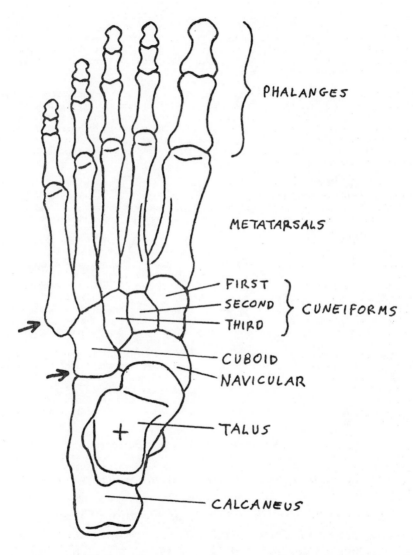

PHALANGES

METATARSALS

FIRST ⎱
SECOND ⎱ CUNEIFORMS
THIRD ⎰

CUBOID
NAVICULAR

TALUS

CALCANEUS

Fig. 3. Bones of the human foot as seen from above. Arrows indicate the locations of the two bony projections on the outside edge of the sole. These same projections in the sasquatch foot bones were for a time thought to have formed the bases for the calloused outgrowths on one crippled foot.

237

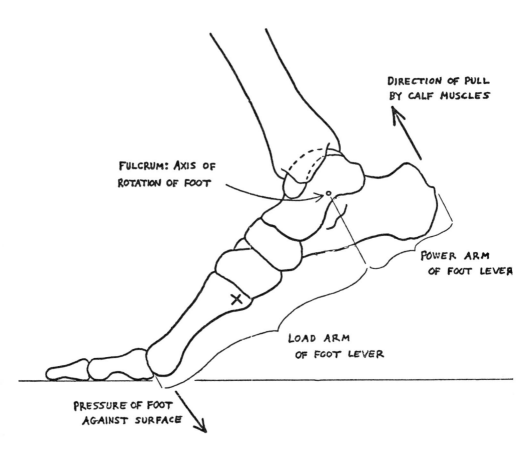

DIRECTION OF PULL
BY CALF MUSCLES

FULCRUM: AXIS OF
ROTATION OF FOOT

POWER ARM
OF FOOT LEVER

X

LOAD ARM
OF FOOT LEVER

PRESSURE OF FOOT
AGAINST SURFACE

Fig. 4. Side view of human foot bones illustrating how they function as a propulsive lever. The sasquatch foot should have a more powerful lifting force at the price of a relatively shorter step-off distance. This would be accomplished by a lengthening of the load arm and a shortening of the power arm of this lever. Given a flattened arch, the posterior end of the first metatarsal (marked with an X) would rest on the ground. Since this bone is relatively much shorter in the sasquatch foot, its two ends are closer together and would form the basis of the double ball.

If the foot segments are altered in this way, the heel section must be correspondingly longer. This is difficult to measure in footprints, but in some cases it is clearly evident. Rather than being simply longer, the heel region is wider as well -- typically one-third of the foot length. Such a general enlargement of the calcaneum (heel bone) should be expected for greater stability and to provide greater breaking strength in proportion to the increased strain put upon it.

The action described above is the step-off where the distal ends of all five metatarsals press against the ground when the heel is lifted. The "push-off" is still another matter where the toe segment is used to lengthen the stride with a final additional push. In man, it is only the big toe or first digit that is significantly involved in this final push-off. The action is not very powerful and many people do not use it at all. If a sasquatch were to try to use this final push-off from the big toe alone, he would not likely have sufficient strength to accomplish anything of the kind. Only by using all five toes in such an action might any possible push be given to his vast bulk.

A five-toed push-off would require at least two anatomical adjustments from the normal human condition which would be visible in footprints. Since the emphasis is not to be on the first toe alone, all five should be more nearly equal in size and strength. Also, in order for them to push in unison, the front of the foot should be more nearly squared-off instead of being strongly tapered as in man (Fig. 2).

Many sasquatch footprints show nearly equal-sized toes lined up almost straight across in a rather nonhuman manner as might be expected. Curiously, there are also several reported bigfoot prints which do not show much of those traits, but appear rather more human in the toes. There are two possible explanations for this. Sasquatch feet may include a great range of variation from a nearly human set of toes at one extreme to the ideal type described above at the other extreme. The second possibility is that some of these prints were faked, at least in part, by enlarging the impression of the first toe to make them look more "convincing." I would rather not choose between these two alternatives at the present time.

In 1969 a number of sasquatch sightings were reported 100 miles north of Spokane, Washington, and late in that year several sets of tracks were seen and recorded by many observers. Casts were made from clear imprints of both feet of this individual and have been studied in great detail. This specimen is especially interesting because its right foot is deformed. The prints of each foot are about 17 inches long, indicating a fairly large creature perhaps in the 700 to 800 pound range (Fig. 5).

The right foot showed only four toes -- the middle one was either missing or held vertically while the adjacent toes turned in, largely filling the gap. More important was a distortion of the whole foot which was bent on its long axis. The origin of this deformity is not clear, but its effects illustrate something of the structure of the foot.

Taking the heel region as stationary, the entire forepart of the foot is turned inward about 30 degrees. The individual did not walk with the foot in this position, but turned it outward somewhat so that its toe-heel line was

239

parallel to that of the other foot. This left both heel and toes twisted inward, while the weight of the leg rested more toward the outside edge of the foot. One effect of this displacement is a slight rise at the instep. This is the only case of an adult sasquatch footprint showing what might be called a raised arch.

Even more interesting is the outer edge of this foot where two lateral projections may be seen on the cast. Both feet appear to be strongly calloused around their edges and this callousing on the right foot extends around these two projections. At first glance these appear to correspond in location to normal bony projections. The anterior one would be the proximal or rear end of the fifth metatarsal. The posterior one would then be a projection on the rear edge of the cuboid bone. If these identifications were correct, the projections would be much farther forward than is normal for a human foot. This would mean the fifth metatarsal is abnormally short, and the calcaneus very large, just as indicated above from other evidence.

Actually the projections do not look like callouses over the bones indicated. The two projections are quite symmetrical and equal in size. Yet the two underlying bones, whether in man or gorilla, are not symmetrical, nor are they the same size. Therefore another interpretation is called for.

The twisting of this foot caused a compression of elements along the inside edge and an extension or spreading of all elements on the outside edge of the foot. Measuring around the outside curve from the base of the little toe to the heel tip, the right foot is almost two inches longer than the left. Unless some bones are enlarged, this means there must be open gaps between several of these bones. Since only three bones form this edge of the foot (fifth metatarsal, cuboid, and calcaneus), there are only two gaps that might have opened. These are in front of and behind the cuboid (Fig. 6).

Gaps between adjacent bones would have to be filled with cartilage or bony material in order to stabilize the foot. This filling would be expected to have grown outward beyond the bone gaps to form the bases upon which callouses developed.

Projections of such gap-fillers would be located just behind the bony processes that were first considered. This means an even shorter fifth metatarsal and longer calcaneus than was previously indicated. It shows an excellent agreement with the short first metatarsal as was deduced from the double ball on the inside edge of the foot.

In general, the sasquatch foot differs from man's in having greatly enlarged ankle bones, especially the heel, very short metatarsals, and a more nearly equal set of toes. These characteristics are all logical requirements for an otherwise human foot adapted to a body weight of 500 pounds or more. These characteristics are also evident in preserved footprints.

In addition, at least two eye-witnesses have added some confirmation to this reconstruction. Roger Patterson has told me his sasquatch appeared to have remarkably thick ankles, although this did not show clearly in his movie strip. If the leg is set relatively farther forward on the foot than in man, then a thick ankle is a consequence. The man who claims to have shot and killed a

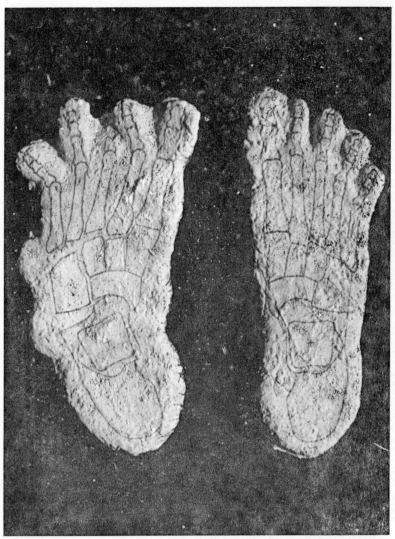

Fig. 6. A duplicate set of casts of footprints from the crippled sasquatch with reconstructed bones drawn in. Compare the relative sizes of the various bones with those of a normal human foot as seen in Fig. 3. Note also the gaps indicated between the bones of the deformed foot where the calloused projections appear. The bones are drawn as if the feet were seen from above. Since the casts correspond to the bottoms of the feet, the right and left feet appear to be reversed.

sasquatch in northeast Washington early in 1970 described the foot to me in some detail. He was most impressed by the relatively short and steeply sloped upper surface of the forefoot.

All good quality bigfoot prints must have been made by one or the other of two possible agencies. Either they are real footprints of a gigantic sub-human primate, or else they are faked as a hoax. (Only very vague prints could be confused with those of bears.)

There are a number of reasons to believe at least certain sasquatch tracks could not have been made by hoaxers. Their obscure locations would mean that perhaps a hundred times as many tracks were laid as have been discovered. Lengths of stride and obstacles stepped over often surpass anything a man can do. Depths of imprints would require a hoaxer to carry many hundreds of pounds of extra weight, thus making the walking accomplishments even more impossible. Independent toe movements as noticed in some tracks would require a special device to accomplish.

To all these must now be added the fact that our supposed hoaxer is an expert on human anatomy with a very inventive mind. He was able to create from nothing all the details of how a foot might be redesigned to support a body weight several times that of a man. And he has continued to plant these tracks over more than a lifetime, always showing only vague hints of these anatomical peculiarities. These include great width of heel, a double ball, and a straighter row of similarly sized toes.

No matter how incredible it may seem that the sasquatch exists and has remained uncaught, it is even more incredible to believe in all the attributes of the hypothetical human track-maker. As Sherlock Holmes put it, "... when you have eliminated the impossible, whatever remains, *however improbable*, must be the truth." Even if none of the hundreds of sightings had ever occurred, we would still be forced to conclude that a giant bipedal primate does indeed inhabit the forests of the Pacific Northwest.

Appendix C
Additional Notes on
Sasquatch (Bigfoot) Foot Anatomy

BY DR. GROVER KRANTZ

Reprinted From Northwest Anthropological
Research Notes—Vol. 6, No. 2

Abstract

Three methods are described which can be used to measure body weights
of the sasquatch. Heel breadths of the footprints, squared, are directly
proportional to weight; level lengths in the reconstructed foot indicate
probable lifting power; and the volume of a filmed subject is determined.
These measurements agree with previously collected data on the approximate
stature to body-weight relationship which is the equivalent of a 6 ft. man
weighing 300 lbs.

In a previous paper, I described several characteristics found in casts
and photographs of sasquatch footprints which argue for the reality of the
animal that has been so often reported (Krantz 1972). An 8 ft. tall, heavily
built hominid would require certain structural modifications in its feet
because of its great absolute body weight. In many cases these same modifications can be detected in the footprints.

My earlier work was concerned primarily with showing in what direction
these modifications should occur, but with little attempt at quantifying
them. This will be remedied here with the description of at least three new
ways of determining body weights from the evidence available at present.
Each of these methods was worked out separately and gave surprisingly
similar results.

Throughout the following discussion, it is necessary to keep clearly in
mind the changing relationships among length, surface, and volume of any
structure as absolute size is increased. When length is increased by a
particular ratio from a standard, surface increases by the square of that
ratio, and volume increases by the cube of that same ratio. This is assuming
that shape is kept constant.

If the human body is doubled in stature (increased by a ratio of 1:2),
then its surface area in increased by four times (1:2 squared is 1:4), and
its volume is increased by eight times (1:2 cubed is 1:8). On a lesser
scale, an increase of half-again-more is a ratio of 1:1.5 for stature, when
square it becomes a ratio of 1:2.25 for surface area, and when cubed it
becomes a ratio of 1:3.375 for volume.

Pulling strength is directly proportional to the cross-sectional area
of a muscle so it increases with the square of the linear dimension.
Breaking strength of tendons and ligaments, and crushing strength of
cartilage likewise increase with surface area. Body weight, however, is a
measure of volume and increases with the cube of a linear dimension. As a
structure such as an animal body is increased in size, its volume (weight)
increases faster than its surface areas (strength), thus making any relationship between weight and strength very much dependent on absolute body size.

There are some aspects of anatomy where a constant relationship must be maintained between volume and surface. When larger versions occur of a particular animal type, then some changes in shape are necessary in order that certain surfaces can keep up with increasing body weights. Articulating surfaces in the joints of the limbs are an outstanding case in point.

All supporting structures in the limbs must do exactly that—support the body. As body weight increases with the cube of linear dimension, cross-sectional areas in the limbs must also increase with the cube of linear dimension. Since surface areas do not normally increase at this rate, certain anatomical changes in design are required in progressively larger animals of a similar type. The limbs of the larger animals are more stoutly built simply in order that their weight-bearing surfaces can keep up with the body weight.

Cartilage surfaces of supporting joints will be damaged if too much weight is applied. On the other hand, a metabolic waste would be involved if the joint surfaces were made larger than the body weight required. A close correspondence ordinarily occurs.

A good example of this relationship in similar animals of different absolute sizes is found in American pronghorn antelope and elk. The elk is four times as heavy as the pronghorn—big healthy specimens weigh about 500 lbs. and 125 lbs., respectively. If they were built exactly the same, joint surfaces in the elk would be only 2.52 times as great. I measured the rather flat articulating surface on the underside of the talus (ankle bone) of both species and found that the elk actually had four times greater area than did the pronghorn—just the same as the ratio of body weights. The elk talus is thus built relatively larger than might be expected in a uniformly enlarged version of the pronghorn.

As a similar test, I measured the upper surface areas of a series of fourteen human tali including European males and both sexes of California Indians. The largest talus had nearly twice the surface area of the smallest, 1,156 sq. mm. as compared with 676 sq. mm. A range of almost 2:1 in body weights (excluding abnormalities) might well be expected in such a sample of people.

The surface area of the sole of the foot (in hominids) may vary greatly in relation to body weight. Elaborations of the epidermis, for example, can differ enough that no close ratio of pounds per square inch can be postulated. The surface area of the talus may be quite another matter, since articulative cartilage has little variation in its crushing strength. My measurements indicate about the same amount of weight per unit area for the human talus as for those of pronghorn and elk, allowing for bipedal versus quadrupedal support.

With each step, the bipedal hominid transmits his entire body weight from one tibia onto the corresponding talus through the cartilaginous surfaces between these two bones. The talar surface is somewhat longer than it is wide, and is broader anteriorly than it is posteriorly. Since the tibia moves over the talus, the latter has the greater surface area. The actual area of contact, at any one moment, can be approximated by measuring

244

the breadth of the mid-talar surface and squaring this figure. The exact procedure of measurement is not critical as long as all comparisons are made in the same manner.

The breadth of the articulating surface of the talus, squared, is directly proportional to the body weight. Thus, a hominid talus with twice the breadth of the average for modern man has four times the surface area and is designed to carry four times the body weight. A talus half-again broader than man's would be designed for 2.25 times the weight, etc.

The upper articulating surface of the talus is not directly imprinted on the ground in a footprint. However, the upper talus breadth appears to be a very nearly constant percentage (about 50%) of the breadth of a bare heel imprint.

Direct evidence is lacking for sasquatch (we have no tali, let alone matching them with footprints) but some reasonable deductions can be made. If the talus were wider than the human in relation to the bottom of the heel, it would be perched upon a comparatively narrow and, presumably, wobbly base. If the talus were relatively narrower than human, then its weight-bearing potential would be less than possible for a given footprint size, and thus rather inefficient in this respect. An exact relationship cannot be demonstrated, but I shall proceed on the assumption that the same breadth ratio of talus to heel exists as in man.

It should now be evident that the squared breadth of a clearly imprinted bare heel is a good indication of body weight. A modern man of average body build and standing 6 ft. tall will weigh about 190 lbs. (the 4-4-4 somatotype of Sheldon 1954). Such men have an average heel breadth of 2.8 in. (my own observation, based on a series of measurements). This may be compared with a commonly reported adult sasquatch heel breadth of 5.5 in. These two heel breadths, squared, are 7.84 and 30.25. This is a ratio of nearly 1:4 which should also be the ratio of the surface areas of the two tali. The sasquatch in question would then weigh almost four times 190 lbs., or somewhat less than 760 lbs.

This reconstructed body weight would refer to normally built and reasonably healthy specimens. It is subject to the same kinds of variation to be expected in any other wild animal. Probably the majority of individuals with 5.5 in. heel breadths would weigh within 10%, more or less, of the indicated body weight, barring seasonal fluctuations.

A series of heel breadths and their corresponding body weights can be calculated on the above basis. I offer the following in English measurements simply because this has been almost exclusively the system used by sasquatch investigators in North America so far. (A table of similar measurements in the metric system is also given below.)

245

Heel Breadth (inches)	Squared (inches)	Weight (pounds)
2.8	7.84	190
3	9	218
3.5	12.25	297
4	16	388
4.5	20.25	491
5	25	606
5.5	30.25	733
6	36	872
6.5	42.25	1,024

Footprints with heel breadths over 6 in. are not very reliably reported. Still, one claim of about an 8 in. heel has been made on correspondingly enormous footprints.   This heel should carry a weight of about 1,550 lbs. if it is correct.

The following is a set of similar measurements in the metric system. The first and last figures are the same as in the list of English measurements, but there is one fewer in between, so these are not equivalents.

Heel Breadth (millimeters)	Squared (millimeters)	Weight (kilograms)
71	5041	86.2
75	5625	96.3
90	8100	138.5
105	11025	188
120	14400	246
135	18225	312
150	22500	385
165	27225	463

Some interesting comparisons can be made of lever lengths in the feet of higher primates. The major lever of the foot is that running from the tip of the calcaneum to the end of the third metatarsal. It is divided by the tibio-talar axis of rotation into a posterior power arm and an anterior load arm. A relative elongation of the posterior, or power, arm gives the foot a greater weight-lifting capacity.

In my previous paper on footprints, there is a photograph of casts of the prints left by a sasquatch with a badly crippled foot. On these casts I had drawn the outlines of the bones as indicated by the deformity of the one foot. Now, two years later, I have measured exactly the lever lengths I had drawn on the normal foot of this pair. Its power arm is 120 mm. and its load arm 223.5 mm. The former is 53.7% of the latter (Fig. 1).

The foot-lever lengths of other higher primates are reported by Schultz (1963:110). Each of these is given here as the percentage that the power arm represents of the load arm, and is compared with "Cripple Foot."

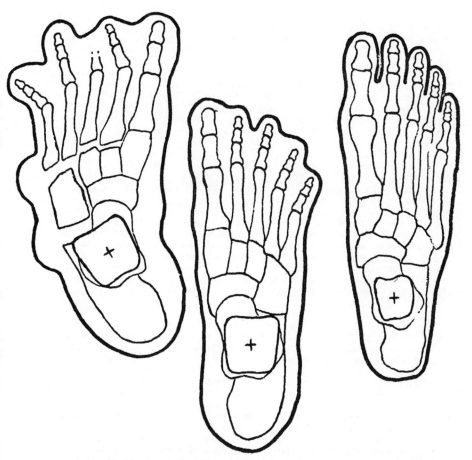

Fig. 1. On the left and center are outlines of the footprint casts of Cripple Foot with reconstructed bones drawn in as they would appear from above. On the right is a normal human foot on the same scale. The sasquatch feet are traced directly from a photograph in an earlier publication (Krantz 1972:102) except that the talar surfaces are enlarged and the tarsal-metatarsal joint is slightly altered. These minor adjustments do not affect the foot-lever lengths as originally reconstructed. These 17 in. long feet are reversed to facilitate comparison with the human foot which was redrawn from Marshal and Lazier (1955:65).

Sasquatch	53.7%
Gorilla	45.2%
Man	38.5%
Chimpanzee	26.8%

Not surprisingly, as body weights increase, so does the relative length of the power arm of the foot lever. As might be expected, the sasquatch foot lever considerably exceeds that of the gorilla in power. The fact that two of these primates are primarily quadrupedal when walking on the ground and the other two are bipedal seems to have no obvious effect on the foot levers.

Macaques and gibbons have still shorter power arms in order of descending weights. The orang-utan has an unusually short power arm (19.4%) considering his weight, but this animal does not walk on his soles and use the foot lever as the others do.

At first glance the difference between the human leverage figure of 38.5% and the sasquatch's 53.7% does not look impressive when one considers the great contrast in body weights. In order just to double the lifting power of the human foot lever, its power arm must be doubled in relative length from 38.5% of the load arm to 77%. The sasquatch power arm extension shows less than half this amount of change. A careful consideration of just how much the sasquatch power arm should be extended came as somewhat of a surprise to me.

The casts of Cripple Foot have heel breadths of 5.75 in. on the right side and 5.5 in. on the left. The average of 5.625 in. can be used to calculate the probable body weight on this individual, and this works out to 767 lbs. by the method described above.

It has been suggested previously (Krantz 1972), and will be repeated below with more evidence, that the sasquatch body build is comparable to that of a 6 ft. man weighing 300 lbs. The following comparison of Cripple Foot's pedal leverage will be that of a modern man of this very stout body build. Such a heavy-set body should have about the same muscular strength per unit weight as a 190 lb. man of the same stature. Still, the comparison should be made with the heavier type because this assumption determines the probable stature of Cripple Foot, which in turn affects his weight-to-strength ratio.

A hominid of 300 lbs. is contrasted with one of 767 lbs with comparable body builds. The larger one is not only heavier, but also has greater muscular strength, though not to the same degree. The ratio by which strength lags behind body weight is equal to the ratio of the cube roots of the weights, as will be seen.

The cube root of 300 is 6.694, and that of 767 is 9.154. The ratio of 6.694 to 9.154 is the difference between the two in linear dimensions. The squares of these numbers (or two-thirds power of the weights) are 44.81 and 83.79, and this is the ratio of surface areas, hence of muscular strength, between the two. When the difference between the weights of the two hominids is reduced by the difference between their strengths, what remains is the ratio of 6.694 to 9.154. So the sasquatch is only 37% heavier, in excess of his strength, than is the stout man.

The foot lever of this particular sasquatch needs to be modified only enough to handle this 37% increase in weight over strength. Where the human foot's power arm is 38.5% of the load arm, in this sasquatch foot the relative length of the power arm should be increased by the ratio of 6.694 to 9.154. This would be an increase from 38.5% up to 52.7% of the load arm. Since this measured percentage of the power arm in my reconstruction of two years ago is 53.7%, or just a trace greater, this is a remarkably close coincidence.

One could also reverse these calculations and deduce from the foot-lever lengths that Cripple Foot should have weighed 814 lbs. This is just 47 lbs., or 6.1%, more than the estimate of 767 lbs. based on his heel breadth.

I had previously argued how improbable it would have been for a track faker to know that the bulges on the edge of the crippled foot should be placed forward of the positions they would occupy in a human foot. To this I can now add that the hypothetical faker somehow also knew almost exactly how far in front to put them.

In October, 1967, the late Roger Patterson obtained a unique movie film in the mountains of northern California. This shows seventeen seconds of what appears to be a heavy-set hairy primate walking past at about 100 ft. away and then off into the forest. It is in color and only slightly out of focus, but the hand-held camera moved a great deal during much of the filming.

Early this year I had the opportunity to view this film about twenty times, forward and backward, and to stop it on any frame for more careful study and measurements. There are two frames which clearly show the full length of the foot together with the anterior-posterior diameter of the ankle. In both of these, the foot length was exactly twice the ankle diameter.

A rough reconstruction of some major foot and ankle proportions from the profile can be made based on an outline of the human foot given by Lewin (1940:51). Allowing for one inch of hair thickness around the ankle accounts for the straight line upward from the heel tip, and also locates the anterior edge of the ankle proper.

With normal internal proportions in this enlarged ankle, one can approximate the position of the center line of the tibia. This line divides the total fleshy foot length so that about 31% of it is in the posterior part. This contrasts with about 25% in the posterior part of the human foot, and appears to be identical with the tibia position in the reconstruction of Cripple Foot. It is clearly indicated that Patterson's movie subject had similar foot-lever lengths. This ankle position shows it was designed for supporting a very great weight, but the details are too imprecise to make any specific estimate (Fig. 2).

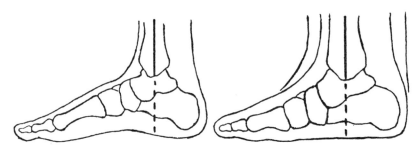

Fig. 2. At the left is an outline of the human foot viewed from the medial side with the bones drawn in from Levin (1940:51). At the right is the same view, drawn to the same length, of the sasquatch foot based on Patterson's 1967 film. The center line of the tibia in the human foot is above 25% forward from the heel tip to the toe tip, but in the sasquatch foot it is 31% forward.

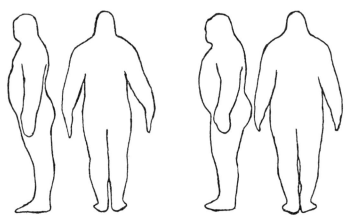

Fig. 3. Outlines traced from photographs of stoutly built men (Sheldon 1954:248) with an allowance for sasquatch-like body hair. Their height to cube-root-of-weight ratios are 10.92 (left) and 10.58 (right) compared with 10.75 estimated for the sasquatch. Both men are of somatotype 4-7-1.

There are still two other methods of estimating the body weight of this particular individual other than by the depth of impression of the footprints which was considerable. I have casts of eight footprints taken from the movie site, three of which are clear enough to measure the heel breadth. Two of these measure almost 4.5 in. and the third about 4.25 in. for an average of 4.41 in. By the method described earlier, this indicates a body weight of 471 lbs., give or take 10%.

The other method is to use the dimensions of all parts of the subject from the film image and to calculate its volume. These dimensions are fairly reliable as the height of the subject is known. The figure is 5.9 times as tall as its foot length, which is known from casts to be 14.25 in. Another check is a duplicate film made from the same camera position of a tall man walking in the old footprints. Both methods show the subject to be almost exactly 7 ft. tall.

From the stature and foot length, Green (1968) has obtained numerous measurements of various bodily parts. I have used these figures, and some taken myself from the film, to determine its total volume, allowing for hair thickness of one inch over virtually the whole body. This volume works out to be 8.44 cu. ft., but this estimate may vary considerably according to the person who makes the calculations. Since the subject is probably just slightly less dense than water, its volume can be multiplied by 60 lbs. per cubic foot, for a total of 506 lbs.

The two figures of 471 and 506 lbs. are acceptably close. Patterson himself called the creature 500 lbs. and he was very good as estimating human weights.

Stature estimates of the sasquatch, which are commonly reported, are often based on fleeting glimpses or are made under emotionally trying circumstances. Other estimates are based on claimed careful observations. These and other, more concrete, lines of evidence can now be combined to form a fairly clear picture of the relationship between heights and weights.

Since volume increases with the cube of a linear dimension, the cube root of the weight will be at a constant ratio to stature for any given body type. Three different body types can be considered here to see how well each fits the most reliable sasquatch data.

1. A body build like that of a typical modern man 6 ft. tall would weigh 190 lbs. This is a stature to cube-root-of-weight ratio of 12.52.

2. The body build of a very heavy-set man 6 ft. tall could weigh 300 lbs. This is a stature to cube-root-of-weight ratio of 10.75.

3. Some investigators who think the sasquatch is extremely heavy because of the depth of footprints would use 400 lbs. for a 6 ft. specimen. Here, the ratio of stature to cube-root-of-weight is 9.77.

The differences among these three ratios can best be illustrated by the three different body weights each would call for at a given stature. (Metric measurements are also given below.)

Stature (feet)	12.52 (pounds)	10.75 (pounds)	9.77 (pounds)
6	190	300	400
7	302	476	635
8	450	711	948
9	641	1,012	1,350
10	880	1,389	1,852
11	1,171	1,848	2,465

(All figures in this chart which are much in excess of 1,000 lbs. can probably be ruled out as being beyond the weight-bearing capacity of the ankle.)

The following is a set of similar measurements in the metric system. The first and last lines are essentially the same as the corresponding English measurements, and those in between are very similar to the English ones.

Stature (centimeters)	Human (kilograms)	Heavy (kilograms)	Heaviest (kilograms)
182.9	86.2	136.1	181.4
215,0	140.0	221.1	295.0
245	207	327	436
275	293	463	617
305	400	631	841
335	530	836	1,115

(All figures in this chart which are in excess of 500 kg. can probably be ruled out as being beyond the weight-bearing capacity of the ankle.)

The best test of the three sets of figures given above is Patterson's movie subject. In this case the height is known to be almost exactly 7 ft. Patterson estimated its weight at 500 lbs., I calculated its body volume which indicated 506 lbs., and its heel breadth calls for 471 lbs. All these weights are acceptably close to the 476 lbs. given in the middle column, and clearly out of range of the other two figures.

In 1884, a wild, hairy, bipedal creature was reported captured in Canada near Yale, British Columbia. A full newspaper account of the event is extant, though there is no information yet known on the ultimate fate of this animal. The most obvious identification is that it was a young sasquatch. Fortunately, its height and weight were measured; it stood 4 ft. 7 in. tall and weighed 127 lbs. (Green 1968).

Compared to adults, very young humans are relatively heavy because their legs are short, while teen-agers are relatively light. The age of the Yale, British Columbia, specimen is unknown; but, if the adults were as tall as 8 ft., it was the equivalent of about a four-year-old human child. This should make it, relatively, a bit heavy as compared with the adult scale. However, since it was measured after capture, possibly by some days or weeks, it could have lost considerable weight. We can only compare its dimensions directly with adult figures.

If the Yale specimen had an average human body build, its height of 55 in. would call for a weight of only 85 lbs. With a body build of 6 ft.—

300 lbs., it should have weighed 134 lbs. If it were built on the scale of 6 ft.—400 lbs., a body weight of 178 lbs. would be expected. Its reported weight of 127 lbs. is only 7 lbs. less than the middle column figure, and over 40 lbs. away from the other two. Its height to cube-root-of-weight ratio is thus very close to that of Patterson's movie subject.

A general consensus of sighting reports tends to center on about 8 ft. as a typical stature of obviously adult specimens. Likewise, what appear to be full-sized footprints have heel breadths of about 5 in. or slightly more. These height and weight tendencies also support the 6 ft.—300 lb. body build.

Some modern men are similarly heavy-set, though with nowhere near the absolute statures claimed for sasquatch sightings. The physical appearance of a 6 ft. man weighing 300 lbs. should approximate that of a sasquatch in terms of bodily proportions. In Sheldon's *Atlas of Men* there are several subjects shown who have nearly the same ratio of height to cube-root-of-weight (10.75) as is indicated for sasquatch.

In Fig. 3, I have traced the outlines of two of these men from Sheldon's photographs with some minor but necessary modifications. The body outlines were drawn just outside the contours on the photographs so that the visual effect of an inch-thick covering of body hair was added. On the head, this same pen line was drawn inside the contours of the brain case to minimize this feature.

These body outlines are remarkably similar to the proportions described by those who claim to have seen sasquatches. Most reports also indicate more massive arms and shoulders than these pictures show, though no adjustment was made here to illustrate this characteristic.

From several quite diverse lines of evidence, height and weight estimates have been made for the reputed sasquatch. Each such item of evidence by itself could easily be dismissed as interesting, but inconclusive. Taken together, however, the close correspondence of all of them to each other appears to be more than can be accounted for by a combination of chance and deliberate faking of evidence. To this might be added the anatomical consistencies found in the handprints (Krantz 1971).

The height and weight of Patterson's 1967 movie subject were each determined by two quite separate methods which gave the same specific ratio between them. The same relationship between height and weight is found in the reported measurements of the specimen captured in 1884 near Yale, British Columbia. Heavily built modern men can have the same relationship between height and weight, and show proportions remarkably similar to the movie subject as well as to descriptions by claimed eyewitnesses.

Lever lengths in the foot have been determined which indicate a weight-lifting ability which agrees closely with the indicated weight. This weight, in turn, can be closely approximated from a different measurement of the heel imprint.
It may be noted that the evidence used in this description comes from only a few sources—two sets of tracks, a movie, an old newspaper item, and some generalizations from sightings and other footprints. These are merely the most definitive items selected from a great mass of data. To this, one could also add the many native American accounts, evidently of this same animal (Suttles 1972).

This is not to say all sasquatch reports are equally reliable. One could safely say that at least one-half of the evidence reported in recent years is in error in some way, or is wholly false. A demonstration of the probable reality of part of the available data does not prove anything about the remainder.

Appendix D

U.S. Army Corps of Engineers
Washington Environmental Atlas 1975, Page 53

SASQUATCH

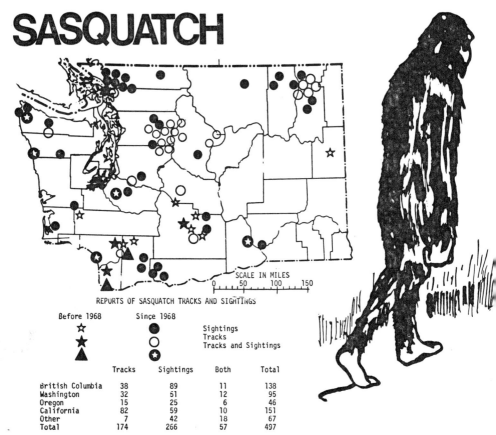

REPORTS OF SASQUATCH TRACKS AND SIGHTINGS

Before 1968	Since 1968	
☆	●	Sightings
★	○	Tracks
▲	✪	Tracks and Sightings

	Tracks	Sightings	Both	Total
British Columbia	38	89	11	138
Washington	32	51	12	95
Oregon	15	25	6	46
California	82	59	10	151
Other	7	42	18	67
Total	174	266	57	497

The very existence of Sasquatch, or "Big Foot" as it is sometimes known, is hotly disputed. Some profess to be open-minded about the matter, although stating that not one piece of evidence will withstand serious scientific scrutiny. Others, because of a particular incident or totality of reports over the years, are convinced that Sasquatch is a reality. Alleged Sasquatch hair samples inspected by F.B.I. laboratories resulted in the conclusion that no such hair exists on any human or presently-known animal for which such data are available.

(continued on next page)

254

Information from alleged sightings, tracks and other experiences conjures up the picture of an ape-like creature standing between 8 and 12 feet tall, weighing in excess of 1,000 pounds, and taking strides of up to 6 feet. Plaster casts have been made of tracks showing a large, squarish foot 14 to 24 inches in length and 5 to 10 inches in breadth. Reported to feed on vegetation and some meat, the Sasquatch is covered with long hair, except for the face and hands, and has a distinctly humanlike form. Sasquatch is very agile and powerful, with the endurance to cover a vast range in search of food, shelter and others of its kind. It is apparently able to see at night and is extremely shy, leaving minimal evidence of its presence. Tracks are presently the best evidence of its existence. A short film of an alleged female Sasquatch was shot in northern California, which, although scoffed at, shows no indications of fabrication.

The Pacific Northwest is generally considered to be the hotbed of Sasquatch activity, with Washington leading in number of reports of tracks or sightings since 1968. However, reports of Sasquatch-like creatures are known from as far away as the Parmir Mountains in the U.S.S.R. and South America.

If Sasquatch is purely legendary, the legend is likely to be a long time dying. On the other hand, if Sasquatch does exist, then with the Sasquatch hunts being mounted and the increasing human population it seems likely that some hard evidence may soon be in hand. Legendary or actual, Sasquatch excites a great popular interest in Washington.

Acknowledgments

Very many people have been associated with and have helped the Academy of Applied Sciences—International Wildlife Conservation Society Bigfoot Project over the past five years and have contributed help that ran the gamut from moral support to field assistance to financial sponsorship. Through their interest, advice, and in many cases, actual physical and financial help, the Bigfoot Information Center has been established, the Bigfoot Exhibition has been built and the *Bigfoot News,* the monthly newsletter of the Center, has been successfully launched. All are to be thanked and I ask to be forgiven if space allows nothing more than a brief mention of their names here. Among those to whom I am grateful are: Anne Adamson, Spike and Red Africa, Len Aiken, Ernie and Dorothy Alameda, Col. Charles Askins, Homer and Phyllis Baker, The Eddie Bauer Company of Seattle for donating some of its excellent camping equipment and cold weather clothing, Al Berry, Herb Beyer, Don Blake, Dr. Geoffery Bourne, John Bauer of the Oregon Bank, Monte and Sue Bricker, Darrell Buckles, Don and Alta Byington, Bryan D. Byrne, Loren Coleman, Ken Coon, Jim Craig, Roy Croft of the *Skamania County Pioneer,* Robert Curley and family, Colin Dangaard of *The National Star,* Marge Davenport of the *Oregon Journal,* Norm and Carol Davis, Jim Day, Ian Des Mares, Harvey Dirmuid, Bob Downing of the *Akron Beacon Journal,* Steve Dunleavy of *The National Star,* George W. Early, Dr. Cortez Enloe, C. W. (Chuck) Ennis, Dick Enright, Lucius Farish, Phillip Fradkin of *The Los Angeles Times,* Katherine Freer, John Fuhrmann, Cleve and Manuela Fuller, Dr. and Mrs. Warren Geiger, Bob and Julie Gimlin, Sandy and Linda Golden, Ray and Susie Goolsby, Bill and Beryl Green and Michael Green, Steven Green of the *Seattle Post-Intelligencer,* John Guernsey of *The Portland Oregonian,* Laymond Hardy, Bill and Margo Harper, George Harrison of the National Wildlife Federation, Donna Henderson, Dr. Bernard Heuvelmans, Mr. and Mrs. Robert Hewes, John Hogan of *Trail Magazine,* the magazine of the International Harvester Company, George and Lo Holton, Jack and Yvonne Hoover,

Conrad and Francis Hudnall, Ralph Izzard, Mike Jay, John Jenkins, David Johnson of *The National Observer*, Mr. and Mrs. George Johnson, David and Carol Jonasson, Edward Killam, Vincent and Mary Killeen and family, Dr. Grover Krantz, Mr. and Mrs. Ernie Kuck, Mr. and Mrs. Bernie Kuhn and family, Dick Lacardi of KMED-TV, Medford, Oregon, Peter Light and Linda St. John, Peter Lipsio, Steve and Vera Matthes, Mr. and Mrs. William Marsh, Ed McClarney of the *Skamania County Pioneer,* Bob and Ardis McClellend, Colleen McKay, Shearn Moody, Steward Mutch, Larry and Ann Nyberg, Mr. and Mrs. Norm Odegaard and family, Mr. and Mrs. William Oden, Ron Olsen, Mr. and Mrs. Dick Park and family, Vern and Barbara Parmentier, Mrs. Pat Patterson, Mike Polesnik, P. J. Reale of the *Quincy* (Massachusetts) *Patriot Ledgers,* Dr. Charles Reed, Grant and Loni Robbins, Warren Robinson, of Fort Belvoir, Virginia, Tim and Trish Ryan, Ivan and Sabina Sanderson of S.I.T.U., Dwane Scott, Mr. and Mrs. Ed Sharp, Peter Shepard, Jeffrey Slusher of Fort Belvoir, Virginia, Dick and Edith Sparke, Chan St. Claire, Sheriff of Stevens County, Washington, Mr. and Mrs. Jon Stewart, Nikki Stevens, Roger St. Hilaire, Stanley Stinson, Steve and Shirley Stone of the Captain Whidby Inn, Whidby Island, Washington, John and Delores Suismehil, Al Stump, of the *Los Angeles Herald Tribune*, Jack and Gail Sullivan. In the city of The Dalles, Oregon, the Chamber of Commerce and its Manager, Bud Hagen; Mayor Donnell and Mrs. Smith and the City Council of The Dalles; Chief of Police Robert Brower and the City Police Department; District Attorney Bernie Smith. Fire Chief Wilson of the City Fire Department, and his staff; Sheriff Ernie Mosier, Sheriff of Wasco County and his department officers, including Deputy Rich Carlson, Deputy Harry Gilpin, and Sgt. Jack Robertson. Father Anthony Terhaar of St. Benedict, Oregon, Bob Walters, Manager of KACI Radio of The Dalles, and his family, Ron and Shirley Ward, Ron and Loren Welch.

A special vote of thanks is owed to certain persons who have generously given more than an ordinary share of help to the Bigfoot project. The time, interest and support that they have provided has enabled us to continue with the project to the present. Among them are: The Directors of the

International Wildlife Conservation Society Inc., of Washington, D.C., in particular Leonard A. Fink and Karl Jonas, M.D. Their expressions of confidence in the long-term project are much appreciated. The Explorers Club of New York, for granting recognition to the project in the form of an Explorers Club flag to myself and Russ Kinne in 1974. Columbia Photo, of Hood River, Oregon and its owners Nicholas and Pam Bielemeier, for much professional photographic advice, work, and equipment and for many overtime hours spent working to assist the project.

For direct support and assistance to the project, the following should know of my appreciation: Frederick Ayer II, Arlie and Polly Bryant, Jack and Ann Bryant, David Chandler, Guy Coheleach, Tim Dinsdale of the Loch Ness Investigation Bureau, John H. Hauberg, Patri Hull, Tom Foley, Bob and Francis Guenette, of Wolper Productions, Los Angeles, California, Nancy Cooke Jackson, Dennis Jenson, Russ and Jane Kinne, Neal and Mary McLanahan, Dr. John Napier, Queen Elizabeth College, University of London, Tom and Mary Page, Ron and Jackie Rosner, Allen Rosse of Washington, D.C. and her son Colin, Marie Roy, Secretary of the Explorers Club, New York, Gerald Russell, Eleanor (Missy) Sabin, Ronald Somers, Lowell Thomas, President of the Explorers Club, Bob and Betty Thomson, Bronson Trevor and for endless hours of patient research, typing, paperwork and field work under all kinds of often difficult conditions to my co-editor of the *Bigfoot News,* confidante and friend, Celia Killeen, very many thanks.

To the International Harvester Company, makers of the four-wheel-drive Scouts that we have been using through all the years of the Bigfoot project, under the most trying weather conditions of extreme heat and bitter cold, in all kinds of terrain in the rugged coastal mountains of the Pacific Northwest, I can only say this: that their vehicles have never let us down, have given excellent service for thousands of miles, and have inspired our confidence. When a better vehicle appears, we will use it. When it does, it will probably be built by International Harvester. Until then we will continue with the toughest vehicles on the market for our kind of work, International Harvester Scouts.

And lastly, a debt of gratitude is owed to Robert Rines, President of the Academy of Applied Science, and his wife Carol, and to the Directors and Members of the Academy for their continuing support of the project, for assistance with equipment funding and sponsorship for which I and all of my associates are indeed grateful.

Index

262

263